ABBA

SONG BY SONG

IAN COLE

FONTHILL

Fonthill Media Language Policy

Fonthill Media publishes in the international English language market. One language edition is published worldwide. As there are minor differences in spelling and presentation, especially with regard to American English and British English, a policy is necessary to define which form of English to use. The Fonthill Policy is to use the form of English native to the author. Ian Cole was born and educated in Australia; therefore British English has been adopted in this publication.

Fonthill Media Limited
Fonthill Media LLC
www.fonthill.media
books@fonthill.media

First published in the United Kingdom and the United States of America 2020
Reprinted 2024

British Library Cataloguing in Publication Data:
A catalogue record for this book is available from the British Library

Copyright © Ian Cole 2020, 2024

ISBN 978-1-78155-785-3

Typeset in 10pt on 13pt Sabon
Printed and bound in England

Acknowledgements

As a pre-teenager in Australia, I first heard ABBA on the radio in 1974, when their Eurovision Song Contest winner 'Waterloo' was a top ten hit. That song did not grab me, but a little over a year later, I heard 'Mamma Mia' at a party, when the hostess played it repeatedly. Something about that song immediately possessed me, and on the car trip home that night, I asked my parents for the *ABBA* album (not the single) for Christmas, which was coming up in a few months. After hearing the full album, I was hooked and became a lifelong ABBA fan, as did thousands of Australian kids on that Christmas Day in 1975.

It has been a longtime dream of mine to write a book about ABBA, with several ideas bouncing around including this one. And so here is *ABBA: Song By Song* in your hands, on paper or on your screen. Many thanks to Jay Slater at Fonthill Media, who reached out in search of a writer for this book and accepted me, based on just two song entries (one of which appears in the book almost exactly as it was first submitted). Thanks also to Joshua Greenland, whose editorial work prepared the book for public consumption.

I owe a huge debt of gratitude to my friend Carl Magnus Palm in Stockholm, Sweden. His research and the books he has published about ABBA over the past twenty-five years, plus the CD and DVD booklets he has written for Universal Music's ABBA releases, have been excellent sources of information for this book and to all ABBA fans, especially his books *ABBA: The Complete Recording Sessions* (originally published in 1994, updated edition 2017) and *Bright Lights Dark Shadows: The Real Story of ABBA* (2001, updated editions 2002, 2008, 2014). His attention to detail has inspired me in my fandom and in writing this book. He graciously offered to read through my drafts, and he served as a sounding board for ideas, a job that I have performed for him many times over the past two decades. He gave me many helpful suggestions, corrections, tips, invaluable information, and support that have made their mark on the book, plus he helped me with my Swedish spelling. Thank you for everything, Carl Magnus.

Special thanks to my friend Marc Andrews (originally from Australia but now based in London, when he is not travelling the world with his husband, Uday);

he has been a music writer for three decades, and as well as writing for *Smash Hits* (Australian and British editions) and *DNA* magazines, he has interviewed dozens of celebrities and published several books based on his thirty-plus years of journalism. His quirky writing style has informed my own writing in this book and elsewhere. Marc also read through the book in draft and offered many suggestions that are reflected in the book, and he helped me find my writing voice.

Thanks also to my friend Christopher Patrick in Australia, for his excellent book *ABBA: Let The Music Speak* (self-published 2008), which inspired me to listen deep into the music, beyond the vocals and the most obvious elements of the recordings.

Quotes and other details throughout the book have been compiled from a number of sources: these are listed in the Bibiliography at the end of the book. This list is far from complete, as I have been collecting information about ABBA for over forty-four years. Many original sources of material are sadly long forgotten.

Many thanks to Roger Holegård and Premium Publishing, Jeff Chandler, David Fyfe, Pepé, Raffe Pohlman, Tina Schuster, and Andy Wetson for sharing fantastic images.

Chart information courtesy of Trent Nickson/ABBA Charts (website currently offline).

Love and thanks: to my beloved husband, Ian Marks. I am so glad you have been by my side for the past twenty-seven years. Our wedding in July 2018 was the happiest day.

To my family: Barry and Beaw, Sue and Garry, Amanda, Ben, Jayden, Dakoda, and Porchè. Surprise! I wrote a book, and you're all in it!

To Roger and Marina Ipaviz, our dearest friends and logical family.

To the friends with whom I have shared the ABBA experience for forty-something years: Allison, Andy, Anita, Brady, Chris, Daniel, David, Dirk, Gavin, Geoff, Geoffroy, Graeme, Greg, Helga, Ice, James, Jason, Jeff, John, Jos, Judy, Julie, Lex, Magnus, Manuel, Marc, Marco, Maria, Mark, Masakazu, Matti, Merrick, Mike, Norma, Pablo, Paul, Pepé, Philip, Raffe, Ray, Richard, Robert, Rod, Roxanne, Sascha, Sean, Sara, Stuart, Tony, and many more.

To the many, many ABBA fans around the world who have been sharing their collective knowledge of ABBA for the past four decades, in the flesh, through pen pal letters, and on various internet forums. Your input is invaluable.

To you, dear reader. I hope you find this book interesting, intriguing, and informative.

Thank you for the music Björn, Benny, Agnetha, Frida, Stig, Micke, Görel, and all the musicians who played on ABBA's records and concerts, plus those artists and designers who projected ABBA's image to the world.

This book is dedicated to the memory of my mother, Christine Cole, who enabled my ABBA addiction, and my best friend Bill Cottingham, who introduced me to music.

Ian Cole
Sydney, Australia
January 2020

CONTENTS

Introduction

'They came flying from far away/now I'm under their spell/I love hearing the stories that they tell.' The first three lines of 'Eagle', the opening track from 1977's *ABBA: The Album*, greeted visitors to the ABBAWORLD exhibition at Sydney's Powerhouse Museum in 2010 and 2011. The quote aptly describes how millions of people around the world feel about ABBA, from distant Sweden.

In the latter half of the 1970s and early years of the 1980s, ABBA was the biggest-selling band in the world. In the UK, they had nine No. 1 singles and eight No. 1 albums. Their *Greatest Hits* was Britain's second-highest selling album of the '70s. In Australia, they had six consecutive No. 1 singles and a fanmania unmatched anywhere in the world; the local compilation *The Best of ABBA* was the nation's first album to sell over 1 million copies—to this day only six albums have outsold it, one of those being another ABBA collection. In West Germany, they had nine No. 1 singles among twenty top ten hits. In the USA, they had fourteen top forty singles and topped the Hot 100 singles chart, plus the Adult Contemporary (twice) and Disco Top 80 charts; an amazing achievement in a country that demands constant touring to maintain visibility, the group only visited briefly for limited television appearances and one concert tour. ABBA sold huge amounts of records and tapes in Eastern European countries behind the Iron Curtain, where access to western music was extremely limited. In Southeast Asia, their records were among the most pirated—a back-handed honour. In their home country Sweden, four of their first five album releases successively broke sales records. In total, worldwide, ABBA had twenty-nine individual No. 1 singles and nineteen No. 1 albums.

As of 2020, ABBA has sold in the range of 400 million records worldwide, according to Universal Music's estimates. The 1992 compilation *ABBA Gold: Greatest Hits*, released ten years after the group ended, was part of a great ABBA revival that continues to this day. That album has sold over 31 million copies, 9 million of those in the US. With sales of over 5.3 million in the UK, it is the biggest selling CD and second-highest selling album. The musical *Mamma Mia!*, based on ABBA's songs, opened in London in April 1999 and is still running, selling tickets well beyond its twentieth anniversary. It has since played in over forty countries (with fourteen years on Broadway), been translated into twenty-one languages, and has been seen by over 65 million people. The 2008 movie version starring a Hollywood A-list cast broke box office records for movie musicals and DVD sales, and the 2018 sequel, *Mamma Mia! Here We Go Again*, came close to matching the first movie's success.

ABBA was awarded the Carl Alan Award for significant contribution to the entertainment industry in 1978, presented to the group by HRH Princess Margaret. ABBA was voted 'Vocal Group of the Year' by the American Guild of Variety Artists in 1981 and was inducted into the Vocal Group Hall of Fame in 2002, the Rock and Roll Hall of Fame in 2010, and the Swedish Music Hall of Fame in 2014. The group received Sweden's Rockbjörnen Lifetime Achievement Award in 2009. In 2015, ABBA's 1976 single 'Dancing Queen' was honoured in the Grammy Hall of Fame. ABBA The Museum in Stockholm opened in May 2013 and is one of the city's top attractions, welcoming over 350,000 visitors per year.

Since ABBA disbanded at the end of 1982, Anni-Frid, Benny, Björn, and Agnetha (the group name is an acronym of the members' first names) have refused all offers to reunite, including a reputed offer of $1 billion (US) in the late 1990s to record an album and perform a 100-concert tour. ABBA made headlines around the world in 2016 simply for standing together on the one stage for just a couple of minutes, not once, but twice. In April 2018, over thirty-five years after their last new record, the group surprised everyone when they announced that they had recorded two new songs, which would be performed by so-called ABBAtars, digital representations of ABBA, for a live concert tour set to premiere in 2020.

ABBA has often been portrayed as a hit-making machine, created by their Svengali manager and record company owner Stig Anderson, but nothing could be further from the truth. ABBA evolved organically from the partnership between two ambitious young musicians, budding songwriters, and record producers, and their popular singer girlfriends, both of whom had developed a love of singing at a young age.

Björn Ulvaeus (born Gothenburg, 25 April 1945) was a member of the folk group the West Bay Singers, who piqued the interest of music publisher Stig Anderson and his record producer partner Bengt Bernhag when they read in a newspaper about the group's audition for a radio talent quest. Renamed Hootenanny Singers, the group's debut record was released in 1963 as the first single on Stig and Bengt's nascent Polar Music label. The band primarily played Swedish folk music and Swedish versions of American folk songs. Inspired by The Beatles' John Lennon and Paul McCartney, Björn tried his hand at writing his own songs, which changed the direction of the band in a more pop-oriented style.

Benny Andersson (born in Stockholm, 16 December 1946) joined the local rock 'n' roll band The Hep Stars in 1964, replacing the band's previous organ player. After a pivotal television appearance in March 1965, they became the biggest band in Sweden almost overnight, inspiring Beatles-style hysteria wherever they went. The band initially played covers of '50s and '60s rock 'n' roll until, like Björn, Benny was inspired by Lennon and McCartney and started writing songs, giving The Hep Stars their biggest hits to date.

The two young men first met on 5 June 1966, when both bands were touring on the annual *folkpark* circuit. *Folkparks*, 'people's parks', were open-air venues in Swedish cities and towns, with stages for concerts, food and drink outlets, and other attractions. During the summer season, popular Swedish artists would tour the *folkparks*, usually performing short sets, sometimes performing at two or three venues per day. The two bands were both scheduled to play that day at the same venue at Alleberg in southern Sweden, and they literally met on the road leading to the venue.

The Hootenanny Singers invited The Hep Stars to a party they were hosting that night after their final show of the day in the town of Linköping. Hitting it off immediately, Björn and Benny, having individually written a few songs for their respective bands, discussed the idea of writing a song together. Just a few weeks later, after the two bands met again at another on-the-road party, the two young men decided then and there to write their first song. 'Isn't It Easy to Say' was recorded by Hep Stars and released on their third, eponymous album in 1966. Over the next few years, the two wrote several more songs, some recorded by Hep Stars or by Björn on singles during a brief solo career, some never made public.

In May 1968, Björn first met teenage singer Agnetha Fältskog (born in Jönköping, 5 April 1950) at a *folkpark* engagement. Agnetha had been the singer with a dance band for a little over a year when she recorded her debut No. 1 single, the self-composed 'Jag var så kär' ('I was so in love') in October 1967. Agnetha had released several self-composed singles and two albums, plus a number of German-language singles for the West German market, then a popular sideline for Swedish artists. A year after their first meeting, Björn and Agnetha met again when both were featured on a television special, and they soon became a couple. They were married on 6 July 1971.

In March 1969, Benny met singer Anni-Frid Lyngstad (born in Ballangen, Norway, 15 November 1945). Having moved to Sweden with her grandmother as an infant, Frida, as she is best known, had been a singer fronting several dance and jazz bands since the age of thirteen in her adopted hometown Eskilstuna. On 3 September 1967, the day Sweden switched from driving on the left side to the right side of the road, she appeared on national television, having won a talent quest earlier in the day. This resulted in a record deal with EMI and her first single, 'En ledig dag' ('A day off', a Swedish version of a 1964 Italian song, 'Weekend in Portofino'). Frida and Benny first encountered each other when they both participated in *Melodifestivalen* (The Melody Festival), the Swedish heats for the Eurovision Song Contest. After another meeting a month later, Benny and Frida embarked on a relationship. They soon became engaged, but did not married until 6 October 1978.

Over the next few years, the four slowly started collaborating, providing back-up vocals, guitar, and piano, as well as writing and producing each other's records: on Agnetha and Frida's solo singles and albums, songs by the recording duo Björn & Benny, and/or songs written and produced by Benny and Björn for other Polar Music artists—the pair became Polar's 'house producers' in 1971.

In October 1970, the first record to feature the combined vocal talents of all four was released: Björn & Benny's single 'Hej gamle man!' ('Hey old man!'), sung by the two men with Agnetha and Frida as the backing choir in the chorus. The song's parent album *Lycka* (*Happiness*) had been intended as a showcase for Björn and Benny's songs, to garner interest from other performers to record their songs.

Following a couple of television and radio appearances, on 1 November, the quartet made its stage debut in the cabaret show *Festfolk* at Trägår'n in Gothenburg, followed by a run at the Strand Hotel in Stockholm in December and a short tour of Sweden in February 1971. The show featured the four singing songs and performing comedy routines. Though that show was deemed a failure, it was the birth of one of popular music's most enduring acts.

About ABBA's Recordings

During ABBA's active years between 1972 and 1982, the group recorded and released an impressive ninety-eight unique songs on eight studio albums (all of which are still available, on CD, LP, download, and streaming) and over thirty singles. Some of those songs were also recorded in languages other than English—their native Swedish, of course, plus German, French, and Spanish. In the main section of this book, I have detailed those ninety-eight songs and their variants on the albums and singles on which they were first released. In Appendix I, I have included some of the songs that got away, songs never released on record, some that ABBA themselves tried to hide, and others that went on to be recycled or remade into other songs. Appendix I also includes details about two brand-new ABBA songs recorded in 2017 (unreleased at the time of writing). Finally, in Appendix II, I have compiled a selection of major compilations, boxsets, live albums, and home video releases where ABBA's music can be found today.

ABBA's recordings were made with a core group of Swedish musicians. In addition to Benny handling piano, synthesizers, and all other keyboard instruments and Björn playing rhythm guitar, the most frequently used musicians were Rolf Alex (drums), Ola Brunkert (drums), Malando Gassama (percussion), Rutger Gunnarsson (bass guitar and string arrangements), Per Lindvall (drums, from 1980), Roger Palm (drums), Janne Schaffer (guitar), Finn Sjöberg (guitar), Åke Sundqvist (percussion), Mike Watson (bass), and Lasse Wellander (guitar).

ABBA's manager, and head of their domestic record label Polar Music, Stig Anderson negotiated deals with different record companies in each country—rather than sign with one multinational—to seek out the company that could offer the best deal and promote ABBA in its own country. ABBA's records were released on Polar in the Scandinavian countries; Epic Records in the UK and Ireland; Atlantic in the US and Canada; Polydor in West Germany, Austria, Switzerland, the Netherlands, and Southeast Asia; Vogue in France and Belgium; Carnaby then later Epic in Spain; Dig It then Epic in Italy; RCA Victor in Australia,

New Zealand, and Central and South America; Philips and later Discomate in Japan; and others, including local labels in Eastern European countries, a rarity for a western group during the Cold War '70s. This led to a non-standard global discography, with the different companies sometimes releasing records with modified tracklists in different packaging, which has created a boon for the ABBA collectors' market. In 1990, Polydor took over the ABBA catalogue worldwide. Today, ABBA's music is released on the Polar Music International label through Universal Music.

All songs were written, arranged, and produced by Benny Andersson and Björn Ulvaeus, except where noted. ABBA's recordings were engineered by Michael B. Tretow. Record releases and single combinations detailed in this book are those released by Polar Music in Scandinavia, with applicable UK and US release dates and chart placings, except where otherwise noted. From 1992 onwards, dates are generally the first recognised international release date.

Ring Ring

Sweden:	26 March 1973
UK:	9 April 1992
US:	1995
Current edition:	Universal Music/Polar CD 549 950-2
Personnel:	Benny Andersson: piano, Mellotron, vocals
	Ola Brunkert: drums
	Agnetha Fältskog: vocals
	Rutger Gunnarsson: bass
	Anni-Frid Lyngstad: vocals
	Roger Palm: drums
	Janne Schaffer: guitar
	Björn Ulvaeus: guitar, vocals
	Sven-Olof Walldoff: string arrangement
	Mike Watson: bass

Recorded at Metronome Studio, KMH Studio, Europafilm Studio, Stockholm: March 1972–March 1973

Duration:	36 minutes

Produced by Benny Andersson and Björn Ulvaeus

Engineered by Michael B. Tretow, with assistance from Åke Eldsäter, Rune Persson, Lennart Karlsmyr (KMH), Björn Almstedt (Europafilm)

Chart position:	Sweden: 2
	UK: —
	US: —

ABBA's first album was released under the group moniker Björn & Benny Agnetha & Frida, a mouthful in anyone's language—the name ABBA had not yet been adopted by the group. Indeed, when the album's first song was recorded in March 1972, the group did not exist. It was only six months after their first single as a quartet, and its domestic success, that they decided to continue the experiment and record a long-playing album.

The album has an eclectic mix of songs, reflecting its creation: some songs had been recorded for a planned second album by the duo Björn & Benny, a follow-up to their 1970 album *Lycka*. It does not sound like the work of a cohesive group; on some songs, the women's voices are relegated to an anonymous-sounding backing choir. Only a few songs contain a hint of the sound that would make ABBA world famous a few years later.

The album was released throughout Scandinavia, but only in a handful of other countries at the time: West Germany, Australia, Japan, South Africa, and Mexico. In Sweden, it was hugely successful, peaking at No. 2 (behind the 'Ring Ring' single on the combined singles/albums chart), but everywhere else it made minimal impact. Only in Australia during the Abbamania phenomenon in 1976 did it become a hit album, reaching No. 10. International releases of the album, including current CD releases, replaced the Swedish version of 'Ring Ring' with the 1970 Björn & Benny single 'She's My Kind of Girl'.

The *Ring Ring* album was not released in the UK until the album's first international CD issue in 1992, and not in North America until 1995.

'Ring Ring'

Written by Benny Andersson, Stig Anderson, and Björn Ulvaeus. English lyric by Neil Sedaka and Phil Cody. German lyric by Peter Lach. Spanish lyric by Doris Band.
Duration: 3.04
Released as a single: 19 February 1973.

Since 1968, Frida, Agnetha, Björn, Benny, and Stig had all made attempts to enter the Eurovision Song Contest as either performers (Frida) or songwriters (the rest). Stig had made his first attempt as early as 1958. Stig had been writing songs and Swedish lyrics for international hits since the late '40s, and he had built his Sweden Music publishing company and Polar Music record label on the back of his songwriting efforts. He claimed to have written over 3,000 lyrics during his career. Stig would write or co-write lyrics for Benny and Björn's songs, including many of ABBA's singles, until 1977.

In the late '60s and early '70s, the international music scene was dominated by artists from the US and UK. Though the occasional hit might come out of continental Europe, few if any lasting international careers were created. Eurovision was seen as the only way to get the attention of an audience outside of Sweden.

In 1973, the Andersson–Anderson–Ulvaeus songwriting team was invited for the second time to submit a song by the Swedish selectors. The previous year, the team had submitted 'Säg det med en sång' ('Say it with a song'), sung by Polar Music artist Lena Andersson, though it was not selected for the contest. Benny and Björn sequestered themselves to come up with a standout tune that could appeal to an international audience and potentially win the contest.

Stig as lyricist worked to come up with a suitable title that would be recognisable to anyone, regardless of what language they spoke. 'It goes without saying that if you take part in an international hit contest you aim to win,' he commented. 'To do this you must have a title that is equally intelligible in Switzerland and Ireland.'

Seeking to give the song a perfect English lyric, or more likely hoping to gain additional publicity for the song, Stig Anderson, through his music publishing contacts (probably American publisher Don Kirshner), approached legendary singer-songwriter Neil Sedaka to write the English lyric. Sedaka and his current lyric-writing partner Phil Cody quickly knocked off a set of new lyrics, based on a rough translation of the Swedish lyric, but adding their own twist: Cody claims the storyline about a girl sitting by the phone waiting for it to ring was his idea.

When it came time to record the song, recording engineer Michael B. Tretow wanted to make the the song outstanding. Having recently read a biography of American record producer Phil Spector, *Out of his Head* by British music journalist Richard Williams, Tretow hoped to replicate Spector's famous 'wall of sound'. But Polar could not afford a studio full of musicians as Spector had used on hits like 'Be My Baby', 'You've Lost That Lovin' Feelin'', and 'River Deep—Mountain High', so he came up with a brilliant idea: he would have all the musicians overdub the full song, essentially doubling the number of instruments. On the second take, he slowed down the tape ever so slightly, an effect which created an enormous sound. Tretow described the scene to writer Carl Magnus Palm in 1994 for the first edition of his landmark book *ABBA: The Complete Recording Sessions*: 'It was like the roof was caving in, Björn and Benny were ecstatic. And I can still remember the chills and how the hair stood up on my arms. It really was something else'.

The song is propelled by an incessant riff, created in the studio by musicians Janne Schaffer (guitarist) and Rutger Gunnarsson (bassist), with Benny and Björn. It is rather curious that the riff bears a strong resemblance to a song from West Germany-based Italian artist and producer Giorgio Moroder, 'Underdog'. The song had even been released on a single in Sweden by Polar Music in 1972, so someone must have been aware of it. Whether that song had a conscious or unconscious influence on the 'Ring Ring' session is unknown.

'Ring Ring' was also recorded in Swedish—titled 'Ring ring (bara du slog en signal)' (if you'd only give me a call)—German, and Spanish. Björn stated: 'We believed a great deal in ourselves and in the prospects for "Ring Ring" internationally'. For long-forgotten reasons, the Spanish version was not released at the time and remained unknown until 1994, when it appeared without notice on the compilation *ABBA Más Oro: Más ABBA Éxitos* (*ABBA More Gold: More ABBA Hits*).

Björn, Benny, Frida, and a heavily-pregnant Agnetha performed 'Ring Ring' in Swedish at the Swedish Eurovision selection, *Melodifestivalen* (The Melody Festival) on 10 February 1973. Alas, the song came third in the jury voting and did not go on to represent Sweden at Eurovision in Luxembourg. Sweden's entry, 'You Are Summer—You Never Tell Me No' by Nova, came fifth.

(For ABBA trivia buffs: one of the members of the duo Nova was Claes af Geijerstam, a friend of the ABBA members, who would be sound engineer on ABBA's concert tours from 1974 through to 1980. His one-time girlfriend, Lena Källersjö, would become Björn's second wife in 1981.)

On the plus side, 'Ring Ring' became a huge hit in Sweden, and a top ten hit across Northern Europe. Famously, for two weeks in April 1973 on the Swedish record sales chart, the Swedish single was at No. 1, the English single at No. 2, and the *Ring Ring* album was at No. 3.

But 'Ring Ring' failed to make an impression on the important British market, where it was belatedly released in October, reportedly selling as few as 500 copies. Stig commented: 'We analysed the problem and came to the conclusion that "Ring Ring" was a hit in the Germanic part of Europe. There is actually a boundary of taste running through the middle of Brussels'. The British single and the Italian single released a couple of weeks later were the first records released under the band name ABBA. See the entry for 'Dance (While the Music Still Goes On)' below for more information on the introduction of the ABBA name.

In 1974, following the chart-topping success of (spoiler alert) ABBA's Eurovision-winner 'Waterloo', Epic Records in the UK instigated a remixed version of 'Ring Ring' as the follow-up single. Additional guitar was added to beef up the sound, and a saxophone riff was added near the end of the chorus, giving the song a bit of a 1974 glam rock sound, and to make it sound more like 'Waterloo'. The vocals sound different from the original, though it is not clear if this was a rerecording or alternate take from 1973. That extra work was to no avail, as the single peaked at a lowly No. 32. A different remixed version appeared on the *Waterloo* album in the US and Canada, with more saxophone riffs throughout the chorus and an overall 'dirtier' sound.

'Another Town, Another Train'
Written by Benny Andersson and Björn Ulvaeus. German lyric by Fred Jay.
Duration: 3.12

'Another Town, Another Train' is the fairly dreary story of a self-pitying man leaving his sleeping partner with a note as he heads off on a train to another town, because he is restless and needs to be free from feeling tied down in one place. It is one of many songs in ABBA's early years featuring a lead vocal by Björn, then still popular at home as an ongoing member of Hootenanny Singers. The recording sounds as dreary as the story; not even the backing vocals from Agnetha and Frida in the chorus can lift the song. Only the flute-like refrain played on a Mellotron (a keyboard instrument that was a precursor to the synthesizer, probably most famously used on The Beatles' 'Strawberry Fields Forever' in 1967) adds any life.

A German version entitled 'Wer im Wartesaal der Liebe steht' ('Who is in the waiting room of love') was released on the B-side of the German version of 'Ring Ring'.

'Another Town, Another Train' was released as a single in Japan and the US, and though it was not a hit, it was included on ABBA's *Greatest Hits* album in 1975 (see Appendix II for details of that album).

'Disillusion'
Music by Agnetha Fältskog, lyric by Björn Ulvaeus
Duration: 3.04

'Disillusion' was one of the final three songs to be recorded for the *Ring Ring* album after the group's performance at *Melodifestivalen* on 10 February, and the birth of Agnetha and Björn's daughter, Linda, thirteen days later. It is the only song on an ABBA record released during the group's lifetime with a melody written by Agnetha, with her husband, Björn, supplying the lyrics. It is the first of only two songs in the ABBA catalogue to feature just one voice, in this case Agnetha solo or double-tracked, singing harmony with herself in the second verse.

Agnetha had been writing sings since she was a child—she wrote her first song, 'Två små troll' ('Two small trolls') at the age of six. She wrote her first hit single, 'Jag var så kär' ('I was so in love'), when she was seventeen in 1967, and she had written many of the songs on her (to this date) four solo albums. Björn and Benny would ask her to write for ABBA, but she only wrote one more song for the group, 'I'm Still Alive', which she performed on ABBA's 1979 and 1980 concert tours, but never recorded for one of the group's albums.

With her increasing commitments with ABBA, and her family duties with baby Linda, Agnetha's songwriting decreased. She would write ten of the eleven songs on her 1975 album *Elva kvinnor i ett hus* (*Eleven women in one house*), including a Swedish version of 'Disillusion', 'Mina ögon' ('My eyes'). But since then, she has composed and released only a handful of songs.

Many of Agnetha's solo songs had themes of heartbreak. 'Disillusion' has a similar theme, and even the recording sounds more like something from Agnetha's solo career than from ABBA. 'I guess I was rather proud that they wanted it on the album, but I [was] a little doubtful that it was good enough,' she remembered. Despite the recording not having the same production values as the rest of the album, it does have a heartbreaking immediacy that is not present on Agnetha's 1975 solo version.

'People Need Love'
Duration: 2.44
Released as a single in May 1972.

Having been collaborating in various combinations on stage, television, radio, and on record since 1969, and with the domestic success of songs like 'Hej gamle man!', the two couples decided it was time to record a song as a full-on quartet.

'People Need Love' was that very first song, though there were no plans to form a permanent group; this was a one-off event, the latest Björn & Benny single featuring guest artists Agnetha & Anni-Frid.

The lyrics are an ode to the peace, love, and harmony, similar themes to recent hits by pop groups such as Blue Mink ('Melting Pot'), the New Seekers ('I'd Like to Teach the World to Sing'), and an early line-up of Brotherhood of Man ('United We Stand'). The vocals during the verses alternated between the two men and two women, with the four joining together in the chorus, declaring the joys of matrimony in a decidedly heterosexual, male-dominant way ('Man has always wanted a woman by his side/a woman needs her man', etc.).

The third chorus is followed by a multi-layered yodelling section, also repeated at the end of the song, devised by Agnetha and Frida in the recording studio. It adds some memorable variety to the song. The opening 'backwards' chord, devised by recording engineer Michael B. Tretow, also heard leading into all subsequent choruses, is another memorable effect on the record that draws the listener in. Years later, Benny said: 'I remember thinking, "Now we've made our first really good record."'

'People Need Love' was released in Sweden in May 1972, in Denmark a little later, and also released in West Germany, Austria, France, and New Zealand, though it made little impact in those territories. The single was released in the US, Canada, and the Phillipines on the Playboy label (yes, an offshoot of the famous men's magazine), billed as Björn & Benny with Svenska Flicka (Swedish girl). The single 'bubbled under' the US Top 100 singles charts—not too bad for a single by an unknown foreign act on a small record label that had little promotion in the world's biggest music market.

The single reached No. 17 in Sweden on the combined singles/albums chart, though if the albums were taken out, the single would have peaked at No. 7. Not the biggest hit, but a good start (coincidentally, The Beatles' debut single 'Love Me Do' had also peaked at No. 17 in their home country).

'I Saw It in the Mirror'
Duration: 2.33

'I Saw It in the Mirror' is a song recycled from Benny and Björn's songwriting and production activities. The original version had been recorded by singer Billy G-son on a Polydor single in 1970. The song was quite bluesy, with a gruff, Joe Cocker-like vocal.

Needing one last track to fill the *Ring Ring* album, Benny and Björn rewrote parts of the song, recorded a new backing track, and sang the song themselves in unison, with Agnetha and Frida chiming in at the end of each verse and in the middle eight. The recording's lower production values show that it was recorded in a hurry, less than two weeks before the album's release date.

'I Saw It in the Mirror' has the dubious honour of regularly being voted as ABBA fans' least-favourite ABBA song.

For historical interest, the Billy G-son version of 'I Saw It in the Mirror' was included as an additional bonus track on the 2012 Deluxe Edition of *Ring Ring*, one of several extra tracks demonstrating ABBA's early development.

'Nina, Pretty Ballerina'
Duration: 2.51

Story songs about unusual characters, usually sung in the third person, were popular in the late '60s and early '70s—The Beatles' 'Maxwell's Silver Hammer' being a prime example of the genre (fun fact: Björn's group Hootenanny Singers recorded a cover of that Beatles track in 1969, entitled 'Ring ring— här är Svensktoppsjuryn' ('Ring Ring—Here is the Swedish Top Ten Jury'). *Svensktoppen* was a top ten chart for songs in Swedish).

ABBA recorded several story songs in the early years, this one being the first. 'Nina, Pretty Ballerina' is the tale of a young, boring office worker who transforms into 'the queen of the dancing floor' on Friday night. There are many who see Nina as a lyrical predecessor of 'Dancing Queen', though in that song, the subject is a teenager, not a working woman, so it is not simply a prequel for the 1976 hit.

'Nina, Pretty Ballerina' could be regarded as the first song that had what would be known as 'the ABBA sound'. The verses feature Agnetha and Frida singing in unison, creating for the first time on record the so-called third voice, creating a sound greater than the sum of its parts, which would become the defining feature of ABBA's records.

There are a few interesting things to listen for in the song. During the verses, there is a repetitive descending bass riff by bassist Rutger Gunnarsson that is unusually dominant. Gunnarsson would be one of ABBA's most frequently used musicians, playing on all their albums, their world tours in 1977 and 1979–80, several post-ABBA projects for all four members, and even played in the orchestra during the Swedish production of the *Mamma Mia!* musical. During the choruses, there is a very fast, incessant piano that is faster than it is possible to play; this was achieved by recording Benny playing the piano with the tape running at a slower speed.

'Nina, Pretty Ballerina' is also one of the few ABBA recordings to use sound effects or 'found sounds'. The song fades in with the sound of a train and its steam whistle; what sounds like the same sound effect opens Electric Light Orchestra's song 'Across the Border' from their 1977 album *Out of the Blue*. A cheering audience can be heard leading from the verses into the chorus and throughout the chorus.

In 1973, 'Nina, Pretty Ballerina' was released as a single in France and Austria, though it was not a hit in either territory. In 1975–76, it was included on *Greatest Hits/The Best of ABBA* compilations around the world and became familiar to listeners everywhere.

'Love Isn't Easy (But It Sure Is Hard Enough)'
Duration: 2.54
Released as a single in June 1973

One of the last songs recorded for *Ring Ring* in 1973, but a bit of a throwback to the first songs recorded by Björn & Benny, Agnetha & Anni-Frid in 1972, 'Love Isn't Easy (But It Sure Is Hard Enough)' features call and response vocals shared between the male and female halves of the group, singing about the difficulties that can come with trying to keep a loving relationship together. The full title is apparently a bit of Swedish humour that does not necessarily translate well into English—'love is not easy, but it is hard'.

The incessant backing refrain 'sweet sweet our love is bitter sweet' bears a passing resemblance to the Beach Boys' 1967 single 'Wild Honey'—not the only time the Californian group would have an influence on ABBA's sound.

'Love Isn't Easy' was the fourth and final single released from the *Ring Ring* album, in Denmark only, though after the massive success of 'Ring Ring', it only reached a disappointing No. 21 on the Danish chart.

'Me and Bobby and Bobby's Brother'
Duration: 2.50

This is the first recorded song in the ABBA catalogue with a solo female lead vocal, in this case Frida (recording predates 'Disillusion' above). It sounds like Agnetha is not present; when the song was recorded, she was in the final month of her first pregnancy.

'Me and Bobby and Bobby's Brother' is a delightful reminiscence of childhood, of a young girl playing with her friend Bobby and his brother. She enjoys a 'heaven of fun' of going to 'football games and such' and climbing apple trees, though as a self-described 'little girl', she does not necessarily relish such boyish activities.

The song is one of the few ABBA songs with a lyric written by Benny. After 1974, he would leave lyric writing to Björn and Stig. Like 'Nina, Pretty Ballerina', 'Me and Bobby and Bobby's Brother' is one of the handful of songs on the *Ring Ring* album that hints at the production values for which ABBA would soon become world famous.

'He Is Your Brother'
Duration: 3.17
Released as a single in November 1972.

Following the domestic success of 'People Need Love', it seemed like a good idea for Björn & Benny, Agnetha & Anni-Frid to put out another single and also record an album. As Björn described it in the book *ABBA: The Complete*

Recording Sessions in 1994: 'The managing director and house producers of the Polar record company had simply decided that it would be much better to make an album with this constellation than with the two boys only, since the girls were much better singers'.

'He Is Your Brother' follows the template of 'People Need Love', with vocals alternating between the two men and two women, in another ode to peace and love for your fellow man. Both songs also share a hint of gospel. Unlike 'People Need Love', which was released in several countries, the single 'He Is Your Brother' was only released in Sweden and, rather bizarrely, New Zealand.

The song became a live favourite on ABBA's concert tours over the next few years. It was the only song from the *Ring Ring* album to be performed during ABBA's European and Australian tour in 1977. A live performance from that tour was included in *ABBA: The Movie* (see Appendix II for more about the film).

Like 'People Need Love' before it, 'He Is Your Brother' uses a musical device to draw the listener into the song; in this instance, the song starts with a downwards glissando on the piano, an effect that would be reused three years later to greater effect on ABBA's biggest hit, 'Dancing Queen'. The glissando appears again at the end of the first chorus to cleverly hide the key change for the second verse.

'He Is Your Brother' was part of the opening medley of the televised *Music For UNICEF* concert held at the United Nations Building in New York in January 1979, with stars of the day including the Bee Gees, John Denver, Earth, Wind & Fire, Olivia Newton-John, Rod Stewart, and Donna Summer singing along with ABBA. See the entry for 'Chiquitita' below for more about that gala event.

'She's My Kind of Girl'

Duration: 2.46
Released as a single in March 1970. Also released on the B-side of 'Ring Ring' 19 February 1973.

The oldest song on an ABBA record is not actually an ABBA song. In 1969, Stig Anderson arranged for protégés Björn and Benny to write and record music for the sexploitation film *Inga II*, filmed in Sweden by American producer Joseph W. Sarno, in the hope of launching an international music career. They recorded three songs: 'She's My Kind of Girl', 'Inga Theme', and the instrumental 'Where Are We All Headin'' (which they would rerecord the following year as 'Nånting är på väg' ('Something is coming') for their album *Lycka*). The former two titles were released as the duo's debut single in Sweden in 1970. Unfortunately the film was delayed and not released until 1971, retitled *The Seduction of Inga* (it was titled *Någon att älska—Somebody to Love*—in Sweden) and the film songs did not lead to a lasting international career for Björn and Benny.

However, in 1972, a Japanese music executive heard 'She's My Kind of Girl' in the office of an industry colleague in Paris—France had been the only country outside

Scandinavia to release the single. The Japanese executive thought the melancholy sound would be popular in Japan. The single was subsequently released by Epic Records in Japan, where it became a hit, peaking at No. 7 and selling a reported 188,000 copies (high figures for non-Japanese artists at that time).

In 1973, 'She's My Kind of Girl' was placed on the B-side of the English version single of 'Ring Ring' in Scandinavia, though Agnetha and Frida do not appear on the recording, and the label credited the song to Björn & Benny only. When the *Ring Ring* album was released outside Scandinavia, 'She's My Kind of Girl' was placed on side two, replacing the English version of 'Ring Ring', which had been moved to side one track one, replacing the Swedish version. This was probably because it had been the single's B-side, rather than for its qualities as a song. Thus, 'She's My Kind of Girl' became a *de facto* ABBA song and remains in place on CD versions of the album today.

Curiously, the song title does not include the word 'just', which is sung in the chorus.

'I Am Just a Girl'
Written by Benny Andersson, Stig Anderson, and Björn Ulvaeus
Duration: 3.02

'I Am Just a Girl' started life in September 1972 as 'Jag är blott en man' ('I am just a man'), written and produced by Benny and Björn, with lyrics by Stig Anderson, recorded by Swedish actor Jarl Kulle for the film *Ture Sventon*. It was released on a Polar single.

The backing track features a small orchestra rather than the usual group of musicians Benny and Björn would use on pop recordings. The orchestral arrangement was written by Sven-Olof Walldoff, who has quite some ABBA history. Walldoff had worked on arrangements for Agnetha's solo recordings since 1968, Björn's Hootenanny Singers in 1969, and also Björn & Benny's *Lycka* album in 1970, and he would go on to arrange the strings for ABBA on 'Honey, Honey', 'Mamma Mia', and 'Dancing Queen'. Most famously, he dressed in a Napoleonic uniform when he conducted the orchestra for ABBA's performance of 'Waterloo' at the Eurovision Song Contest in 1974.

At some point within the following six months, needing another track for their debut album, Björn, Benny, Agnetha, and Frida recorded new English vocals over the same backing track. 'I Am Just a Girl' is one of the few songs that features the four ABBA members singing the majority of song in unison and harmony, only broken when Agnetha takes the solo vocal in the middle eight. Like 'People Need Love', this girl lives in a male-dominated world, she sees herself as nothing special, until a man finally reciprocates her 'luff' (love), as Agnetha so charmingly expresses it. Björn and Benny would eventually improve in writing from a female perspective.

Swedish group Family Four recorded a version in 1973 for a single released by RCA Records, with a new Swedish lyric by Stig Anderson entitled 'Kalla't vad du vill' ('Call it what you want'), using the original backing track.

Like 'I Saw It in the Mirror' above, Kulle's original version 'Jag är blott en man' was included as an additional bonus on the *Ring Ring* Deluxe Edition in 2012.

'Rock'n Roll Band'
Duration: 3.09
Released on on the B-side of 'Ring Ring' [English version] internationally in 1973.

With the success of 'She's My Kind of Girl' in Japan, Björn and Benny had recorded several songs aimed at that market, and released another single, 'En Carousel' (see 'Merry-Go-Round' below). After that single failed to excite the Japanese record-buying public, Epic Records Japan sent a tune written by local composer Koichi Morita for the next single, for which the duo wrote lyrics entitled 'Love Has It's Ways' (*sic*.). The recording of that song did not feature Agnetha and Frida.

For the B-side, Björn & Benny recorded their own composition, 'Rock'n Roll Band'. Alas, upon release in November, the single was another flop, and that was the end of Björn and Benny's Japanese career, for now.

Later, 'Rock'n Roll Band' became another song revisited for the group's album. An additional guitar riff and long guitar solo were added, new vocals recorded that swapped two lines of the lyric and deleted lines the led into the choruses, and strong backing vocals by Agnetha and Frida were added. The guitar solo over the final choruses is probably the most interesting thing on the recording.

In most of the world, 'Rock'n Roll Band' was released on the B-side of the English 'Ring Ring' single; it was also the closing track on the *Ring Ring* album. It seems an odd choice to release such a wildly different song on the B-side of the group's first true international single release rather than another song that highlights the best the band can offer, but there was probably a method to the madness; in the late '50s and early '60s, American producer Phil Spector would issue rubbish tracks on the B-side of singles, so there was no mistaking the intended hit side. It is plausible that Polar was employing this same trick.

When ABBA performed 'Rock'n Roll Band' on their European concert tour between November 1974 and January 1975, and their Swedish *folkpark* tour in June and July 1975, Frida took the lead to more evenly spread the songs with solo lead vocals.

The title is a curiosity. 'Rock'n Roll Band' reads like an abbreviation of 'rocking roll band' rather than the intended 'rock and roll band'.

Non-Album Tracks, 1972–1973

'Merry-Go-Round'
Written by Benny Andersson, Stig Anderson, and Björn Ulvaeus.
Duration: 3.24
Released on the B-side of 'People Need Love' in May 1972.

'Merry-Go-Round' was the second attempt by Björn and Benny as a follow up single to 'She's My Kind of Girl' in Japan (see 'Santa Rosa' below). The vaguely oriental-sounding introduction was written specifically to appeal to Japanese record buyers. However, the single was a flop, and it was the beginning of the end for Björn & Benny's Japanese career—just one more single would be released, and that song would be composed by another songwriter.

'Merry-Go-Round' was issued as the B-side of 'People Need Love' in all territories where the single was released. The label credits only Björn & Benny, though Agnetha and Frida may be the vocalists on the 'merry, merry, merry, merry' coda. A Swedish version, 'En karusell', was released as a single by Björn & Benny in Scandinavia. The Swedish lead vocal was obviously recorded over the English version—at the end, the backing vocal 'merry, merry, merry, merry, merry-go-round' can clearly be heard.

Curiously, the Japanese single had the Swenglish title 'En Carousel' taken from the title of the Swedish version. The mix released in Japan was different to the B-side version, with more echo and an early fadeout during the final chorus.

'Santa Rosa'
Duration: 2.59
Released on the B-side of 'He Is Your Brother' in November 1972.

Looking to capitalise on their success in Japan with 'She's My Kind of Girl', Björn and Benny took a song they had started writing several years earlier, originally entitled 'Grandpa's Banjo', and created 'Santa Rosa' as a potential follow-up single. Already having the line 'I'd give anything to be back home in', the song's title was simply chosen from a map, though it should be noted that Spanish-sounding titles were popular at the time (for example, 'Is This the Way to Amarillo' by Tony Christie).

Though Björn and Benny had used their partners Agnetha and Frida on backing vocals on several recordings in the previous couple of years, the two women did not feature on 'Santa Rosa'. Despite the song being created especially for the Japanese market, it appears the marketers at Epic Records were not impressed, and the song was not released in Japan. Regardless, Björn and Benny, along with Agnetha and Frida, performed 'Santa Rosa' at the World Popular Song Festival in Tokyo in November 1972.

The recording did not go to waste, being released on the B-side of the second Björn & Benny, Agnetha & Anni-Frid single, 'He Is Your Brother'. Agnetha and Frida are credited on the label, though they do not sing on the recording at all. 'Santa Rosa' did not receive an international release until 1994, when it was included on the ABBA boxset *Thank You for the Music*.

'Åh, vilka tider'

Written by Benny Andersson, Stig Anderson, and Björn Ulvaeus.
Duration: 2.31
Released on the B-side of 'Ring ring (bara du slog en signal)' (Swedish version) 19 February 1973.

'Åh, vilka tider', which directly translates as 'oh, such times' but is better expressed as 'those were the days', was recorded in June 1972 for a planned second Björn & Benny album. Several Björn & Benny singles had been released since the duo's *Lycka* album in 1970, but as activity for the quartet Björn & Benny, Agnetha & Anni-Frid increased, the duo album was cancelled, leaving several recordings in limbo, many of which remain unreleased to this day.

Like many Björn & Benny tracks recorded in 1971 and 1972, 'Åh, vilka tider' features strong backing vocals from Agnetha and Frida. It is a typical *schlager* of the period. *Schlager* is a particularly syrupy form of popular music primarily in the northern parts of Western Europe, it is a German word that directly translates as 'hit song'. The lyrics are a look back to a past that may be remembered as more idyllic than it really was.

In February 1973, the song was released on the B-side of the Swedish version of 'Ring Ring' in Scandinavia. 'Åh, vilka tider' holds the distinction of being the only commercially-released song in ABBA's *oeuvre* not to have been recorded in English. As such, it did not achieve international release until 1994 on the *Thank You for the Music* boxset.

Waterloo

Sweden:	4 March 1974
UK:	17 May 1974
US:	July 1974
Current edition:	Universal Music/Polar CD 549 951-2
Personnel:	Benny Andersson: piano, moog, Mellotron, vocals
	Ola Brunkert: drums
	John 'Rabbit' Bundrick: keyboards
	Christer Eklund: saxophone
	Agnetha Fältskog: vocals
	Malando Gassama: congas
	Rutger Gunnarsson: bass
	Anni-Frid Lyngstad: vocals
	Per Sahlberg: bass
	Janne Schaffer: guitar
	Björn Ulvaeus: guitar, vocals
	Sven-Olof Walldoff: string arrangement

Recorded at Metronome Studio, Stockholm: September 1973–February 1974

Duration:	38 minutes

Produced by Benny Andersson and Björn Ulvaeus

Engineered by Michael B. Tretow

Chart position:	Sweden: 1
	UK: 28
	US: 145

Waterloo was the first ABBA album released in much of the world. By now, the group was officially known as ABBA, but the album sleeve featured the four individual names in parentheses, to remind listeners that this was the same group that had released *Ring Ring* the year before, which seems fairly pointless as most of the world outside of Northern Europe was completely unaware of the group Björn & Benny, Agnetha & Frida.

ABBA were coming closer to finding their own sound, but like *Ring Ring* the year before, *Waterloo* contains an eclectic mix of songs, with attempts at pop, rock, *schlager*, reggae, and funk. Like the previous album, there were as many songs with male lead vocals as female, though unlike that album, all the songs on *Waterloo* sound as if they were recorded by the same group.

During recording of tracks for the album, the songwriting team Andersson–Anderson–Ulvaeus was invited again to submit a song for the Eurovision Song Contest in 1974. They would pull out all stops to create a memorable sound, with an image to match. ABBA are seen on the album sleeve dressed in the glam costumes they had created for the song contest, with Napoleon lurking behind them—actually bassist Mike Watson in hat and cape.

Scandinavian copies of the album opened with the Swedish version of the title track, with the English version as the last track on side two. Most international versions and modern CD releases dropped the Swedish version, and moved the English version to side one, track one. Some countries tagged 1973's 'Ring Ring' on to the end of side two, either the original English-language version, or (in North America) a unique 1974 remix.

At the time of release, some critics assumed that the album had been quickly thrown together to capitalise on the Eurovision win. ABBA had in fact spent six months recording the album, and it was actually released a month before the song contest. In countries where the Eurovision connection was slight or even unknown, the reaction was more favourable. In *Rolling Stone* magazine, reviewer Ken Barnes wrote: 'With their concise, upbeat pop creations, Abba is much closer to the essential spirit of rock & roll than any number of self-indulgent hotshot guitarists or devotional ensembles handing down cosmo-dynamic enlightenment to the huddled masses'. Despite such enthusiastic reactions, and although the title track was a worldwide top ten hit, the *Waterloo* album was a minor international success.

'Waterloo'

Written by Benny Andersson, Stig Anderson, and Björn Ulvaeus. German lyric by Gerd Müller-Schwanke. French Lyric by Alain Boublil.
Duration: 2.45
Released as a single 4 March 1974.

Having failed to make it to the Eurovision Song Contest in 1973 with 'Ring Ring', Björn, Benny, and Stig set their sights on the 1974 contest to introduce ABBA to the world. Though the group had been successful in some countries, mostly in the northern half of Europe (remember Stig's earlier comment that there was a 'boundary of taste running through the middle of Brussels'?), so far they had failed to gain traction in the UK, no longer had a record deal in North America, and had made little impact in the rest of the world. Björn recalled: 'In one way it was an advantage having to wait another year before winning, because in the meantime we learned quite a lot about how things worked in other countries'.

Just as the year before, Björn and Benny sequestered themselves in their soon-to-be-famous songwriting cabin on the holiday island of Viggsö in the Stockholm Archipelago, east of the city, to come up with an ultra-catchy tune to conquer Eurovision and the world (the two ABBA couples and Stig all had summer homes on the island). Once the melody was completed, it was up to Stig to come up with a title and lyric. 'Thinking up a title is not just a kind of cynical mathematics; you have to be very careful to make the title fit the song,' he observed. 'You have to make it seem as though the title and lyric were born at the same moment as the tune.'

'I thought a long while, at least a week. I had a number of different ideas. One was "Honey Pie". I searched through my wife's cookbooks for honey pie, but still this wasn't quite right,' Stig recalled. 'In order to obtain additional ideas, I browsed through collections of quotations, and then I spotted Waterloo. "This is a great title," I thought, "a generally accepted term, even internationally."' Waterloo refers to the famous battle named for the nearby town in modern-day Belgium, which saw the defeat of Napoleon Bonaparte's French army by the British forces led by the duke of Wellington, and the Prussian army under the command of the Prince of Wahlstatt.

In 2018, Swedish actress Rebecca Ferguson (*Mission: Impossible—Fallout*) claimed that her British-born mother, Rosemary, had helped to translate the lyrics of 'Waterloo' from Swedish to English. Her Swedish husband was in the music industry and friends with Stig and ABBA. This is probably an exaggeration: Björn said in interviews during the '70s that though he and Benny were fluent in English, they had a native speaker cast their eyes over the lyrics, to ensure they were okay. It is more likely that this was Rosemary's contribution, if indeed there is any truth in the story.

ABBA worked long and hard in the studio to create a song that would captivate television audiences across Europe. They were clearly influenced by the glam pop movement then at its peak. Benny, Björn, and Micke (as Michael B. Tretow is known to friends) spent days and days in the studio, adding and removing instrumental and vocal elements, and even editing out half of the third chorus to keep the song under three minutes, the maximum length mandated in Eurovision rules.

In addition to the song, ABBA wanted their performance to stand out visually. 'I thought let's make a mark, let's be as different as possible so that at least, even if we end up ninth, people will still remember us,' Björn said. The group commissioned glamorous costumes from Swedish designer Inger Svenneke, with epaulets and chains to give a slight military look to tie in with the Napoleonic theme of the song. As a surprise element for the contest, which would be held in Brighton, England, Björn had guitar maker Göran Malmberg build him a silver star-shaped guitar, which would be kept hidden during rehearsals until it was revealed on the night of the song contest.

On 9 February 1974, 'Waterloo' easily won the Swedish selection contest, *Melodifestivalen*, with 302 points, ninety-one points ahead of the runner up. The single and similarly-titled album were released one month later, allowing for maximum exposure before the contest. First pressings of the Polar English-language single had a rough early mix, which was quickly replaced when the mistake was discovered. This version is a bonus track on the 2014 *Waterloo* Deluxe Edition CD.

The Eurovision Song Contest was held on 6 April 1974 at The Dome, part of the nineteenth-century complex built by the Prince Regent (later King George IV) in the seaside town. ABBA performed 'Waterloo' eighth of seventeen entries, and won the contest with twenty-four points, six points more than second place. 'We thought we had a good song but we also thought maybe it was a little out of style for the Eurovision Song Contest but as it turned out, everything went fine,' Benny said.

Following the win, 'Waterloo' went on to be a No. 1 single in much of Europe, including the UK. It was also a No. 4 hit in Australia, No. 6 in the US, and No. 7 in Canada, countries where the contest was little-known at the time. In Sweden, 'Waterloo' equaled the record set by 'Ring Ring' the previous year, with the album at No. 1, and the Swedish and English singles at Nos 2 and 3. By 1978, the song had reported worldwide sales of close to 6 million copies.

Eurovision may have introduced ABBA to the world, but 'Waterloo' also introduced Eurovision to a world beyond the reach of the European Broadcasting Union (EBU). Though a few songs from the contest had been hits around the world, the song contest itself was mostly unknown outside Western Europe, but today it is shown all over the planet. Björn said in 1980: 'We weren't particularly happy about being launched as a Eurovision group, but at that time it was virtually our only chance to reach outside Sweden. Being a Swedish group meant that nobody would listen to you'. Today, thanks to ABBA breaking down the proverbial doors, Sweden is the third-biggest supplier of popular music (after the US and UK), thanks to its in-demand songwriters and producers, supplying everyone from American idols to K-Pop superstars.

ABBA also recorded 'Waterloo' in Swedish, German, and French. A Spanish version was to be recorded during a promotional visit to Madrid in the wake of the contest, but it seems that this never happened. Aside from the Swedish version, the foreign language versions were not successful, as record buyers seemed to prefer the English version. The German version reportedly sold 1/25th the number of copies of the English version. 'Waterloo' would be the last time ABBA would record in a language other than English until 1979.

At some unknown time later in 1974, ABBA recorded new lyrics for the chorus for a thirty-second jingle for the BBC's Radio 1. It is not known if the jingle was played at the time; it resurfaced in a radio broadcast in 2015.

'Sitting in the Palmtree'
Duration: 3.39

Still in search of a signature sound, with 'Sitting in the Palmtree', ABBA try their hands at light reggae. The lyric, sung by Björn, is the rather odd story of a man who, having been rejected by his girlfriend, Ginny, climbs a palmtree and insists on staying at the top until she takes him back.

When performed in concert on ABBA's 1977 tour of Europe and Australia, Björn would jokingly introduce the song as being based on a true story that happened to a friend, sometimes identifying the friend as guitarist Lasse Wellander.

Benny has often been critical of his older songs, but this is a rare case where he has positive thoughts: '... nice song, nobody cares [for it], but I still like it,' he said in 2018.

'King Kong Song'
Duration: 3.14

ABBA's early albums are littered with quite quirky songs, perhaps none more so than 'King Kong Song'. The first verse, sung by Björn, tells the tale of a man watching the classic 1933 movie *King Kong*, becoming inspired to perform a new song with his band about a 'big, black, wild gorilla'. For the rest of the song, we hear just that, as Agnetha and Frida sing of turning the venue into a jungle and making everyone dance like gorillas. It is quite a clever trick, turning the song on itself, to become the subject of the song that is being sung. Lyricist Björn may not have even realised that is what he wrote.

The song led to one of ABBA's most embarrassing on-stage moments at a 1975 concert at Konserthuset in Stockholm. Björn recounts the story: 'When we came to one of the percussion breaks in the song, one of the girls started singing in the wrong place. One half of the band followed her, the other half played on like it was supposed to be, and after a while it was just chaos'. To add shame to embarrassment, many music insiders and friends were in the audience, including legendary American concert promoter Sid Bernstein (Bernstein had promoted The Beatles' tours in the US in the '60s, and wanted to do the same for ABBA).

In early 1977, 'King Kong Song' received quite a lot of radio airplay in Australia, thanks to the recent cinema release of the Dino De Laurentiis *King Kong* remake. As it had been the B-side of the 1974 single 'I've Been Waiting for You', the song actually entered the singles chart, peaking at No. 94 in Australia and No. 8 in New Zealand, where the single was listed as a double A-side.

Today, 'King Kong Song' is not held in high esteem by ABBA members. Benny frequently nominates the song for inclusion on the mock ABBA compilation *ABBA Wood*, a collection of ABBA's 'lesser' songs. Despite Benny's opinion, it is one of those fun songs that make the early ABBA such a treat to explore.

'Hasta Mañana'

Written by Benny Andersson, Stig Anderson, and Björn Ulvaeus. Spanish lyric by Buddy and Mary McCluskey.
Duration: 3.05

'Hasta Mañana' was the last song recorded for ABBA's *Waterloo* album. The title and lyric came to Stig Anderson while on holiday in the Canary Islands. He had taken a tape of the backing track to try to write a lyric to the new song. Everywhere he went he heard the phrase '*hasta mañana*', a Spanish phrase meaning 'until tomorrow', a common way of saying goodbye. He realised 'Here is a title'. Once he completed the full lyric, he then had to phone back to Stockholm, shouting the lyrics down a dodgy long-distance phone line, much to the amusement of passersby.

With the lyrics completed, ABBA were having trouble finding the best way to interpret the vocal. 'We discovered rather quickly that none of us could sing the song and had given up after a while,' Agnetha recalled. 'I was alone in the studio playing around with it and it occurred to me that I could sing it like ['50s balladeer] Connie Francis. So I sang it very sensitively and it began to take shape.'

At one stage, Benny, Björn, and Stig considered 'Hasta Mañana' a contender for the 1974 Eurovision Song Contest, as it was in the same vein as the previous few years' winners, a solo female ballad. Stig recalled 'I had already decided for "Waterloo". "Let me decide this," I said to Björn and Benny, "and if this is a disaster, you can cut my throat afterwards."' It is incredible to think that after so much work had gone into making 'Waterloo' a standout for submission to Eurovision that they might even consider another song. But in the end the trio wisely decided that 'Waterloo' would be a better showcase for the group.

Though the Spanish feel and title of the song would seem to make 'Hasta Mañana' an ideal candidate for release as a single in Spain, it was not released in that format there. However, it was released as the follow-up single to 'Waterloo' in Italy, where it peaked at No. 30, and South Africa, where it reached No. 2.

In Australia, 'Hasta Mañana' was placed on the B-side of the late-1974 single 'So Long' (see what they did there, putting two songs with titles that are forms of saying 'goodbye' on the one single). In 1976, at the height of Australian Abbamania in the wake of the broadcast of the record-breaking TV special *The Best of ABBA* (aka *ABBA in Australia*), it would be an Australian top twenty chart single, while across the ditch in New Zealand, it reached No. 9.

Six years after the song was recorded, Agnetha and Frida entered the studio with Michael B. Tretow to record vocals in Spanish for an album for release in Latin America, *Gracias Por La Música* (Thank You for the Music). 'Hasta Mañana' was an obvious choice due to its Spanish title and *schlager* feel.

In the twenty-first century, 'Hasta Mañana' is one of several ABBA songs in the repertoire of Benny Anderssons Orkester, Benny's big band that has recorded several albums and tours Sweden most summers. It can also be heard in the movie sequel *Mamma Mia! Here We Go Again*, sung by BAO vocalist Helen Sjöholm, during a party scene late in the film.

'Hasta Mañana' was subject to two high-profile cover versions in the '70s. In 1976, Australian singer Judy Stone released a cover that charted alongside ABBA's original version. Reportedly, Ms Stone was less than happy that ABBA's version was taking attention away from her single. The following year, American singer Debbie Boone (daughter of '50s crooner Pat Boone) released a version as the B-side of her million-selling single 'You Light Up My Life', exposing ABBA's song to a wider audience, for those who bothered to flip the single.

'My Mama Said'
Duration: 3.14

As we have seen, for their second album, ABBA was still in search of their own sound. On 'My Mama Said', they experimented with a funky jazz sound, one they would not return to. The guitar solo by Janne Schaffer, the first one to appear on an ABBA song, is one of the few times an ABBA record features truly improvised playing

The lyric is another childhood story, this one detailing the fight between a teenage girl and her mother about the girl's boyfriend, Fred, and being allowed to go out with him. The verses feature a high, soft unison vocal from Agnetha and Frida, singing the part of the young girl, while Björn joins them on the lower-toned choruses, with the mother's responses. A similar vocal device had been used on Cat Stevens' 1970 single 'Father and Son'. The lyric is quite bleak for ABBA, especially in the final chorus where the mother thinks that her daughter would rather see her dead.

'Dance (While the Music Still Goes On)'
Duration: 3.05

Following the success of the 'Ring Ring' singles and album in Scandinavia and parts of Europe, and a successful eighty-stop Swedish *folkpark* tour during the summer of 1973, the decision was made for the quartet to record a second album, with this track being the first song recorded for that project. By this time, the group had acquired the name ABBA, an acronym of their first names, first coined by Stig Anderson, who had gotten tired of rattling off the four names whenever talking about the group. There had been some resistance to the name within the group, as Abba was the name of a Swedish canned fish manufacturer. Björn and Benny particularly did not want to be associated with fish products. In fact, though the name ABBA had been used informally for the previous six months, the studio documents for the first recording session for this song in September 1973 still list the group moniker Björn & Benny, Agnetha & Frida, but this would change for the next recording session the following month.

'Dance (While the Music Still Goes On)' is the first of several ABBA songs to break the usual pop song structure of verse/chorus/verse/chorus/middle eight/chorus. It opens with a short eight-bar passage sung by Agnetha, which is repeated in the middle eight, followed by the chorus: there is no verse. The first chorus is sung by Björn and Benny, with Agnetha and Frida joining in on the second and subsequent choruses. With layers and layers of vocals, and a drum beat similar to the Ronettes' 1963 multi-million seller 'Be My Baby', 'Dance' is one of ABBA's best examples of applying a Spectoresque Wall of Sound.

The recording is one of only two in ABBA's catalogue to feature a musician other than Benny playing keyboards (the other being 1973's 'I Am Just a Girl'). Guitarist Janne Schaffer had brought his friend, American keyboardist John 'Rabbit' Bundrick to the recording studio. Bundrick was an in-demand session player, who had played with names like Johnny Nash, Bob Marley, Free, Sandy Denny, and Donovan, and would later play on *The Rocky Horror Picture Show* soundtrack, and work with The Who, Joan Armatrading, Eric Burdon, Roger Waters, and Mick Jagger, among others. Bundrick ended up playing the keyboards on 'Dance', but for unknown reasons was not credited on the album sleeve.

Though 'Dance (While the Music Still Goes On)' was never a single, it was included on ABBA's first *Greatest Hits* volume—every other track on the album had been a single in at least one country. However, it was the B-side of 'Honey, Honey' in North America, Australia, and New Zealand, and of 'Fernando' in France and Belgium (though that came after its inclusion on those countries' *Greatest Hits* album).

'Honey, Honey'

Written by Benny Andersson, Stig Anderson, and Björn Ulvaeus.
Duration: 2.55
Released as a single *circa* June 1974.

The ABBA sound is finally starting to gel on 'Honey, Honey', recorded in October 1973. Agnetha and Frida sing together with their famous third voice, while the middle section of the song features a double-tracked Björn vocal. The whole recording has been sped up ever so slightly, raising the pitch.

'Honey, Honey' is another song with an unusual structure. It features verses and a middle section that is double the length of the usual middle eight, but it does not really have a chorus. The song fades out on a repeat of the first verse. In the 2006 book *Mamma Mia! How Can I Resist You*, Benny talks about the song's structure: 'It is something of a strange song because it has no end really. Normally a song would have a beginning, a middle and an end or it would have a verse, chorus, verse, chorus and so on. "Honey, Honey" doesn't do either of those things. It just starts and goes on but it has no ending'.

'Honey, Honey' was the follow-up single to the Eurovision winner 'Waterloo' in most of the world, excluding the UK, where a new remix of 1973's 'Ring Ring' was released instead. ATV Music, the British publishers of 'Honey, Honey' saw the hit potential and arranged for a cover version to be recorded by the male/female duo Sweet Dreams, who were rewarded with a top ten hit. The cover version was also a minor hit in Australia, alongside ABBA's original version, while in the US and Canada, ABBA's version was a bigger hit, thanks to a push by Atlantic Records.

ABBA also recorded the song in Swedish for the B-side of the Swedish language 'Waterloo' single.

In the 1990s, recording engineer Michael B. Tretow recorded a quirky cover version with his daughter, Sofia, handling the lead vocals. Tretow's version cleverly incorporated musical motifs from thirteen other ABBA songs, including 'Mamma Mia', 'Dancing Queen', 'Gimme! Gimme! Gimme! (A Man After Midnight)', and 'The Day Before You Came'. The Tretows' version was released on the American CD *ABBA—A Tribute: The 25th Anniversary Celebration* in 1999.

That same year, 'Honey, Honey' was featured as the first full song in the stage musical *Mamma Mia!*, based on ABBA's songs. The musical, set on an idyllic Greek island, tells the story of a single mother, Donna, and her daughter, Sophie. Sophie is about to marry her fiancé, Sky, and wants to invite the father she has never met. She finds her mother's diary from the summer before her birth, and discovers that there are three men who could be her father, so she invites them all. Shenanigans ensue, set to a soundtrack of twenty-two ABBA songs.

'Watch Out'
Duration: 3.46
Released as the B-side of 'Waterloo', 4 March 1974.

'Watch Out' was another attempt at a rock song, and possibly the most un-ABBA-like recording in the entire ABBA catalogue. With Björn's gruff lead vocal, Agnetha and Frida's shrieking backing vocals, roaring guitars, squealing synthesizers, inexplicably ending with a booming thunderclap and the sound of falling rain, it almost works. The recording is just not loud enough. Considering the pop and *schlager* that ABBA was creating at the time (recording started in the same sessions that birthed 'Waterloo', 'Sitting in the Palmtree', and 'Hasta Mañana'), one wonders what the inspiration for this song was.

Polar Music put this song on the B-side of the 'Waterloo' single. Like 'Rock'n Roll Band' on the back of 'Ring Ring', it was probably so no one would confuse it with the Eurovision contestant and take attention from 'Waterloo'.

'What About Livingstone'
Duration: 2.54

'What About Livingstone' refers to David Livingstone, the nineteenth-century Scottish missionary and explorer famed for searching for the source of the River Nile in central Africa. He is best remembered in the quote 'Doctor Livingstone, I presume?'

In 1866, Livingstone embarked on his third expedition in Africa. After several years with no contact from the expedition, the *New York Herald* sent explorer Henry Morton Stanley in search of the famed explorer. Upon finding Livingstone in 1871 (in Ujiji in modern-day Tanzania), Stanley uttered that world-famous phrase.

NASA's manned moon missions were still quite topical in the news in 1973, when 'What About Livingstone' was recorded in October. Apollo 17, the sixth moon landing, had taken place in December 1972. There had been much criticism of the continuing moon missions, watching astronauts hitting golf balls and driving moon-buggies, with seemingly little benefit for great expense. Public interest in the moon missions was decreasing, and though further missions were planned, Apollo 17 would be the last.

The year 1973 also marked the centenary of David Livingstone's death. Coincidentally, in July and August, Swedish television broadcast the 1971 British docu-drama series *The Search for the Nile*. Livingstone featured in three of the six episodes, with episode five, *Find Livingstone*, focused on Stanley's search for the explorer. Around the same time, daily newspapers advertised a set of collectable medallions featuring ten world explorers, including David Livingstone, with the advertisement headed *De tio som upptäkte världen åt oss* (the ten who discovered the world for us). It seems likely that either the television series or the medallion set—or both—came to lyricist Björn's attention.

'What About Livingstone' compares the discoveries of explorers of past centuries with the astronauts as modern-day explorers. The song's narrator overhears some men reading the newspaper and laughing at the thought of men flying to the moon, wondering 'what's it good for anyway.' She counters their negativity, explaining that explorations of this kind, like Livingstone's expeditions to Africa, are of great benefit to the world.

'Gonna Sing You My Lovesong'
Duration: 3.35

This charming and wistful Frida-sung ballad was the last recorded ABBA song to feature lyrics written by Benny. The lyric could have been inspired by real-life events. When Benny and Frida first got together in 1969, Benny was still in a relationship with another woman, though it was essentially over. That relationship indeed came to an end shortly afterwards, and the new couple was soon living together.

The musical backing features a Mellotron, a cheap way of getting the effect of orchestral strings on a recording, which Benny had previously played on 'Another Town, Another Train'. Though the potential single 'Honey, Honey' featured real strings, 'Gonna Sing You My Lovesong' seemed always destined to remain an album track.

'Suzy-Hang-Around'
Duration: 3.11

Another oddity in the ABBA catalogue, 'Suzy-Hang-Around' is the only ABBA song with a lead vocal by Benny. He often said that he could 'sing in tune, but it is an ugly sound', so he preferred others to sing the songs he had written.

Like 'Me and Bobby and Bobby's Brother' on *Ring Ring*, 'Suzy-Hang-Around' is another tale of childhood remembrance. But this time the boys do not want to play with the young girl (who might be the narrator's sister; Benny does have a younger sister, Eva-Lis), despite admonishments from his mother. And like that song, the lyric was written by Benny. 'It's a pretty good tune though, and the recording is quite nice,' he once proudly declared.

ABBA

Sweden:	21 April 1975
UK:	7 June 1975
US:	28 August 1975
Current edition:	Universal Music/Polar CD 549 952-2
Personnel:	Benny Andersson: piano, clavinet, synthesizer, vocals
	Ulf Andersson: saxophones
	Ola Brunkert: drums
	Agnetha Fältskog: vocals
	Bruno Glenmark: trumpet
	Rutger Gunnarsson: bass
	Björn J'son Lindh: string and horn arrangements
	Anni-Frid Lyngstad: vocals
	Roger Palm: drums
	Janne Schaffer: guitar
	Finn Sjöberg: guitar
	Björn Ulvaeus: guitar, vocals
	Sven-Olof Walldoff: string arrangement
	Mike Watson: bass
	Lasse Wellander: guitar
Duration:	37 minutes

Recorded at Glenstudio, Stocksund; Metronome Studio, Stockholm: August 1974–March 1975

Produced and arranged by Benny Andersson and Björn Ulvaeus

Engineered by Michael B. Tretow

Chart position:	Sweden: 1
	UK: 13
	US: 174

ABBA finally found their sound with their third, self-titled album. Almost gone are the experiments in musical genres that populated the first two albums. Those albums had featured an almost equal distribution of vocals between the male and female halves of the group. On *ABBA*, Agnetha's and Frida's voices dominate, with almost half of the eleven songs sung by the two women in unison, creating what became known as the famous 'third voice', three songs with solo leads by either Agnetha or Frida, only two lead vocals from Björn, and for the only time on an ABBA record, an instrumental piece led by Benny. The album was a showcase for the entire group.

For the first time, Benny and Björn did not feel rushed to put an album out to a fixed timetable. They worked on the recordings until they felt they were ready, continuing to record overdubs and rework some songs over several months. Also for the first time, songs were attempted during the recording sessions that were destined for the so-called vault, never to be released. The album's release date was pushed back several times from an initial scheduled date of late 1974, until *ABBA* was ready in April 1975.

Lead single 'I Do, I Do, I Do, I Do, I Do' was a major European and Australian hit, but it was the next two singles, 'SOS' and 'Mamma Mia', that saw Abbamania explode, particularly in Australia and the UK, and those songs proved to the world that ABBA was not a one-hit wonder.

The album's sleeve was a wry comment aimed at ABBA's domestic critics, showing the group living a champagne lifestyle in a limousine and the foyer of a high-class hotel, ironically luxuries the group could not afford at the time.

In 1975, Mats Olsson wrote in Swedish newspaper *Expressen* 'ABBA has polished their style and become more daring. There are no weak songs here'. Phil Alexander wrote in American music magazine *Cash Box* 'One of the most expertly engineered and mixed collaborations of its genre. That genre lies somewhere between the structural integrity of Bela Bartok and the rockability of Elton [John]'.

In the wake of the huge international success of 'SOS' and 'Mamma Mia', the album massively outsold the previous two. It was the first ABBA album to top the charts somewhere outside of Scandinavia, when it reached No. 1 in Australia in December 1975. Uniquely, every song from the album appeared on a single side somewhere in the world.

The Deluxe Edition released in 2012 came with a bonus DVD that featured the record-breaking television special *ABBA In Australia*.

'Mamma Mia'

Written by Benny Andersson, Stig Anderson, and Björn Ulvaeus. Spanish lyric by Buddy and Mary McCluskey.
Duration: 3.32
Released as a single in November 1975

ABBA excelled at producing happy, cheerful-sounding songs with an undercurrent of melancholy. Perhaps none more so than 'Mamma Mia'. It is the happiest sounding song in the world, but the lyric tells the tragic tale of a protagonist whose lover repeatedly cheats on her, making her 'angry and sad', repeatedly breaking up with him, but she's not strong enough to resist him and 'could never let [him] go'.

For the recording of 'Mamma Mia', Benny and Björn moved away from the 'wall of sound' aesthetics that had been used on many recordings since 'Ring Ring' in 1973, though that production style would continue throughout the ABBA era. '1975 was when we learned what to do,' Benny recalled in *ABBA: The Official Photo Book* in 2014. '"Mamma Mia" was the first song we arranged tightly. Almost all the songs after that had the same type of arrangement. All the instruments contribute something that deviates from the melody line. Listen to the marimbas, listen to the guitars. They're playing their own defined lines.'

Everything about the song draws the listener in from the get-go. Benny explains, 'The opening of "Mamma Mia", that "tick-tock, tick-tock" is played on a marimba, which is an instrument of wood blocks, like a larger version of a xylophone, really.' The melody of the guitar riff is repeated in the second half of the verse. The third voice created by Agnetha and Frida singing in unison. 'On the chorus we stripped everything out,' Björn remembered. 'Suddenly the chorus stood right out, thanks to something as simple as that.' Recording engineer Michael B. Tretow has said of 'Mamma Mia': 'It's the whole idea of ABBA put together in one track'. *Rolling Stone* described the song as 'a greatest-hits album in three and a half minutes'.

'Mamma Mia' was the last song recorded for ABBA's third album. It was the opening track, but unbelievably this stand out song was not planned as a single.

Coinciding with the release of the album, ABBA made four promotional film clips with director Lasse Hallström: 'Mamma Mia', 'SOS', 'Bang-A-Boomerang', and 'I Do, I Do, I Do, I Do, I Do'. The four clips were made not necessarily to promote singles, but to promote the album as a whole as well as the band itself. Indeed, the four clips were played as a television special in Sweden titled *4 × ABBA*. 'I Do, I Do, I Do, I Do, I Do' was released as a single with the album, while 'SOS' was planned as the follow-up.

In August, the promotional film clip for 'Mamma Mia' was played on the Australian music television programme *Countdown*. Reaction was immediate, with viewers flooding the television station, record shops, and RCA, ABBA's Australian record company, with requests to buy the single. RCA contacted Polar Music for permission to release 'Mamma Mia' as a single, but Stig Anderson declined, saying that 'the Australians had already released so many singles' (there had been five in the previous twelve months after 'Waterloo', plus a four-track EP).

Under increasing public pressure, eventually Stig relented, and ABBA was rewarded with a No. 1 single for ten weeks. 'That we finally did give permission depended upon a desire to test "Mamma Mia", to see just how strong it was,' Stig recalled. 'The fact that it was the first song on the album certainly indicated that we had great confidence in it. And we were still a little doubtful. That which happened in Australia far exceeded our wildest expectations. "Mamma Mia" proved to be considerably stronger than we thought.'

As a result, the single was released around the world, and in January 1976 became ABBA's first British chart-topper since 'Waterloo' over eighteen months earlier. Björn reminisced for the Australian ABBAWORLD exhibition in 2010: 'We had an uphill struggle after "Waterloo" and our follow-up singles didn't do well. Then the Australians came to our rescue. They released "SOS" and "Mamma Mia" and both songs made the charts in a big way down under. Suddenly everyone else around the world realised there was life in the band that was supposed to be dead. I'm forever grateful to the Australians for that'.

'Mamma Mia' would go on to revive ABBA again, not once but twice. In 1994, it featured in the two Australian films *The Adventures of Priscilla, Queen of the Desert* and *Muriel's Wedding*, during the ABBA revival of the early '90s following the release of the compilation CD *ABBA Gold*. Five years later, the song gave its title to the musical based on ABBA's songs, which opened in London 'coincidentally' on the twenty-fifth anniversary of ABBA's Eurovision win. The musical has since spread around the world, playing to over 65 million people and has been translated into twenty-one languages. Of course, the song would also be included in the 2008 film version, sung by three-time Oscar winner Meryl Streep, and in the 2018 sequel *Mamma Mia! Here We Go Again*, where it was sung by Lily James, playing the younger version of Streep's character Donna.

In 1980, 'Mamma Mia' was an obvious choice for the Spanish-language album of ABBA hits *Gracias Por La Música*.

'Hey, Hey Helen'
Duration: 3.16

'Hey, Hey Helen' is one of two songs recorded for the *ABBA* album with minor political overtones. Divorce was a controversial and much-discussed topic during the '70s, with no-fault divorce laws introduced in some countries and a subsequent rise in the divorce rate.

The lyric may have been partially inspired by the 1973 British television series *Helen: A Woman of Today*. The thirteen-episode series about the struggles of a recently divorced woman had aired in Sweden between January and April 1974, a few months before the song was recorded, though lyricist Björn has claimed that he does not remember the series. The song's lyric even features part of the programme's title in the line 'and the price you pay/to be called a woman of today'.

The backing track was one of ABBA's last attempts at glam rock, with strong drums and percussion, grinding guitars and bass, and a funky keyboard break. Listen for the two piano notes after each line in the chorus—in each chorus, they follow a different pattern, mostly descending but sometimes ascending. Another one of those special treats hidden in ABBA's songs.

'Tropical Loveland'
Written by Benny Andersson, Stig Anderson, and Björn Ulvaeus.
Duration: 3.05

After 'Sitting in the Palmtree' on *Waterloo* the year before, ABBA tried their hand at reggae styles one more time with the delightful 'Tropical Loveland'. The lyric is a fairly generic love song, inviting a lover to join the singer at an unnamed tropical getaway. Despite the inconsequential tone, Frida's sincere vocal invites the listener along.

This song would be Frida's only solo lead on the *ABBA* album, compared to Agnetha's two leads, 'SOS' and 'I've Been Waiting for You'. In later years, Benny and Björn would say that they tried to equal out the solo leads between the two women, but it also depended on the voice that was best suited to the song. 'Tropical Loveland' is also a rare opportunity to hear Benny play one of his favourite instruments, the accordion, on an ABBA record. His father and grandfather had taught him to play the instrument at a young age, giving him his first accordion for his sixth birthday. The three would entertain family and neighbours as 'Benny's Trio'.

Though 'Tropical Loveland' would never be a single A-side, ABBA performed the song on two television specials in early 1976 in West Germany and Australia. Perhaps coincidentally, 'Tropical Loveland' would be the B-side of the then brand-new single 'Fernando' in both countries.

'SOS'
Written by Benny Andersson, Stig Anderson, and Björn Ulvaeus.
Duration: 3.22
Released as a single in June 1975.

'SOS' is widely regarded as ABBA's first truly classic song, even by ABBA members: '"SOS" was probably our first really good song,' Benny said in 2006. With its piano-led opening and synth-riff that appears throughout the song, Agnetha's pleading lead vocal in the verses, and its strong two-part chorus, it is an obvious stand out on the *ABBA* album, especially when sandwiched between the pleasant but inconsequential 'Tropical Loveland' and the Björn-led pseudo-funk of 'Man in the Middle'.

Pete Townshend of The Who told *Rolling Stone* magazine in 1981: 'I remember hearing "S.O.S." on the radio in the States and realizing that it was Abba. But it was too late, because I was already transported by it. I just thought it was such a great sound, you know—great bass drum and the whole thing. They make great records'. Similar comments attributed to John Lennon are probably apocryphal and mixed up with Townshend's—by the time the single was on the airwaves in the US, where the former Beatle had relocated in 1971, Lennon had retired from public life and was not speaking to the media, except about important personal milestones.

Amazingly for a song that sounds like an instant hit, 'SOS' was the third single released from the *ABBA* album, in September 1975, five months after the album. 'SOS' would restore ABBA's fortunes in the UK, where each ABBA single following 'Waterloo' in 1974 had charted progressively lower, until 'I Do, I Do, I Do, I Do, I Do' in mid-1975 slightly reversed that trend. Six weeks after entering the singles chart, 'SOS' peaked at No. 6. Björn said in the official *ABBA Magazine* in 1980 'After ["Waterloo"] we had a struggle convincing people that we were no one-hit wonders because disc jockeys and reporters had made up their minds that this was something that wasn't going to last for more than half a year'.

In Australia, 'SOS' would be ABBA's third No. 1 single, where it followed 'I Do, I Do, I Do, I Do, I Do' and 'Mamma Mia' at the top of the chart, giving ABBA fourteen consecutive weeks at No. 1 from October 1975 to January 1976.

A curious feature can be heard in the third chorus, one of many of those hidden treats that make ABBA's songs special. Rather than just repeating the chorus, the line 'the love you gave me' was changed to 'and the love you gave me'. Most cover versions miss this trick, though it did appear in the version performed in the movie version of the musical *Mamma Mia!*, sung by actors Meryl Streep and Pierce Brosnan and produced by Benny.

Other artists have been inspired by 'SOS'. Sex Pistol Glen Matlock admitted to taking inspiration from 'SOS' for the band's third single 'Pretty Vacant', though he has given contradictory details of which section of the song was 'taken' from 'SOS'—either the song's introduction, based on the piano riff in the introduction of 'SOS', or the chorus, based on the 'when you're gone' section—and whether it was an homage that he snuck past the other band members, or a pisstake on the perceived simplicity of ABBA's song.

A more obvious inspiration is found in the refrain in the 1983 Dolly Parton–Kenny Rogers duet 'Islands in the Stream', written by The Bee Gees, which bears resemblance to the 'when you're gone' melody. Picking up on the resemblance, when Australian singer and avowed ABBA fan Kylie Minogue performed 'Islands in the Stream' in a BBC radio broadcast concert to launch her 2018 album *Golden*, her backing singers sang ABBA's 'when your gone' lyrics during this section of the song.

The song's quiet verse–loud chorus structure may have been an influence on the grunge movement of the '90s. Nirvana frontman Kurt Cobain was a professed ABBA fan; that group's breakthrough hit 'Smells Like Teen Spirit' and other songs certainly follow that template.

Controversially, the chorus of the 1988 dance hit 'Bring Me Edelweiss', by Austrian dance act Edelweiss, took the chorus melody of 'SOS'. Stig Anderson as publisher and co-writer had given the band permission, claiming that he wrote that particular part of the song, but had not gotten permission from songwriters Benny and Björn, who subsequently sued Stig for lost royalties.

Despite that drama, Benny and Björn approved a sampling of 'SOS' in 2015 on a track entitled 'Coupé in C Minor', on a free download album *Peace Tracks*, created by the Talking Peace Festival collective to commemorate International Peace Day on 21 September. The track also featured American minimalist composer and musician Philip Glass, Melissa Auf der Maur, a former member of the rock band Hole, and musicians from seven African and Asian countries. *Peace Tracks* featured another track that sampled ABBA's 1981 song 'Soldiers' from *The Visitors* album.

Agnetha recorded a Swedish version of 'SOS', using ABBA's backing track, for her 1975 solo album *Elva kvinnor i ett hus* (*Eleven women in one house*), at the insistence of her record company, CBS Cupol. This album would be her last for the company, as her contract would expire at the end of the year. Agnetha had been with Cupol as a solo artist since her first single in 1968. Indeed, all ABBA records released before 1976 included the credit 'Agnetha by courtesy of CBS-Cupol' on the sleeves and labels. The album had been long-delayed, with sessions going on for almost eighteen months, and her previous album having been released in 1971. With only one compilation album and a couple of singles in the interim, none of which were particularly big sellers, Cupol wanted one guaranteed hit with some ABBA magic on the album.

'Man in the Middle'
Duration: 3.00

In mid-'70s Sweden, ABBA were under constant criticism from members of the so-called *progg* movement for creating music simply for 'entertainment', for not being political in their music. *Progg*, derived from the word 'progressive', was a left-wing anti-commercial movement that rose in the late '60s. Unlike British and American prog rock, with overblown, pompous recordings and songs with esoteric themes, Swedish *progg* was anti-elitist, with an attitude of 'anyone can have a go', probably more in keeping with the burgeoning punk movements in London and New York.

'Man in the Middle', with its critique of a rich fat cat riding around in his limousine, eating lobster and caviar and drinking champagne with a pretty young girl, while 'the rest of us drink a beer', is probably the closest to a political statement in an ABBA song until the *Super Trouper* album five years later. The song itself is another attempt at funk, though it is a little too pop to be really funky.

Björn sings lead on this song, which appeared on side one of the *ABBA* album, and was also on the B-side of the 'SOS' single.

'Bang-A-Boomerang'
Written by Benny Andersson, Stig Anderson, and Björn Ulvaeus.
Duration: 3.04

Following ABBA's triumph in the Eurovision Song Contest in 1974, the Andersson–Anderson–Ulvaeus team was invited to submit a song for the 1975 Swedish selection. Logic dictated that though ABBA would not enter the competition again, having achieved their goal of launching the group into the world, the songwriting trio would submit another Polar act, Svenne & Lotta. Svenne Hedlund had been the lead singer of Benny's pre-ABBA group Hep Stars;

Lotta, his wife, joined the band as co-lead singer in 1968, as the band transitioned from rock 'n' roll to '60s pop to *schlager*. The song 'Bang-A-Boomerang', which Benny and Björn were working on in late 1974 for the next ABBA album, was passed on to the duo for their Eurovision bid.

'Bang-A-Boomerang' originally had a different melody for the verse and slightly different melody in parts of the chorus. Benny and Björn were not happy with the original version, so they scrapped it, wrote a new melody for the verse, and tweaked the chorus. Curiously, the original version made it out into the world, when Danish singer Ulla Pia recorded a cover version 'Som en boomerang' ('Like a boomerang') in 1975. It seems that a copy of the early version had been supplied to the singer's record company, EMI, by mistake, on which her recording was based. As it was released as the B-side of a single ('Til et solgyldent land'), it seems that it went unnoticed for decades.

When Svenne & Lotta came third in *Melodifestivalen*, and thus failed to qualify for the Eurovision Song Contest, Benny and Björn decided 'Bang-A-Boomerang' was too good a song to waste and had Agnetha and Frida record new vocals on the existing backing track for *ABBA*. Svenne & Lotta were not happy with this development, as their version was subsequently seen by many as a cover of the ABBA song.

The lyric uses a boomerang, the returning throwing tool most famously used by Australian aborigines, as a metaphor for love: if you give love, you will get love in return.

ABBA obviously had faith in the song's potential; it was one of four tracks from the *ABBA* album for which they made promotional films (known today as music videos) in April 1975. 'Bang-A-Boomerang' was only released as a single in France, which was never one of ABBA's biggest markets, with only three No. 1 singles. This was one of the least successful, peaking at a lowly No. 59.

'I Do, I Do, I Do, I Do, I Do'
Written by Benny Andersson, Stig Anderson, and Björn Ulvaeus.
Duration: 3.15
Released as a single in April 1975.

'The whole feel of "I Do, I Do, I Do, I Do, I Do" is inspired by the sound of Billy Vaughn,' Benny says. 'He was an American bandleader who had a number of hits in Europe through the 1950s, numbers like "Sail Along Silv'ry Moon" and "Twilight Time". And one of Billy Vaughn's trademark sounds was using two saxes playing in harmony. So the two saxes on "I Do, I Do, I Do, I Do, I Do" [overdubbed by Ulf Andersson] are a deliberate homage to his music.'

With such obvious strong potential hits 'SOS', 'Mamma Mia', and even 'Bang-A-Boomerang', it is surprising that this '50s big band throwback was released as the single to launch the *ABBA* album. Though perhaps not: pop culture was going through a '50s revival at the time, in the wake of the 1973 American film *American Graffiti*, the British film *That'll Be The Day* the same year, and the television series *Happy Days* that premiered in 1974 and ran for ten years. Though those films featured '50s rock 'n' roll soundtracks, there was a general interest in '50s culture, so perhaps it was not so strange after all.

Björn said 'this is a very commercial song. We did that because it had a chance to get into the charts in England.' Despite Björn's confidence, the single barely dented the British top forty, peaking at No. 38. However, elsewhere is was quite a hit, reaching the top ten across Europe, No. 12 in Canada, No. 15 in the US, and becoming ABBA's first chart topper in Australia and New Zealand.

The original recording featured two verses that were edited out of the song before release: 'Let's get together/every day will be better/I love you/I do, I do, I do, I do, I do/Leave it or take it/I believe we can make it/don't you too?/I do, I do, I do, I do, I do'. The two verses were replaced by a saxophone break. Curiously, the lyrics for these lost verses were included in all sheet music folios and lyric sheets.

'I Do, I Do, I Do, I Do, I Do' would make a memorable appearance in the 1994 Australian film *Muriel's Wedding*, the story of a young, lonely, ABBA-loving woman. Having transformed herself and finally having her fantasy wedding, the song is played during her walk up the aisle, much to her groom's and the congregation's surprise and obvious discomfort.

'Rock Me'
Duration: 3.03
Released on the B-side of 'I Do, I Do, I Do, I Do, I Do' in April 1975.

The *ABBA* album would feature only two lead vocals from Björn, the least so far on an ABBA album. Subsequent albums would include at most just one Björn lead.

'Rock Me' was originally recorded as 'Baby', with lead vocals by Agnetha (see 'ABBA Undeleted' in Appendix I for more about that song). Björn and Benny were not happy with that version, so wrote a new lyric that would be sung by Björn. The original backing track was retained, in a key slightly too high for Björn. It is likely that varispeed was utilised to allow him to record within his vocal range, though you can still hear the strain in his voice on the higher notes. 'Rock Me' features a trick also used on 'Mamma Mia', when most of the backing instruments stop playing during the third chorus, though this was much more effective in the latter song.

'Rock Me' was released on the B-side of 'I Do, I Do, I Do, I Do, I Do' almost simultaneous with the *ABBA* album in April 1975. In 1976, during the era of rampant Abbamania 'down under', the single was flipped and 'Rock Me' became a chart hit in its own right in Australia (peaking at No. 4) and New Zealand (No. 2). 'Rock Me' was ABBA's last stab at '70s glam rock.

'Rock Me' is one of the few songs that would be performed on all of ABBA's concert tours from 1975 onwards. It would also be included on *Greatest Hits Vol. 2* in 1979, thanks to its status as a top ten hit in Australia and New Zealand—the only pre-1976 song on ABBA's second official compilation album.

'Intermezzo no 1'
Duration: 3.48

ABBA's only truly instrumental recording started life under the title 'Bach-låten' ('the Bach tune'), named for eighteenth-century composer Johann Sebastian Bach. 'Classical rock' or 'pomp rock' had endured some popularity in the late 1960s and early 1970s: well-known examples include Mason William's single 'Classical Gas', Deep Purple's live album *Concerto for Group and Orchestra* with the Royal Philharmonic Orchestra, and concept albums *The Six Wives of Henry VIII* and *Journey to the Centre of the Earth* by Rick Wakeman.

'Intermezzo no 1' was Benny's attempt to bring his classical music influences into a pop idiom. On the album sleeve, the track was billed as 'Intermezzo no 1 featuring Benny Andersson', a unique solo credit for Benny on an ABBA record.

The strings and horns on the track were arranged by Swedish musician and composer Björn J:son Lindh, who also arranged the horns on 'Man in the Middle'. J:son Lindh would also play the distinctive flute refrain on the 1984 hit single 'One Night in Bangkok', from Benny and Björn's first post-ABBA project, the musical *Chess*.

Under the working title 'Mama', the piece was performed during ABBA's concert tour of Europe in November 1974 and January 1975. Sound engineer Claes af Geijerstam tells a story of how the title came about on the tour: he had marked the song as 'intermission' on his copy of the setlist, as it came midway through the concerts and did not require any microphones. Benny saw this, and from there it was a short jump to the musical term 'intermezzo'. Benny relates a slightly different story: he played the recorded track to Geijerstam and Claes declared 'That's an intermezzo!' 'No 1' was added to give the piece a bit of gravitas, and hinted it could be the first of many such pieces.

'Intermezzo no 1' would become a staple of ABBA's concert repertoire, being one of only three songs performed in all concerts on ABBA's subsequent tours (the other two being 'Waterloo' and 'Rock Me', though 'Waterloo' was not played on all dates in 1979). A performance in Australia in March 1977 was featured in *ABBA: The Movie* (possibly recorded at the second concert in Sydney), while another live recording is included on the 2014 album *ABBA Live at Wembley Arena*, recorded in London in November 1979.

'I've Been Waiting for You'
Written by Benny Andersson, Stig Anderson, and Björn Ulvaeus.
Duration: 3.39
Released on the B-side of 'So Long' 18 November 1974.

Agnetha was given a second lead vocal on the *ABBA* album with this beautiful ballad. 'I've Been Waiting for You' was first released as the B-side of the glam rocker 'So Long' in November 1974. In Australia, that single was spilt into two separate singles, released simultaneously. 'I've Been Waiting for You' achieved some radio airplay and reached No. 49, while 'So Long' bombed, just a few months before the country was struck with Abbamania.

'I've Been Waiting for You' is another pining love song from Agnetha, but this time she is thrilled and excited that she has found the object of her affection.

In the '90s, PolyGram, having taken control of the ABBA catalogue at the start of the decade, had plans to produce an ABBA remix album. 'I've Been Waiting for You' was one song that Benny was keen to remix, as he is not fond of the harsh sound of the recording. But that project never came to fruition.

After years of relative obscurity, 'I've Been Waiting for You' found new audiences in the movie sequel *Mamma Mia! Here We Go Again*. In the second film, Sophie (Amanda Seyfried) is preparing to reopen her late mother's hotel after extensive renovations, while the story of how mother Donna first met the three men who could have been Sophie's father in 1979 is told in flashbacks. Björn wrote new lyrics for the film, in which (spoiler alert for those who may not have seen it) Sophie sings of the love she has for her unborn child.

'So Long'
Duration: 3.06
Released as a single 18 November 1974.

'So Long' was the first single released from sessions for ABBA's self-titled third album. Interestingly, the label of the Polar single in Sweden shows that the song is 'From ABBA's LP "ABBA" POLS 262'; though the album would be another five months away, it had already been given its title and catalogue number. It shows that ABBA wanted the new album to be a showcase for ABBA as an entity, rather than a vehicle for the hit single, as the previous two albums had been titled.

The song bears quite a sonic resemblance to 'Waterloo'—indeed, the guitar riff in the chorus originated in the chorus of the Eurovision winner. In late 1974, ABBA's international record licensees felt that of the new songs completed so far, it had the best chance of becoming a hit, especially as it would be recognisable as ABBA to listeners familiar with 'Waterloo'. Though the single was released in November 1974, while ABBA were in the middle of a European concert tour, the promotional opportunity was missed, and the single would be ABBA's worst performing international single.

There are a couple of interesting things to note in the recording. The song opens with an arresting noise that sounds like a jet engine rising in pitch. This was achieved with one of guitarist Janne Schaffer's effects boxes, a Morley echo (the effect is repeated before the final chorus). In the coda, there is a solo trumpet played by Bruno Glenmark, owner of GlenStudio where much of the *ABBA* album was recorded. Just as the song starts to fade, we hear some delightful piano ad-libbing from Benny. It is a pity we do not hear more of this in ABBA's catalogue.

6

Non-Album Tracks, 1975

'Crazy World'

Duration: 3.47
Released on the B-side of 'Money, Money, Money', 1 November 1976.

'Crazy World' had a long history before its eventual release. It was recorded during sessions for the *ABBA* album in 1975, but the recording was never completed and the song was shelved. In 1976, it was resurrected for possible inclusion on the next album, *Arrival*, but again it was left off. Instead, it was relegated to the B-side of the 'Money, Money, Money' single, released in November 1976, a month after *Arrival*, two years after the song was recorded.

The maudlin performance matches the lyric. Sung by Björn, the song is the story of a self-pitying man who thinks that the unknown man he has seen with his girlfriend is her secret lover. In the end, she informs him that it is in fact her brother, Joe, who had returned to town, so 'you'll be seeing a lot of him'. The best feature of the song is the backing choir in the middle eight, added by Agnetha and Frida during additional recording in 1976.

'Medley: Pick a Bale of Cotton—On Top of Old Smokey—Midnight Special'

Tradtional, arrangement by Benny Andersson and Björn Ulvaeus.
Duration: 4.15
Released on the album *Stars im Zeichen eines guten Sterns* in West Germany, September 1975. Also on the B-side of 'Summer Night City', 6 September 1978.

The so-called folk medley is the only recording in the entire ABBA catalogue not to have been written by any ABBA members. The medley was recorded in May 1975 for the West German charity album *Stars im Zeichen eines guten Sterns*

(*Stars [artists] Under the Sign of a Good Star [celestial body]*), originally without the word 'medley' as part of the title: this was added when the song was released on the B-side of 'Summer Night City' in 1978. Stig Anderson said in 1994 'the Germans asked us to record a medley of so-called free tunes, whose royalties would go to charity'. The other tracks on the album were similar medleys of public domain songs.

'Pick a Bale of Cotton' controversially dates back to the slave days in the cotton plantations in the southern US during the eighteenth and nineteenth centuries. This song became known to a wider audience in the 1930s, when it was recorded by blues singer Leadbelly. Today some would question the wisdom of a white Swedish group recording such a song.

'On Top of Old Smokey' originated in the mountain ranges of North Carolina, eastern Tennessee, and southwest Virginia, possibly in the first couple of decades of the twentieth century, though the song may actually be much older. Its first popular hit version was recorded by folk quartet The Weavers in 1951. The same year, Swedish singer Brita Borg recorded a Swedish version (in 1969, Borg would record Benny, Björn, and Stig's song 'Ljuva sextital'—'Sweet Sixties').

'Midnight Special' was another song that became well-known from a recording by Leadbelly in 1934, though there were recordings by other artists in the 1920s and the song itself is probably older. The 'midnight special' of the title was a train, which could be heard through the bars of a southern prison as it passed by late at night, symbolising freedom to the prisoners. In modern popular music, the song is most familiar by Creedence Clearwater Revival's 1969 recording on the album *Willy and the Poor Boys*.

The charity album went mostly unnoticed at the time, even in West Germany. It was released in September 1975, but did not enter the charts. Most ABBA followers were unaware of the medley until it appeared on the 'Summer Night City' single.

7

Arrival

Sweden:	11 October 1976
UK:	5 November 1976
US:	4 January 1977
Current edition:	Universal Music/Polar CD 549 953-2
Personnel:	Benny Andersson: piano, keyboards, vocals
	Ola Brunkert: drums
	Lasse Carlsson: saxophone
	Anders Dahl: string arrangement
	Agnetha Fältskog: vocals
	Malando Gassama: percussion
	Anders Glenmark: guitar
	Rutger Gunnarsson: bass, string arrangement
	Anni-Frid Lyngstad: vocals
	Roger Palm: drums
	Janne Schaffer: guitar
	Björn Ulvaeus: guitar, vocals
	Sven-Olof Walldoff: string arrangement
	Lasse Wellander: guitar
Duration:	34 minutes

Recorded at Metronome Studio, Stockholm: August–December 1975, March–
September 1976
Produced by Benny Andersson and Björn Ulvaeus
Engineered by Michael B. Tretow

Chart position:	Sweden: 1
	UK: 1
	US: 20

ABBA's first truly classic album, *Arrival*, was ABBA's first international hit studio album, following the success of compilation albums *Greatest Hits/The Best of ABBA* (see Appendix II).

The album's sleeve, featuring the four members crammed into the cabin of a Bell 47 helicopter, became an iconic image and one of the world's most recognised album covers (visitors to ABBA The Museum in Stockholm can recreate the experience themselves). It was also the first official ABBA album to use the famous ABBA logo, with the first 'B' reversed, designed by art director Rune Söderqvist, who would design all of ABBA's album sleeves and most of their singles from 1975's *Greatest Hits* to the posthumous *ABBA Live* in 1986. The logo had first appeared on the 'Dancing Queen' single released in August, and also on French and West German compilations released a few months earlier.

Upon the album's release, critic Bob Woffinden wrote in *NME*: 'Operating in a rarefied atmosphere where the only true competition is their own previous standards, Arrival matches expectations and is their most accomplished to date'. In 2018, *Classic Pop* magazine enthused: 'Their most accomplished album of all time? Probably'. Standalone single 'Fernando' was recorded during sessions for *Arrival*, but was released seven months before and not included (though it was added to the tracklist in Australia and New Zealand). Today, 'Fernando' is an essential bonus track on CD editions of the album. *Arrival* was the first ABBA studio album to be a chart-topper around the world, not just in the Scandinavian countries.

The Deluxe Edition, released on the album's thirtieth anniversary in 2006, came with a DVD that included the classic television special *ABBA-dabba-dooo!!*, produced by Swedish Television, which introduced the *Arrival* album to television viewers in late 1976.

'When I Kissed the Teacher'
Duration: 3.00

'When I Kissed the Teacher' harks back to a more innocent time, a throwback to the girl group songs of the late '50s and early '60s when a young girl with a crush on an older boy or male adult, in this case her teacher, might take advantage of their closeness and sneak in a kiss on the cheek. With its sparkling acoustic guitars, vibrant vocals, singalong melody, and catchy backing vocals, 'When I Kissed the Teacher' made a perfect opening track for ABBA's fourth album.

An early mix with minor differences was used as the soundtrack of a film clip made for the *ABBA-dabba-dooo!!* television special. In the first chorus, the echoed 'they dreamed' and the rumbling build-up of sound under the lines 'nearly petrified 'cause he was taken by surprise' are missing, and there are minor differences in the whole song. This version can be heard in the television special on the DVD with the *Arrival* Deluxe Edition.

'When I Kissed the Teacher' was the first big number in the movie sequel *Mamma Mia! Here We Go Again* in 2018, and it was also the lead track released from the soundtrack album. Björn tweaked the lyrics in the middle eight (the 'one of these days' section) to be sung by a female teacher, rather than a male, to avoid an awkward key change. It has also been widely assumed that this was done to make the lyric more suitable in the #metoo era. The song, sung by Lily James, reached No. 40 on the British singles chart in the weeks before the film's opening.

'Dancing Queen'

Written by Benny Andersson, Stig Anderson, and Björn Ulvaeus. Spanish lyric by Buddy and Mary McCluskey.
Duration: 3.50
Released as a single 16 August 1976.

'My life is as good as an ABBA song. It's as good as Dancing Queen.' That line, uttered by Toni Collette in the 1994 Australian film *Muriel's Wedding*, sums up how millions of people around the world feel when they hear ABBA's biggest hit.

'Dancing Queen' took a full year from the first recording session to its release as a single. Like 'Waterloo' in 1974, ABBA worked extremely hard on 'Dancing Queen' to create the perfect recording, adding more and more layers of instruments and vocals, editing out one verse, even rearranging the order of the verses, and still laying more on top of that. The song has one of the most arresting openings of any ABBA song, or even of any popular song ever. The descending piano glissando, the refrain with Agnetha and Frida's wordless vocalising synchronous with Benny's synthesizer, leading to the exciting climax of the chorus, all in the first forty-five seconds. *Rolling Stone* brilliantly describes it: 'That opening piano swirl can trigger a pheromone rush in any human who knows what it means to (1) dance (2) jive, and/or (3) have the time of their life, on a floor'.

Benny and Björn always intended 'Dancing Queen' to be a disco song—early to mid-'70s disco being rather different from the frenetic four-on-the-floor music of the disco boom following the 1977 movie *Saturday Night Fever*, slightly fewer BPM (beats per minute) but still eminently danceable. They were inspired for the feel and the rhythm by George McRae's international hit of 1974 'Rock Your Baby'. The idiosyncratic drum beat created by drummer Roger Palm was inspired by New Orleans' musician Dr. John, particularly his 1972 album *Dr. John's Gumbo*. 'It's different from what we've done before. We like to give people nice surprises,' Björn said. The working title of the backing track was 'Boogaloo', which may have been inspired by ex-Beatle Ringo Starr's stomping 1972 hit 'Back Off Boogaloo', whose title in turn had been inspired by a favourite saying of Starr's friend, British glam rocker Marc Bolan.

Everyone knows 'Dancing Queen'. It is the tale of a seventeen-year-old 'looking out for a place to go' on Friday night, to dance and perhaps to find a man (or 'king', as the lyric would have it), though not necessarily in search of a long-term relationship. 'She only lives when she's in the disco, dancing,' Björn said.

Twenty-first-century interpretations cast a different view—in 2016, Simon Goddard wrote in *Pitchfork*: 'Perhaps this is a song of someone who wants to be Esmerelda but knows they are Quasimodo*.... The dancing queen could be an isolated young girl alone in her bedroom, too scared, too shy, almost certainly believing herself too hideous to step out of Friday night; her one happiness her unrealistic fantasy that she could find love amongst the beautiful people on the dancefloor'. Even more bleakly, in 2018, Angus Harrison wrote in *Vice*: 'Our narrator has realised she is no longer the Dancing Queen. She is no longer young, no longer sweet, no longer 17. Now, instead, she watches from the bar: the dancefloor a maelstrom of lost faith, memories and missed opportunities. She was once 17, and as such was totally oblivious that the moment would never end'. He concludes: '"Dancing Queen" is a song about death'. A long way from Björn's stated vision of a girl who only lives for the disco.

During recording, the song lost its original first verse, which can be heard on the *Arrival* Deluxe Edition DVD, in rare footage of ABBA in the studio. The verse was probably cut out to tighten up the song and possibly also because the lyric ('baby baby, you're out of sight/hey you're looking alright tonight/when you come to the party/listen to the guys/they've got the look in their eyes') was not very good. At the same time, the verses were rearranged. What had been the third and fourth verses (the verses starting with 'Friday night and the lights are low' and 'Anybody could be that guy') became the first and second, the original second verse ('You're a teaser') became the third verse, after the chorus.

The strings rising up beneath the line 'having the time if your life' never fail to raise chills up the spine. Interestingly, this part of the arrangement was always part of the song. Footage of the recording session shows Benny and Björn playing the first take of the backing track for Frida and Agnetha, with the two men singing what would become the melody of the string arrangement.

Even before the single was released, ABBA performed 'Dancing Queen' at a gala concert in June on the eve of the wedding of Sweden's King Carl XVI Gustav to German-born Silvia Sommerlath. The title and the occasion led many commentators to believe the song had been written for the occasion, though it was almost a year old, and the future queen at thirty-three was not quite 'young and sweet, only seventeen'.

'Dancing Queen' was released in August 1976 and became a worldwide No. 1 hit. 'When we recorded the vocals, I remember we both had the chills,' said Agnetha. 'The hair stood up on our arms.' Frida recalled: 'I thought it was one of the best things we had done'. It would be ABBA's only American No. 1 single on the Hot 100 (popular singles) chart in April 1977. Thanks to its enduring popularity as a party song and as a gay anthem, 'Dancing Queen' has become ABBA's biggest hit.

'Dancing Queen' also inspired the contemporary generation of New Wave artists: Elvis Costello freely admits to cribbing the descending piano chord sequence in his single 'Oliver's Army', and Chris Stein of Blondie once admitted to wanting to replicate 'Dancing Queen' for that band's single 'Dreaming'.

A Spanish version, 'Reina Danzante' (a sort-of literal translation of the title), was recorded in 1980 for the album *Gracias Por La Música*. Curiously, it has the full unedited backing track with the four verses, as the backing track was copied from the original master tape, before it had been copied, edited, and subjected to further overdubs. In the Spanish version, the lyrics from the second verse are repeated in the fourth. In 1993, when *Gracias Por La Música* was repackaged as *ABBA Oro*, the Spanish version was retitled 'La Reina Del Baile' ('The queen of the dance').

In 1990, Stig Anderson sold his Sweden Music empire, including the Polar Music record company, to Dutch/German conglomerate PolyGram. Looking to capitalise on their new investment, in 1992, the company put together the compilation CD *ABBA Gold: Greatest Hits*, collecting nineteen of ABBA's biggest international hits. It was self evident that 'Dancing Queen' would be rereleased as a single to promote the album. The single was a top forty hit across the world all over again, its highest placement at No. 6 in Switzerland.

'Dancing Queen' is one of several songs to be revisited by ABBA members. In 1992, Björn and Benny joined Irish band U2 on stage at Globen in Stockholm for a reverential performance of the song. The following year, Frida sang a version with *a cappella* singers The Real Group, which was performed in a concert celebrating Queen Silvia's fiftieth birthday and recorded on the group's album *Varför får man inte bara vara som man är* ('Why aren't you allowed to be just as you are'). Twice Benny has played 'Dancing Queen' on piano accompanying reknowned Swedish organist Gunnar Idenstam in organ recitals in 2012 and 2016.

'Dancing Queen' would also be the centrepiece of the aforementioned film *Muriel's Wedding*, about a lonely twenty-something woman who finds solace in ABBA's music. In the film, we first hear the song when the lead character Muriel is at a low point, playing the song on cassette, alone in her bedroom. Later, after she has run away to the life she thinks she wants to live, she says that now-immortal line about her life being as good as an ABBA song to her friend Rhonda. At the end of the film, the song is heard again in exultation as Muriel and Rhonda escape both their repressed home lives and also the fantasy life that Muriel had been living.

It was a foregone conclusion that ABBA's biggest hit would be a highlight of the *Mamma Mia!* stage musical, the 2008 film based on the musical, and its 2018 sequel *Mamma Mia! Here We Go Again*. In the films, the song is an all-singing, all-dancing crowd pleaser and, particularly in the first movie, a rallying call of female empowerment.

'Dancing Queen' became embroiled in controversy when British musical pranksters The JAMS (aka The Justified Ancients of Mu Mu, aka The KLF—the Kopyright Liberation Front) used an unauthorised sample of 'Dancing Queen' for the track 'The Queen and I', on their album *1987 (What the Fuck is Going On?)*; the track also sampled Sex Pistols' 1977 single 'God Save the Queen'. After legal action from ABBA and Britain's Mechanical-Copyright Protection Agency, the album was withdrawn from sale. The band dramatically disposed of most copies by burning them in a bonfire in the middle of a field, with remaining copies thrown overboard from a ferry into the North Sea.

Australian singer Kylie Minogue celebrated Australia's reignited and enduring love for ABBA when she sang 'Dancing Queen' at the closing ceremony of the Olympic Games in Sydney in September 2000. It was the only non-Australian song performed on the night. Benny and Björn were so pleased with Ms Minogue's performance that they sent her a congratulatory telegram. Blogger Varmstad wrote after viewing the performance: 'There is nothing more Australian than an unhealthy relationship with ABBA'. The quote was thought so appropriate that it was displayed on a wall at the ABBAWORLD exhibition in Sydney in 2010.

* the two central characters in Victor Hugo's classic 1831 novel *Notre-Dame de Paris* (aka *The Hunchback of Notre-Dame*).

'My Love, My Life'
Written by Benny Andersson, Stig Anderson, and Björn Ulvaeus.
Duration: 3.52

Agnetha's heartfelt lead vocals are wrapped in one of ABBA's lushest productions, backed throughout the song by an angelic choir, a sound inspired by British group 10cc's 1975 hit 'I'm Not In Love'. Indeed, Agnetha's is the only identifiable voice in the song. The song was actually introduced as 'Agnetha's latest solo hit' in the Australian television special *ABBA From The Beginning*, a localised version of the Swedish special *ABBA-dabba-dooo!!* The singer pines as her lover moves on, 'like an image passing by'.

Like several other songs on the *Arrival* album, 'My Love My Life' went through major changes between its initial conception and final version. The first recording, in a higher key and in a French chanson style, was titled 'Monsieur, Monsieur', also sung by Agnetha. The lyric told the story of a youthful romance in France, a theme revisited in 'Our Last Summer' on *Super Trouper* in 1980. A portion of this early take was played on the Swedish radio special *A för Agnetha* (*A for Agnetha*) in December 1976, though it is obscured by dialogue between Agnetha and interviewer Ulf Elfving.

More recently, both Björn and Benny have hinted that they felt 'My Love, My Life' was overproduced, and could have been arranged differently. Benny has also said that it was 'almost one of my absolute favourite songs'. So perhaps it is no surprise that he selected 'My Love, My Life' as one of six ABBA songs he recorded for his 2017 album *Piano*, a collection of his own compositions for ABBA, the musicals *Chess* and *Kristina från Duvemåla*, and more, played solo on piano.

In 2018, 'My Love, My Life', appeared in the penultimate scene of the film *Mamma Mia! Here We Go Again*. The song's arrangement was similar to the version on the *Piano* album, with subtle strings added to Benny's piano. Björn wrote new lyrics, making it a song expressing the love between a mother and daughter. It was sung by actors Lily James and Meryl Streep, portraying younger and older versions of the mother character, Donna, and Amanda Seyfried as Donna's daughter, Sophie.

'Dum Dum Diddle'
Duration: 2.53

A popular album track upon in its original release, 'Dum Dum Diddle' has been much maligned over the years for its lyrics, not least by their author Björn, who has said that the song may as well have been titled 'dumb dumb diddle'. Nonsense words in an alliterative, onomatopoeic title and a few perhaps dodgy rhymes aside (smilin'/violin), there is really nothing wrong with the lyric.

The song tells the story of a woman pining for a musician, wishing that she could receive as much attention as he pays to his violin, though she is too shy to actually approach him. He may be a stranger, a neighbour, or even her neglectful lover. However you interpret it, the song is a poignant tale of unrequited love. Agnetha and Frida sing in unison with gusto, one of the prime mid-period examples of ABBA's third voice effect.

The refrain heard in the introduction, after the first chorus and in the fadeout, and the counter-melody played during the chorus, are the first obvious influences of Benny's love of traditional Swedish music in ABBA's recordings. Folk influences would make their way into future ABBA recordings, most overtly in the title track of the *Arrival* album.

In addition to Björn's criticism of the title, Frida has described 'Dum Dum Diddle' as 'a silly song.' In the book *ABBA: The Complete Recording Sessions*, Björn explained that he had been up all night the day before the recording studio was booked to record the vocals and came up with the lyric at around 5 a.m. 'I expected the others to reject [it]—but they didn't,' he said.

Though they might have disparaged the song in recent years, ABBA obviously thought enough of it at the time to perform it live on the television special *ABBA-dabba-dooo!!* and in their concerts on the 1977 tour, when Benny played the folkish refrain on the instrument of his childhood that introduced him to his love of music, the accordion.

'Knowing Me, Knowing You'
Written by Benny Andersson, Stig Anderson, and Björn Ulvaeus. Spanish lyric by Buddy and Mary McCluskey.
Duration: 4.02
Released as a single 18 February 1977.

The first song from concentrated sessions for ABBA's fourth album in March 1976, immediately following a promotional visit to Australia. 'Knowing Me,

Knowing You' is the first ABBA song with a distinctly adult flavour. It is definitely the world of adult relationships, with the protagonist 'walking through an empty house/tears in my eyes' following a marriage separation. Pete Townshend of The Who observed in *Rolling Stone*: '… what's quite interesting is that Abba was one of the first big, international bands to actually deal with sort of middle-aged problems in their songwriting. And it was quite obviously what was going on among them—that song, "Knowing Me, Knowing You"'.

Though the song was sung by Frida, the lyric is a decidedly male point of view. In the '70s, it was most common for children to remain with their mother following a divorce. Björn wrote in 2014: 'I don't think I've ever had such a vivid image in my head when writing a lyric. I saw the rooms and I saw cardboard boxes piled up against the walls. There were no carpets on the floors and my steps echoed the way they do in an empty house. I say "my steps" because I was the man walking through those rooms even though in reality I was a happily married man at the time'.

The chorus is one of ABBA's most complex. Frida and Agnetha sing the melody with ascending and descending harmonies, while Björn and Benny sing a counter melody backing vocal that complements the lead. And, of course, the famous 'aha' after the title, one of the most memorable gimmicks in popular music. Take out any of those elements, as many cover versions do, and the song falls flat.

There is a lot to listen for in the instrumental refrain after the chorus. There are two guitars playing the solo in harmony, but buried in the mix and only just audible is a glockenspiel playing a counter melody. The glockenspiel can be heard more clearly on the live recordings in the television special *ABBA in Concert* and the album *Live at Wembley Arena*. The recording originally opened with the the riff that appears in the released version between 2.53 and 3.00: in the introduction, it was played twice, and it also appeared twice in the place in the song where in the released version it is heard just once. These were edited out of the released recording.

'Knowing Me, Knowing You' was the third single released from *Arrival*. It was the biggest hit of 1977 in the UK, but in Australia, it was the first sign of a decline in the group's popularity after the intense period of adulation, fanmania, and overexposure over the previous eighteen months. Though it was released on the eve of ABBA's Australian tour, after six consecutive No. 1 singles, it peaked at a comparatively lowly No. 9.

British comedian Steve Coogan took the title for a comedy series satirising television talk and variety shows, hosted by his alter ego Alan Partridge in 1994, using the 'aha' refrain as a catchphrase. The show spun off a Christmas episode in 1995 punningly entitled *Knowing Me Knowing Yule*.

A Spanish version, 'Conociéndome, Conociéndote' (a direct translation of the song title) was recorded for *Gracias Por La Música* in 1980.

'Money, Money, Money'

Duration: 3.05
Released as a single 1 November 1976.

Like 'My Love, My Life' discussed above, 'Money, Money, Money' is another song that went through different ideas before the best concept stuck. Björn's first dummy lyric even had the title 'Money, Money, Money', but feeling that was clichéd, that there were already enough songs about money, he came up with a lyric titled 'Gypsy Girl'.

After recording the backing track, Benny and Björn felt that the 'Gypsy Girl' idea was not really working and returned to the original 'money' concept. The tack piano and single violin (actually a holdover from the 'Gypsy Girl' lyric) are reminiscent of the 1930s Berlin cabaret scene, as depicted in the 1972 movie musical *Cabaret*, which also featured a song about money. 'This is Benny and me going back to our European roots. It is almost a tango,' Björn says in the book *Mamma Mia! How Can I Resist You*.

Frida takes the lead vocal, which tells the story of a woman seeking a wealthy man to give her an easy life, but failing that, she will try to win a fortune in the casinos of Las Vegas or Monaco.

The chorus offers some curious things to listen for: Agnetha sings the melody one full octave above Frida. Benny said: 'There is an octave harmony in the background of the chorus; it is quite soft so you can't really hear it'. The bass guitar follows the melody line 'money, money, money/must be funny/in the rich man's world'. Hidden in the mix after the first chorus is a repeated 'oo-ee-oo-ee' vocal. Though it is pretty much inaudible in ABBA's recording, it was restored in the *Mamma Mia!* musical.

'Money, Money, Money' contains one of those infamous ABBA grammatical clangers, though one is less discussed than some others. In the chorus, the lyric explains that life 'must be funny/in the rich man's world'. ABBA did not mean to say that the life of the wealthy is hilarious, but that it must be fun to have enough money not to worry about earning a living. The Swedish word 'roligt' means both fun and funny, depending on its context. The same misused word appears in 1975's 'Tropical Loveland' and 1979's 'Does Your Mother Know'.

Benny has singled out 'Money, Money, Money' as one of ABBA's best songs and recordings. He has said that it is a song he can imagine other people singing (as would happen in *Mamma Mia!*), and that the recording was not overproduced, as he feels today that many ABBA songs were. In 2018, he recorded a solo piano version for a deluxe reissue of his 2017 solo album *Piano*.

'Money, Money, Money' was released as a single around the same time as the *Arrival* album, though Björn does not seem to remember that it was an international hit single, saying that he thought it had 'limited release'. It was ABBA's sixth consecutive No. 1 single in Australia (excluding older singles and B-sides that had also charted during 1976), and the fifth consecutive No. 1 in West Germany. In the UK, it peaked at No. 3, breaking what would otherwise have been a streak of seven chart-topping singles.

'That's Me'

Written by Benny Andersson, Stig Anderson, and Björn Ulvaeus.
Duration: 3.15
Released as the B-side of 'Dancing Queen', 16 August 1976.

'That's Me' is notable as the first ABBA recording to feature Benny's new Polymoog synthesizer. Previous synthesizers, such as the Minimoog used on so many previous recordings, had been monophonic, only playing one note at a time. The Polymoog was polyphonic, able to play more than one note, so it was able to play chords. This can be most clearly heard in the introduction, in the descending sequence before the vocal starts (heard between 0.08 and 0.15).

Agnetha and Frida sing the song together, splitting to harmonies as the verse progresses. The lyric is about a woman who might not be the kind of woman a man would want to get into a relationship with. She's 'Carrie not the kind of girl you'd marry'. A similar theme, expressed from the other side of the relationship, is covered in the next track on the album, 'Why Did It Have to Be Me'.

'That's Me' was first released on the B-side of 'Dancing Queen' in August 1976, and then included on side two of *Arrival*. In Japan, 'That's Me' was released as a single in its own right, where it became one of ABBA's most popular hits, reaching No. 7, ABBA's highest-charting Japanese single. Agnetha has said that it is one of her favourite ABBA songs, leading to her 1998 solo compilation CD being titled *That's Me—The Greatest Hits*.

'Why Did It Have to Be Me'

Duration: 3.20

'Why Did It Have to Be Me' has a long, complex history, and demonstrates Benny and Björn's work ethic: how they would continue to work with a melody until they felt it had been given the right treatment. Their original demo was a boogie song with Björn singing nonsense lyrics built around the phrase 'why did it have to be me'. When it came time to record the song, they felt it should have a Hawaiian feeling. Stig Anderson came up with lyrics titled 'Happy Hawaii', the story of a woman heading to the airport to fly to a Hawaiian holiday, to get away from the rain, seeking fun in the sun, and maybe romance.

After Agnetha and Frida's joint vocals had been recorded and the song was mixed, Benny and Björn were not entirely happy with the song. They started again, this time recording a country-style backing track with lyrics titled 'Memory Lane', though it appears that no vocals were recorded for this version. They did not think the 'Memory Lane' concept was right either, and eventually came to the conclusion that the original demo idea best suited the song.

In 'Why Did It Have to Be Me' Björn sings the part of a man who cannot help falling in love with a woman despite her reputation as a maneater. Agnetha and

Frida reply in unison as the woman, singing that all she wanted was 'a little love affair', but he would be better off forgetting about her. A bit like Carrie in 'That's Me', which preceded this song on *Arrival*.

The recording of 'Why Did It Have to Be Me' was subjected to heavy editing before release. An additional verse, a repeat of the instrumental break, and a repeat of the first verse in a higher key were all edited from the latter part of the original recording.

On the first two ABBA albums, vocal duties had been shared almost equally between the male and female halves of ABBA. On *ABBA* in 1975, songs with a male lead were reduced to two. From *Arrival* onwards, Agnetha's and Frida's voices would dominate ABBA's output, either together or individually. For the sake of variety, most subsequent ABBA albums would feature one Björn lead vocal showcase.

ABBA performed 'Why Did It Have to Be Me' live on the television special *ABBA-dabba-dooo!!* The song would become a highlight of ABBA's concerts, where it was transformed into a duet between Björn and Frida, giving Agnetha a short break and opportunity to change costume, and is one of a handful of songs to be performed on all of ABBA's international concert tours in 1977, 1979, and 1980.

In 2005, Benny Anderssons Orkester added 'Why Did It Have to Be Me' to their concert repertoire, sung by Tommy Körberg and Helen Sjöholm, adding the introduction and coda from 'Happy Hawaii'. The song also featured in the film *Mamma Mia! Here We Go Again*, and was so popular it entered the British singles chart.

See the entry for 'Happy Hawaii' below for more on what happened to that song and 'Memory Lane'.

'Tiger'
Duration: 2.55

In the '70s, many of the world's big cities were regarded as dangerous places, with certain streets and whole areas that people would avoid at night, or even during the day. In the song 'Tiger', the dangerous city is likened to a jungle, with danger brought to life in the form of a predatory animal. The frenzied vocals of Agnetha and Frida evoke a wild, stalking animal, setting fear in the hearts of the city's citizens and the listener. Reviewer Simon Goddard brilliantly described 'Tiger' in 2016: 'A fabulously unsettling psycho-pop thriller of urban dystopia and Droogish violence* not so very far away from [David Bowie's] Diamond Dogs'.

Around the time the *Arrival* album was released, there were reports that 'Tiger' was under consideration for release as a single. Alas, that was not to be, though it did have release in 7-inch form in Japan, on the B-side of 'Dancing Queen', and in Argentina, coupled with another *Arrival* track, 'Dum Dum Diddle'.

'Tiger' would make the fitting climax of the *Arrival* album, where it was followed by the sedate, stately title track. The following year, it would be the suitably exciting, rocking opening number for ABBA's concerts in Europe and Australia, which can be seen in the feature film *ABBA: The Movie*.

* a reference to *A Clockwork Orange*, the 1962 novel by Anthony Burgess, made into a controversial feature film by Stanley Kubrick in 1971. 'Droog' was a slang term for the members of the lead character's violent gang.

'Arrival'
Duration: 3.00

Even more overtly than 'Dum Dum Diddle', 'Arrival' displays Benny's love of Swedish folk music. The original title for the near-instrumental piece was 'Ode to Dalecarlia', the English exonym for Dalarna, a region of central Sweden. The track was renamed 'Arrival' after the album, which itself had been named after the sleeve photo concept, rather than the usual method of naming an album after a song.

The melody is repeated three times and is dominated by Benny's many keyboards and synthesizers, though there are strings in the recording. The first time is fully instrumental, the second time wordless vocals from Agnetha and Frida can be heard, while the third time their vocals are heard at full volume, with gorgeous multi-layered harmonies. The strings were arranged by Swedish violinist Anders Dahl, who in 1979 recorded an album of instrumental versions of twelve ABBA songs, *Anders Dahl and his Magic Strings Play ABBA*, at ABBA's Polar Music Studios.

In 1983, French composers Alain and Daniel Boublil put together the musical *ABBACADABRA* for a television production, using ABBA's songs with all new French lyrics telling a story featuring famous fairytale characters. Frida sang the duet 'Belle' with French singer Daniel Balavoine, using the tune of 'Arrival'. Later in the year, an English version was staged in London, and Frida again recorded a duet with the 'Arrival' melody for single release entitled 'Time', with British singer B. A. Robertson, though she did not appear in the stage production.

In the late 1990s, Björn wrote lyrics for 'Arrival', intended for the musical *Mamma Mia!*, which would have appeared near the end of the musical (roughly serving the same purpose as 'When All Is Said and Done' in the 2008 movie version), but the song was dropped while the musical was still in development. In 2008, British singer Sarah Brightman recorded this version for her album *A Winter Symphony*, stating in interviews that Björn had given her the lyrics, though when asked, Björn said he had no idea how she got the lyrics.

British multi-instrumentalist Mike Oldfield recorded a cover version for his 1980 album *QE2*. The single sleeve parodied the *Arrival* album sleeve, with Oldfield in a helicopter similar to the one on ABBA's sleeve, and the 'K' in Mike reversed, mimicking the reversed 'B' in the ABBA logo.

8

Non-Album Tracks, 1976

'Fernando'

Written by Benny Andersson, Stig Anderson, and Björn Ulvaeus. Spanish lyric by Buddy and Mary McCluskey.
Duration: 4. 15
Released as a single in March 1976. Added to the album *Greatest Hits* in 1976.

'Fernando' started life as a Swedish-language recording by Frida, for her solo album *Frida ensam* (*Frida alone*), produced by Benny, which was released in November 1975. The original Swedish lyric by Stig Anderson had been a fairly straightforward love story, with Frida singing 'long live love' to her best friend, 'darling Fernando'.

Realising the song's hit potential, Björn set to writing an English lyric, which was subsequently recorded for release as ABBA's next single in March 1976. He kept the title 'Fernando', but wrote a story that he described as 'two old revolutionaries, reminiscing' about a 'fight for freedom'. 'The name together with the music suggested Mexico to me,' he said. Benny added that there was no plot agenda: 'The text provides the atmosphere itself to the music'.

In a note in the boxset *The Singles* (released in 2014), Björn wrote 'On a beautiful summer night I was lying flat on my back on the jetty at my country house. I was looking at a starry, completely unobscured sky and it was as though the words were handed to me from above. I only had to reach out and grab them—"there was something in the air that night..."'

English speakers will often latch onto a perceived 'grammatical error' in the line 'since many years I haven't seen a rifle in your hand'. Critic Simon Goddard has observed: 'The members of ABBA could learn and sing in English, but they still thought like Scandinavians. Their phrasings made grammatical sense but their assembly of words were not the natural choices of any lyricist for whom English was a first language'. Though the line might technically be not quite correct English, it clearly conveys its meaning, and isn't that what matters?

During ABBA's lifetime, 'Fernando' was the group's biggest selling hit single, reportedly having sold over 6 million copies by 1978. In Australia, now in the grip of Abbamania, 'Fernando' would top the singles chart for fourteen consecutive weeks, a record that equalled The Beatles' 'Hey Jude' in 1968. 'Fernando' would remain the country's highest selling single for over two decades (usurped by Elton John's tribute to Diana, Princess of Wales, 'Candle In The Wind '97'), and hold its achievement of most weeks at No. 1 until 2017, when it was overtaken by Ed Sheeran's 'Shape of You' with fifteen (non-consecutive) weeks at the top. In the US, 'Fernando' topped the Adult Contemporary Chart, making it ABBA's first American No. 1 single ('Dancing Queen' would top the Hot 100 chart the following year).

In most countries, 'Fernando' was included on compilation albums released under titles such as *Greatest Hits* or *The Best of ABBA* in 1976, also featuring songs from the first three ABBA albums. There was no worldwide release, each country compiled their own with twelve, fourteen, or fifteen tracks, though they all featured songs selected from the same pot of fifteen songs. In Australia and New Zealand, 'Fernando' had not been included on the local compilation *The Best of ABBA* but instead was added to the *Arrival* album when it was released in November, inserted as track four on side two. In recent years, 'Fernando' is included as a bonus track on all CD reissues of *Arrival*.

In August 1976, ABBA recorded new lyrics for an advertising campaign for Japanese electronics manufacturer National (now Panasonic) for the Australian market. The one-minute jingle featured the song's second verse and the chorus and was used in television and radio advertisements for several years. The lyrics were mostly written by a copywriter from the George Patterson advertising agency.

The first take of Frida's Swedish version was included in the 'ABBA Undeleted' medley of studio outtakes released in 1994 on the boxset *Thank You for the Music*. This version has a stiffer musical backing with a bit of a tango rhythm—indeed, its working title was 'Tango'.

Given the Latin title and theme of 'Fernando', it was an obvious choice for ABBA to record in Spanish for the *Gracias Por La Música* album in 1980.

Though 'Fernando' was one of the few top-tier ABBA hits not included in the *Mamma Mia!* musical, aside from a couple of lines absent-mindedly sung by lead character Donna in both the stage and film versions, it was shoe-horned into the sequel film *Mamma Mia! Here We Go Again*. There it is sung by music and screen legend Cher and was the highly-anticipated second song released from the soundtrack album in the lead up to the film's July 2018 premiere. The American star enjoyed making the film so much that she recorded an album of ten ABBA songs entitled *Dancing Queen*, which became a chart-topping hit.

'Happy Hawaii'

Written by Benny Andersson, Stig Anderson, and Björn Ulvaeus.
Duration: 4.22
Released as the B-side of 'Knowing Me, Knowing You', 18 February 1977.

As detailed above, 'Happy Hawaii' had been one of the ideas for the melody that eventually became 'Why Did It Have to Be Me'. Despite Stig's interesting story lyric, and the strong vocal recorded by Agnetha and Frida, the Hawaiian treatment was not felt right and the recording was shelved. A country-style version of the tune entitled 'Memory Lane' was attempted, before Benny and Björn finally came up with the version of the song with which they were fully satisfied, and 'Why Did It Have to Be Me' was what buyers heard on the *Arrival* album in late 1976.

With the release of *Arrival*, it seemed that 'Happy Hawaii' and 'Memory Lane' would be consigned to the vault, never to be heard by the general public. But executives from RCA Australia had heard 'Happy Hawaii' while visiting Sweden during the album sessions, and asked why such a good song was left unreleased. Benny and Björn took another look at the song, decided it was not that bad, so they put final touches on the recording and released it on the B-side of 'Knowing Me, Knowing You' in February 1977. Upon release, they announced: '"Happy Hawaii" is a "jest" on our part. We think it is fun to show our public how we conceived the song from the beginning. And besides, many people who had heard "Happy Hawaii" on the demo tape wondered what happened to it'.

A cartoon short of 'Happy Hawaii' was created by an Australian production company for a proposed ABBA cartoon television series (a film of 'Money, Money, Money' was also produced). The series was abandoned, and the film was rarely seen until its release on DVD with the *Arrival* Deluxe Edition in 2006.

Meanwhile, the 'Memory Lane' backing track was also heard in public, played underneath interviews on the Swedish radio documentary *B för Björn (B for Björn)*, one of five episodes in a series on the four members with the fifth concentrating on the group, in December 1976.

9

ABBA:
The Album

Sweden: 12 December 1977
UK: 13 January 1978
US: 24 January 1978
Current edition: Universal Music/Polar CD 549 954-2
Personnel: Benny Andersson: keyboards, vocals
                   Ola Brunkert: drums
                   Agnetha Fältskog: vocals
                   Malando Gassama: percussion
                   Rutger Gunnarsson: bass, string arrangements
                   Anni-Frid Lyngstad: vocals
                   Roger Palm: drums
                   Janne Schaffer: guitar
                   Björn Ulvaeus: guitar, vocals
                   Lasse Wellander: guitar
Recorded at Marcus Music, Metronome Studio, Glenstudio, Stockholm; Bohus
                   Studio, Kungälv: May–November 1977
Duration: 41 minutes
Produced and arranged by Benny Andersson and Björn Ulvaeus
Engineered by Michael B. Tretow
Chart position: Sweden: 1
                   UK: 1
                   US: 14

Recorded after ABBA's concert tour of Europe and Australia in the early months
of 1977, *ABBA: The Album* was ABBA's most ambitious yet, with more mature
lyrical themes and longer songs than previous ABBA albums. Earlier in the year,
Björn said: 'Admittedly, our lyrics were once written in school-book English,
but lately we've been putting more stress on the lyrics because people actually

listen to them. Before they were just a complement to the music'. The album sleeve features a special credit: 'STIG ANDERSON helped us with the lyrics on "The Name Of The Game", "Move On", and "I Wonder (Departure)"'—it would be the last time that Stig would make lyrical contributions to Benny and Björn's songs.

ABBA: The Album's release coincided with the concert film *ABBA: The Movie*, mostly filmed during the Australian leg of the tour. As Stig said at the time: '… the album promotes the movie which promotes the album'. The album's cover art was also used as the poster for the film. A painting showing ABBA's faces, in a typical group pose, surrounded by images relating to the songs and the film: a bird flying in the sky and a marionette, representing the songs 'Eagle' and 'I'm A Marionette'; kangaroos, sheep, and palm trees common to Australia; a running figure with microphone and tape recorder, indicating the reporter character in the film; and a plane and taxi, both modes of transportation that featured in the film.

Early plans were to release a double album, with a second disc of live recordings from the Australian tour. Some reports of the album's impending release said it would include *ABBA—The Book*, a biographical picture book. Both ideas were dropped.

'Eagle'
Duration: 5.51
Released as a single in May 1978.

Björn has said that he was inspired to write the lyric by the sense of freedom he felt when reading the novella *Jonathan Livingston Seagull* by Richard Bach. The book had been published in 1970, after originally appearing as a series of short stories in *Flying* magazine in the late '60s, and it became a bestseller. In 1973, a film adaption was released, with Grammy-winning score and songs by American singer-songwriter Neil Diamond. Due to the ABBA song's title and its acoustic, soft rock feeling, critics at the time assumed that the song was a tribute to Californian country-rock band Eagles, though there is nothing in the lyric that gives that impression.

'Eagle' was the strong opening track on ABBA's fifth album. It also featured in *ABBA: The Movie* in a rather bizarre sequence near the end of the film. For any reader who has not seen the movie, the following is a major spoiler: the film shows an inept radio DJ, Ashley Wallace, following ABBA's tour around Australia, trying to secure an exclusive 'dialogue' with ABBA for a radio special. Having finally scheduled an interview, he unfortunately sleeps in and misses the appointment. The group's Australian tour is over, they have left their hotel, and are heading to the airport to fly home to Sweden. Ashley returns to his hotel, and the elevator doors open, revealing ABBA. As the elevator rises, Ashley gets his interview, but instead of seeing the interview, we see ABBA singing 'Eagle'.

Why are ABBA at Ashley's hotel, and why did they not exit the elevator when it reached the ground floor?

'Eagle' was released as the third single from *The Album* in many countries, but the five-minute, fifty-one-second-long song was edited to a shorter radio-friendly four minutes and twenty-three seconds by editing out the instrumental break and two chorus repeats. Some markets shortened the song even more to three minutes and thirty-six seconds by fading the outro early. In some territories, the single charted as a double A-side with 'Thank You for the Music'.

'Take a Chance on Me'
Duration: 4.05
Released released as a single in January 1978.

For this classic ABBA hit, Björn was inspired while out jogging. A repetitive rhythmic 'tecka cha' sound ran through his head, which he expanded to 'take a chance'. The backing vocals during the choruses—'take-a-chance, take-a-chance, take-a-take-a-chance-chance'—echo that jogging rhythm. Björn wrote in *The Singles* boxset in 2014: 'My running pace was in rhythm with the melody that went through my head over and over again. My feet pounded the blacktop relentlessly at a steady rhythm and I found myself not quite singing, but half whispering percussive sounds in time with that rhythm'.

When the song was performed in concert in 1979 and 1980, those backing vocals were played back from a prerecorded tape, sung by Björn, Benny, and backing singer Tomas Ledin. It would have been impossible to sing that repetitive chant live. It was the only time that ABBA used such 'cheating' technology in concert—all other singing and playing was fully live.

An early take of the instrumental backing track, originally titled 'Billy Boy', was included in the medley of previously unreleased takes 'ABBA Undeleted' in 1994 (see Appendix I for details). At this early stage, the song had a more rock feel than the released version. The final version was more pop, but Benny points out another influence: 'The guitar playing is more country music-like. There is definitely a country music feel to this song'.

The single was another multinational No. 1 hit. In the US, it was reported as being ABBA's biggest-selling single, though it only reached No. 3 in the Hot 100. It was a beneficiary of Atlantic Records' ABBA Month in May 1978, which also saw the parent album become ABBA's highest-charting American album, peaking at No. 14. See the entry about the *Olivia!* television special in Appendix I for more details.

'Take a Chance on Me' was also included in *Mamma Mia!* on stage and in both films. In the first film, it is a fun scene sung by British actor Julie Walters and Swedish actor Stellan Skarsgård, while in the sequel, it appears in a post-credits gag scene with a surprise gay twist.

'One Man, One Woman'
Duration: 4.25

Frida sings this song about a troubled marriage. It is another adult situation: here we have a wife and husband hitting a rough patch in their relationship. The story opens with silence over breakfast, then the husband leaves for work. The wife despairs over the love that seems lost between them. Later, she hears his key in the front door, he comes in smiling, and she realises there is still hope for the future. Some critics have hinted it could be a semi-autobiographical look inside Björn and Agnetha's marriage at the time, though when the song was recorded, they were expecting their second child, and their separation was almost eighteen months in the future.

The majestic instrumental coda sneaks up on the listener. The strings playing during the chorus increase in volume in each chorus repeat, until the coda when they are released from hiding behind the vocals. The string arrangement was written by bassist Rutger Gunnarsson, who would write most of the string arrangements for ABBA for the next three years, until the last song to feature a real orchestra, 'The Winner Takes It All', in 1980.

'The Name of the Game'
Written by Benny Andersson, Stig Anderson, and Björn Ulvaeus.
Duration: 4.54
Released as a single 17 October 1977.

'The Name of the Game', the first new song recorded after the release of the *Arrival* album in October 1976 and the concert tours of Europe and Australia between January and March 1977, marks a turning point for ABBA and the start of the second half of the group's career. A more mature, adult sound, previously only heard in 'Knowing Me, Knowing You', would come to dominate ABBA's output from this point, even on those songs that might be considered 'lighter' pop material.

Between the tour and the first recording sessions for what would be *ABBA: The Album*, Benny, Björn, and engineer Michael B. Tretow visited Los Angeles to investigate recording equipment to outfit their own recording studio, which was under construction at this time and would open in May 1978. As well as looking for recording equipment, Benny and Björn were inspired by the 'soft rock' music coming out of America, which would influence several of the songs recorded during the year.

'The Name of the Game' was ABBA's most complexly constructed song to date. Its melody contains six distinct sections that are all very different from each other, but due to the song's production, and Agnetha's and Frida's voices, the song holds together. Its most distinct feature is the opening synthesizer riff.

Writer Carl Magnus Palm makes the observation in his biography *Bright Lights Dark Shadows: The Real Story of ABBA*: 'The song is centred around a bass and synthesizer riff which sounded like a slowed-down cousin to its counterpart in Stevie Wonder's "I Wish"', a 1976 hit. Björn responded in the book *Mamma Mia! How Can I Resist You?*: 'I don't personally make any connection with that song'. The American soft rock influence can be perceived in the chorus; the chord sequence in the first part of the chorus ('What's the name of the game/does it mean anything to you') resembles the chord pattern in the chorus of east coast band Boston's 1976 breakthrough hit 'More Than a Feeling'. Another striking feature is the high piccolo trumpet sound heard during the chorus, inspired by The Beatles' 1967 single 'Penny Lane', which in turn had been inspired by Bach's 'Brandenburg Concerto No. 2'. This recording is an excellent example of Benny and Björn's ability to bring together diverse influences to create something new and unique.

The song is one of only three in ABBA's released catalogue to feature solo vocal sections from both Agnetha and Frida, though other parts of the song are sung in unison or harmony (the other two being 'Midnight Special' in 1975 and 'The Way Old Friends Do' in 1979).

The inspiration for the lyric is most unusual. Björn relates the story: 'The lyric for "The Name of the Game" was written for Lasse Hallström. He needed a song for one of the scenes in *ABBA: The Movie*, which he was directing. The storyline featured a reporter who was meant to be chasing us all around Australia while we were on tour there, trying to get an interview with us. And in the movie there's a short sequence where he has a dream that he is a psychiatrist and is listening to Agnetha lying there, pouring out her feelings for him'. Which came as a surprise to his songwriting partner: 'I only found out in 2006 that Björn had written the lyric for Lasse's movie,' Benny responded. Contrary to popular belief, it is not a song about the state of Björn and Agnetha's marriage at that time.

ABBA's more mature sound took some getting used to. The only country to send the single to the top of the charts was the UK, though it was top ten across Europe, and top twenty in North America. In Australia, it marked the end of Abbamania, crawling up the singles chart to peak at No. 6 three months after release.

A 3.56 edited version appeared on the 1982 compilation *The Singles: The First Ten Years*, and other compilation albums, right up to the 1997 remastered CD *ABBA: The Album*. This edit, which removed the whole second verse, originated with a promotional single for Atlantic Records in the US in 1977. Inexplicably, the edit was created at Polar Music by editing the single's master tape, which was later used for compiling those releases. Later compilations and re-releases of *ABBA: The Album* included the restored full-length version.

In 1996, American hip-hop group Fugees used a sample from 'The Name of the Game' on their track 'Rumble in the Jungle', for the film soundtrack *When*

We Were Kings. For the first time, Benny and Björn approved a sample from an ABBA recording. Benny commented 'it was flattering that they wanted to use "The Name of the Game", because here was this incredibly hip American band wanting to use our track from the 1970s'. To date, they have only approved samples on three other occasions, the others being 'Gimme! Gimme! Gimme! (A Man After Midnight)' in 2005 and 'SOS' and 'Soldiers' in 2015.

'Move On'
Written by Benny Andersson, Stig Anderson, and Björn Ulvaeus. Spanish lyric by Buddy and Mary McCluskey.
Duration: 4.42

'Move On' was the final song recorded for *ABBA: The Album*. The song is an ode to the journey of life. The first verse features a spoken word passage from Björn, backed by a humming melody; the second verse is sung by Agnetha solo; while on the third verse Frida joins Agnetha with a harmony vocal.

Due to Agnetha's advancing pregnancy, she was not always able to participate in recording sessions for *ABBA: The Album*. Though Agnetha has a lead vocal in two of the verses of 'Move On', it is hard to hear her in the chorus melody and harmonies, which are dominated by Frida's voice—it is quite likely she is not there at all, but Agnetha's voice can be heard in the 'la-la-la' backing that increases in volume during each chorus, until it overwhelms the final chorus repeats.

Agnetha and Björn's son, Christian, would be born in 4 December, just a week before *ABBA: The Album* was released.

'Move On' was the last ABBA song to feature a songwriting co-credit for Stig Anderson, though by this stage of ABBA's career, apparently his contribution was limited to titles. He said later: 'I don't miss writing lyrics. It is extremely demanding. Granted it contributed to the business, but it isn't the kind of burden you want to carry for too long a period of time'.

A Spanish version entitled 'Al Andar' ('When walking') was recorded in 1980 for the *Gracias Por La Música* album, but with Benny and Björn overseas in Barbados on a songwriting trip while Agnetha and Frida were recording the Spanish vocals, Agnetha sang the first verse, replacing Björn's spoken word verse. When that album was repackaged as *ABBA Oro* in the 1993, the title was modified to 'El Andar' (Walking).

'Hole in Your Soul'
Duration: 3.41

On an album that is filled with downbeat songs and mature themes, 'Hole in Your Soul' stands out as a bright spot on side two of *ABBA: The Album*. It is a party song, an ode to a rock 'n' roll lifestyle.

Like several of ABBA's previous attempts at a rock song, there is something that is not quite right with 'Hole in Your Soul'. Like 'Watch Out' on the *Waterloo* album in 1974, the electric guitars are not loud enough, and it does not have the 'four on the floor' drum pattern of a typical rock song, instead bongo drums drive the rhythm. When performed in concert on ABBA's 1979 and 1980 tours, the song works a lot better.

The centre section of the song ('aha, you paint your world and use all colours' etc.) uses the melody of part of the chorus of 'Get on the Carousel', an unrecorded song that ABBA had performed in concert on the tour earlier in the year, as part of the ambitious mini-musical *The Girl with the Golden Hair*. 'Hole in Your Soul' was originally much longer than the version that was released. An additional verse and a repeat of the 'aha' breakdown section were edited from the song.

Apparently the names mentioned in the second verse are a tribute to real people known to ABBA: Sam the chauffeur was ABBA's driver during a trip in the US; Jerry who works in the office is Jerry Greenberg, head of Atlantic Records, ABBA's North American licensee; Annie who goes to school was his daughter; and Sue who lies by the pool was the secretary of the British ABBA Fan Club.

The highly-percussive opening, which includes some vamping on electric piano from Benny and a descending guitar riff from Lasse Wellander, was used over the opening titles of *ABBA: The Movie*.

Polar Music's original plan was to release 'Hole in Your Soul' as the lead single from *ABBA: The Album*. RCA Records in Australia had even assigned the single a catalogue number in anticipation of the first new ABBA release since the concert tour in March. Björn and Benny recorded a promotional message to be sent to Polar Music's international licensees, promoting the song as the single. But somewhere along the way plans were changed and 'The Name of the Game' was released instead, probably because it featured in a major scene in the forthcoming *ABBA: The Movie*, leaving 'Hole in Your Soul' as a highlight of the album.

'Hole in Your Soul' makes a short appearance in the film *Mamma Mia! Here We Go Again*, sung by the Greek taverna band during a party scene towards the end of the film.

The Girl with the Golden Hair—3 Scenes from a Mini Musical

For the climax of ABBA's concerts in Europe and Australia in 1977, Björn and Benny created a four-song sequence they described as a mini-musical, *The Girl with the Golden Hair*. It was an age when concerts were becoming more theatrical, notably by artists like David Bowie and Alice Cooper. In concert, Agnetha and Frida were dressed identically in gold and white costumes and blonde wigs, both portraying the titular girl. Agnetha sang the first song, 'Thank You for the Music', Frida sang the second, 'I Wonder (Departure)', and the two women came together for the remaining two songs, 'I'm a Marionette' and 'Get on the Carousel', with audiences unable to distinguish between them. The songs were linked with music, and narration by British actor Francis Matthews.

Years later, Benny commented: 'I suspect the whole thing was probably quite weird for the audiences: they just wanted to see ABBA,' adding that 'it was not a good choice for a tour'. Some critics acknowledged that ABBA were brave to include something so ambitious in their concerts.

Only three of the mini-musical songs were recorded for *ABBA: The Album*. The final song, 'Get on the Carousel', was not recorded in the studio but did appear in some form to the public. See the entry for that song in Appendix I.

'Thank You for the Music'
Written by Benny Andersson and Björn Ulvaeus. Spanish lyric by Buddy and Mary McCluskey.
Duration: 3.48

In 'Thank You for the Music', the girl with the golden hair, portrayed by Agnetha, is singing about how she loves to dance and sing and how music brings such joy to her life. '"Thank You for the Music" is a deceptive song,' Benny says. 'Although it sounds simple on the surface, there are a lot of chords in there. You don't realise until you try to play it. This is the perfect song to play on the piano; it sits easily on the keyboard.'

The lyrics in the second verse were rewritten for the studio recording. In the original concert version, Agnetha thanks 'the guys who bring the sweet memories into our lives', namechecking The Beach Boys' songwriting genius Brian Wilson, '50s rock 'n' roll legend Chuck Berry, and The Beatles' John Lennon and Paul McCartney.

At the end of the 1977 concerts, a reprise of the chorus was performed, with ABBA and all their backing musicians and singers lined up across the front of the stage.

An earlier attempt at recording this song was released on the four CD boxset *Thank You for the Music* in 1994. It has been dubbed the Doris Day version, due to Agnetha's singing in the style of the iconic American singer and actress of the '40s, '50s, and '60s.

Unlike the other songs in the mini-musical, 'Thank You for the Music' has had a long second life outside its original concept. Though it was never a major international single (in 1978, it was the B-side of 'Eagle'), the song is regarded by many as one of ABBA's signature songs, thanks to its inclusion on compilations such as *Greatest Hits Vol. 2* and *ABBA Gold*, in ABBA's 1979 and 1980 concerts, its release as a single in some countries in 1983 to promote local compilation albums, and in the *Mamma Mia!* musical. It was also recorded in Spanish as the title track of the album *Gracias Por La Música* in 1980.

It is a song that Benny has returned to frequently. He has played a solo piano version on television, on radio, in concert (most recently in December 2019, at a Swedish festival in Hong Kong), and on the menu screen for the 2005 DVD release of *ABBA: The Movie*. He has even played it to a room full of ABBA fans when he made a surprise appearance at the annual International ABBA Fan Club Day at ABBA The Museum in 2016. It is also one of six ABBA songs he recorded for his solo album *Piano* in 2017, and in promoting the album, he has played it on several television programmes and also made a music video, filmed in his Riksmixningsverket Studio in Stockholm.

'I Wonder (Departure)'
Written by Benny Andersson, Stig Anderson, and Björn Ulvaeus.
Duration: 4.33
Released on the B-side of 'The Name of the Game', 17 October 1977.

In the second song of *The Girl with the Golden Hair* Frida sings about being torn between the bonds to her friends, family, and home town and leaving to pursue her dream of becoming a famous star. 'We wanted a sad ballad and as always the melody came first. I felt that it would provide the vehicle for explaining this girl's trepidation, the worry that surrounds any departure, the feeling of what's going to happen to me,' Björn remembered. In some aspects, the lyric reflects Frida's own life, when she left her husband and children in 1969 to pursue her singing career in Stockholm.

A live recording taped at one of ABBA's concerts in Sydney, Australia, in March 1977 was included on the B-side of 'The Name of the Game' single. Unlike most of ABBA's released live recordings, the only studio overdub was Benny's delightful piano solo following the first chorus, which replaced the soprano saxophone solo performed in concert. Many listeners feel that the immediacy and emotion of the live recording make it a more compelling listening experience than the studio version. Today the live version can be heard on the CD boxset *Thank You for the Music*, or on the Deluxe Edition of *ABBA: The Album*.

In early rehearsals for the concert tour, 'I Wonder' had a completely different lyric, possibly titled 'So Simple'. Instead of expressing her concerns at leaving her old life behind, in the early version Frida sings of her doubts about forming a relationship with a man. Such a lyric does not really progress the story from small town girl who wants to sing to famous star trapped by fame, which is probably why it was rewritten as heard in the song we know today.

'I Wonder' is another of the six ABBA songs Benny plays on his 2017 album *Piano*, though oddly he omitted the piano break after the first chorus. It was also recorded for the film *Mamma Mia! Here We Go Again*, serving the same function as in *The Girl with the Golden Hair*. The song was cut from the film, but appears on the soundtrack CD and as an extra on DVD, Blu-ray, 4K, and digital releases.

'I'm a Marionette'
Duration: 3.54

In 'I'm a Marionette', the girl with the golden hair has become a star but feels trapped in her fame, with others pulling the strings controlling her (like a marionette): her management, the media, and fans, and she feels completely out of place. Björn describes the story: 'This girl was in the big city and had made it, and now she was starting to feel that everyone wanted a piece of her, that events were outside her control. Although it had not been exactly like that for us, even though most of the song was fiction, there was still a little bit of truth about our situation'. It made for a rather depressing finale for ABBA's fifth studio album.

Unusually for an ABBA song, 'I'm a Marionette' changes tempo and time signature. The verses start in 4/4, or common time, four beats to the bar, before switching to 3/4, or waltz time, while the chorus is primarily in 3/4, switching to 4/4 for a couple of bars, and has a slower tempo than the verses. The song was restructured for the studio recording, with a twenty-six-second-long, bass-led introduction, and a one-minute-long free-form guitar solo.

10

Voulez-Vous

Sweden:	23 April 1979
UK:	4 May 1979
US:	6 June 1979
Current edition:	Universal Music/Polar CD 549 955-2
Personnel:	Rolf Alex: drums
	Benny Andersson: keyboards, synthesizers, vocals
	Ola Brunkert: drums
	Lars O. Carlsson: saxophones
	Anders Eljas: string arrangements
	Agnetha Fältskog: vocals
	Joe Galdo: drums
	Malando Gassama: percussion
	Rutger Gunnarsson: bass, string and horn arrangements
	Paul Harris: bass
	Nils Landgren: trombone
	Ish Ledesma: guitar
	Anni-Frid Lyngstad: vocals
	Roger Palm: drums
	Halldor Pálsson: saxophone
	Arnold Paseiro: bass
	Jan Risberg: Oboe
	Janne Schaffer: guitar
	Johan Stengård: saxophone
	George Terry: guitar
	Björn Ulvaeus: guitar, vocals
	Mike Watson: Bass
	Lasse Wellander: guitar, banjo
	Katjek Wojciechowski: saxophone

International School of Stockholm Choir: vocals on 'I Have a
Dream'

Duration: 42 minutes
Recorded at Polar Music Studio, Marcus Music, Stockholm; Criteria Studio,
Miami: April 1978–March 1979
Produced and arranged by Benny Andersson and Björn Ulvaeus
Engineered by Michael B. Tretow
Chart position: Sweden: 1
                    UK: 1
                    US: 19

ABBA's disco-flavoured sixth album was recorded in difficult circumstances. With Benny and Björn suffering from writer's block, and the breakdown of Björn and Agnetha's marriage, it took longer to record than any other ABBA album. Its contents continued the maturation of ABBA's songs, with more adult themes and openly sexual songs. Benny said at the time of the album's release: 'We didn't rush to make a disco record so that we could keep up with everyone else, just that when you hear a good record you get inspired to create one that's equally good of your own. We found that disco-based rhythms suited and enhanced our music so naturally we used them'. Though, in later years, he has said that he thought it was a mistake for ABBA to go down the disco road.

The title track was ABBA's only studio recording not recorded in Sweden. There were many songs attempted but dropped during sessions for *Voulez-Vous*. 'For a while nothing really happened. Then we threw a lot of songs away,' Benny said. The 1978 single 'Summer Night City' was originally slated for inclusion on the album, but it was dropped due to bad feelings about the recording from Benny and Björn. Both it and the single released several months after the album, 'Gimme! Gimme! Gimme! (A Man After Midnight)', have become welcome inclusions on CD reissues.

In keeping with with the disco theme of the album, the sleeve was photographed at Alexandra's Disco, one of Stockholm's trendiest nightspots, with Benny, Björn, Frida, and Agnetha dressed for a glamorous night out.

Reviewer David Brennan wrote in 2018: '… it may not be their gloomiest album … but *Voulez-Vous* is surely, beneath its mirror-ball glitz, the bleakest, a catalogue of empty trysts, seedy nightlife and emotional manipulation'.

The DVD with the 2010 Deluxe Edition included the 1979 international co-production *ABBA in Switzerland*, which featured half of the album's songs.

'As Good As New'
Duration: 3.22

The opening track on ABBA's sixth studio album is driven by a strong disco beat, contrasted with a string figure that opens the song and supports the chorus. After 1977's fairly glum *ABBA: The Album*, here was ABBA back 'as good as new'.

The song features one of the strongest and most strident vocals Agnetha ever recorded. Here is a woman who realises she was wrong to leave her lover and is returning, begging for forgiveness and declaring that her love is 'takin'' on a new dimension'. A rather curious lyric, considering the recent breakdown of the marriage between lyric writer Björn and singer Agnetha. The couple had been growing apart for some time, and their separation was announced at the start of 1979, two months before the song was recorded. When performing 'As Good As New' in concert on ABBA's tour of North America and Europe between September and November 1979, Björn would introduce Agnetha with the slightly crass 'my ex-wife' or the rather odd 'my old friend'.

At the time *Voulez-Vous* was released, twenty-year-old aspiring dancer and singer Madonna Ciccone was living in Paris, on her long road to superstardom. Reputedly, she fell in love with the album and played it frequently. Seven years later, her song 'Papa Don't Preach', the opening track of her third album *True Blue*, featured a dramatic string opening, apparently inspired by 'As Good As New'. Madonna would later be inspired by 'Gimme! Gimme! Gimme! (A Man After Midnight)' and 'Like an Angel Passing Through My Room'.

'Voulez-Vous'
Duration: 5.11
Released as a single 3 August 1979.

The title track of ABBA's sixth studio album, 'Voulez-Vous' is the only ABBA song to be recorded outside of Sweden (excluding live concert recordings).

In January 1979, Benny and Björn travelled to the Bahamas for a songwriting holiday. With only half the songs required for the next ABBA album, several attempted recordings being deemed unsuitable, and feeling the symptoms of writer's block, they felt a trip away would recharge their batteries. In the Bahamas, they would have access to American top forty radio and could seek inspiration from the latest sounds.

Having written a disco-inspired tune, and being close to the hub of disco music, they felt the urge to record the track as soon as possible. Björn recalled: 'The Bahamas is really only half-an-hour away from Miami. So we had this idea when we were down there, why don't we go over to Miami to record it just for fun'. They contacted Atlantic Records to make arrangements and booked the world-famous Criteria Studios in Miami, where artists such as the Bee Gees, Fleetwood Mac, Eric Clapton, the Eagles, and KC & the Sunshine Band had recorded in recent years.

Local musicians, including members of the band Foxy, were hired to record the backing track. Foxy had formed in 1976 and released their biggest hit, 'Get Off', in 1978. Several legendary American record producers, including Tom Dowd and Ron and Howard Albert (known as the Albert Brothers)*, took part in the recording session. 'We had a great time doing that and it would be nice to repeat the experience with people like Tom Dowd and the group Foxy,' Benny said. Many years later, Björn agreed, with reservations: 'It was great fun, but it felt a little awkward and a bit scary because we were not only working with unfamiliar musicians but also unfamiliar surroundings'. Engineer Michael B. Tretow flew in from Sweden to ensure the recording was compatible with Polar Music Studio's equipment.

On return to the Polar Music Studios in Stockholm, the vocals and additional instruments were recorded, not least the catchy horn riff played throughout the choruses.

Björn's lyric sets the song in a discotheque, where hormones run high and dancers flirt in the dark: 'What I had in mind before I even had the title was a kind of nightclub scene, with a certain amount of sexual tension and eyes looking at each other'. Agnetha and Frida share the lead vocal. Listen closely to the phrase 'Voulez-vous, ah!' at the end of the first and third choruses: buried way down in the mix among the harmonies is the line sung as a high-pitched scream, slightly off-key.

The completed recording was so strong that 'Voulez-Vous' gave its title to ABBA's sixth studio album, and the song's aura gave the album its reputation as ABBA's so-called disco album, though only four or five of its songs could really be classed as 'disco'. It was also released as the third single from the album, backed by 'Angeleyes'. In some countries, the single was marketed as a double A-side.

An extended remixed version was created for a US promotional single for distribution to disco disc jockeys. It is the only ABBA song to be subject to an official remix. The remix was first released commercially on the compilation CD *The Definitive Collection* in 2001, and is also included on the *Voulez-Vous* Deluxe Editon CD.

'Voulez-Vous' featured as the dramatic closing number of Act One of the stage musical *Mamma Mia!*, where it was a huge all-cast dance number. It had the same function in the 2008 motion picture.

* By 1979, Dowd had produced or engineered dozens of artists since 1959, mostly for Atlantic Records or its affiliates, including The Drifters, Wilson Pickett, Solomon Burke, Dusty Springfield, Aretha Franklin, Iron Butterfly, Cher, Lulu, Dr. John, Delaney & Bonnie, the Allman Brothers Band, Eric Clapton, Rod Stewart, Lynyrd Skynyrd, and Bette Midler. The Albert Brothers, based at Criteria Studios, had produced artists including Dr. John, Sutherland Brothers & Quiver, Wishbone Ash, Crosby, Stills & Nash, Procol Harum, and Johnny Cougar (John Mellencamp), as well as a stack of disco hits as Fat Albert Productions.

'I Have a Dream'
Written by Benny Andersson and Björn Ulvaeus. Spanish lyric by Buddy and Mary McCluskey.
Duration: 4.44
Released as a single in December 1979.

The last song recorded for the *Voulez-Vous* album in March 1979, 'I Have a Dream' would also be ABBA's final single of the '70s, the decade they came to embody.

Björn remembers: 'The night I finished the lyric for "I Have a Dream", Benny was having a party over at his place'. Benny continues: 'I told the guests, "we have a new song." I played it to them and they simply thought it was a great tune…. We ended up with everybody there at the party singing that song'.

'I Have a Dream' features the International School of Stockholm Choir on the third verse, highlighting the sing-along quality of the song. 'We had specifically wanted British and American children, so that they had the right enunciation, and Swedish kids that young would seldom be totally fluent in English,' Björn said. It is the only time that any voices other than the four ABBA members are heard singing on an ABBA record.

As well as the choir, 'I Have a Dream' features another unusual sound never heard before on an ABBA record. Janne Schaffer plays the introduction and refrain on an electric sitar, adding to the international flavour of the song. Though the sitar is an Indian instrument, the way it is played here sounds more like a bouzouki. Indeed, the versions featured in the two *Mamma Mia!* musical films feature that Greek instrument.

Though envisaged as a general uplifting anthem, about personal strength, overcoming obstacles, and having a positive view of the future, there are many who see the song as a hymn. The song is popular with church choirs and Christian groups, often mistitled 'I Believe in Angels'. It is not known how Björn (an atheist) feels about this development. Some listeners connect the song with American civil rights activist Martin Luther King's famous 'I have a dream' speech in Washington, DC, in August 1963, but Benny says 'I didn't make any connection with Martin Luther King at all, and I still don't.'

In September, following the success of a Spanish version of the earlier single 'Chiquitita' in Latin America, ABBA recorded a Spanish version of 'I Have a Dream', entitled 'Estoy Soñando' ('I am dreaming'). The lyrics were written by Buddy and Mary McCluskey, who had been responsible for the Spanish lyric of 'Chiquitita'. Like the English version, the Spanish version also features a children's choir.

ABBA would perform 'I Have a Dream' in concert on their tours of North America, Europe, and Japan in 1979 and 1980. At each concert, a choir from a local school or community group would join ABBA on stage for the third verse and a reprise. In Japan, the choirs sang in Japanese, much to the delight of local audiences.

After the European leg of the tour finished, 'I Have a Dream' was released as a single, backed with a live recording of 'Take a Chance on Me' from Wembley Arena in London. In the UK, West Germany, and France, the single was packaged as a special souvenir edition, with a seasonal message from ABBA on the back of the sleeve. It was a top ten hit in several countries, topping the charts in Belgium and the Netherlands. In the UK, it was held off the top spot by Pink Floyd's 'Another Brick in the Wall, Part II', coincidentally another song featuring a children's choir. Twenty years later, 'I Have a Dream' finally reached No. 1 on the British singles chart, when Irish boy band Westlife covered the song.

'I Have a Dream' is a song that Frida has returned to in the years after ABBA. In May 1984, she sang the song at a televised concert in Geneva, Switzerland, Gala de l'ONU (United Nations Gala), backed by a children's choir, where she embarrassingly muddled the words but forged on ahead, smiling. In November the same year, Frida appeared on a French variety programme, promoting her solo album *Shine*. Greek singer Nana Mouskouri was another guest on the same programme, closed the show with her French cover of 'I Have a Dream', 'Chanter la vie' ('Sing the life'). Nana wandered through the all the show's guests who had lined up on stage, and at one point shared the microphone with Frida, though Frida sang along in English. Frida also recorded a version of 'I Have a Dream' in 2003 with her friend, Swiss entertainer and restauranteur Dan Daniell (real name Urs Biner) for a single in support of their children's charity.

'Angeleyes'
Duration: 4.20
Released as a single 3 August 1979.

'Angeleyes' is the story of a dumped lover dealing with being alone, though typically for ABBA, the glum story is hidden behind a happy, upbeat song. Here, the protagonist is out walking 'by the river' when she sees her ex-lover out with a new 'young girl'. She feels the urge to approach the new girl and tell her that despite external appearance, her man is not all that he seems. This leads to her reminiscing about the 'good times' they had in the past, and that she cannot forget him though it brings her pain.

As with several recordings in this era, the availability of ABBA's own recording studio could be seen as a blessing or a curse—in this case, more and more was loaded onto the recording. The verses are sung in harmony an octave apart, making the melody line too high or too low to comfortably sing along, while multiple harmonies and melodies in the chorus disguise the actual melody. In the film *Mamma Mia! Her We Go Again*, Benny created a less over-produced version, sung by Christine Baranski, Julie Walters, and Amanda Seyfried, which was a surprise highlight of the film.

'Angeleyes' was released on single in 1979, backing the title track 'Voulez-Vous'. In the UK and Ireland, 'Angeleyes' was the preferred side of the double-A side single, peaking at No. 3. In the US, in advance of ABBA's tour of the country, 'Angeleyes' was pushed by Atlantic Records after 'Voulez-Vous' had failed to entice record buyers. 'Voulez-Vous' had stalled at No. 80, though 'Angeleyes' did not fare that much better, peaking at No. 64.

'The King Has Lost His Crown'
Duration: 3.30

Hidden by Frida's sultry lead vocal, 'The King Has Lost His Crown' is actually a quite bitter song. The narrator is addressing a man who has recently been dumped by his 'new girl'. But rather than consoling him, she seems to be quite sarcastic in addressing his pain, as she sees him as a self-styled king of women who has lost his crown. Frida said of the song: 'It has a nice atmosphere, something new I think for ABBA, something we haven't created before'.

As well as closing out side one of the *Voulez-Vous* album, 'The King Has Lost His Crown' would be placed on the B-side of the non-album single 'Gimme! Gimme! Gimme! (A Man After Midnight)' later in the year.

'Does Your Mother Know'
Duration: 3.13
Released as a single in April 1979.

'Does Your Mother Know' was released as a single in conjunction with the *Voulez-Vous* album. It was the first time a song with a Björn solo lead had been released as an ABBA single. Early singles and the previous year's 'Summer Night City' had featured shared vocals or alternating sections, but this was his first (and only) solo single lead. Frida recalled: '... he made a demo tape of this song and it sounded very, very good, so we thought it might be a good idea to let him do the lead vocal ... and I think it worked out very, very well'.

The lyric is set in another nightclub scene, where a man is being approached by a much younger woman. 'I had read a newspaper article about relationships between men and young girls,' Björn recalled. 'I had the idea of reversing the situation and creating a song about a man who, instead of trying to pick up a girl, turns round and says, "Oh, what are you doing out tonight, does your mother know that you're out?"' Thanks to that line featuring in the chorus, which can be taken to mean being out of the closet, 'Does Your Mother Know' has joined the ranks of ABBA's gay anthems.

Listen closely to the break between the first chorus and second verse: very faint shouts can be heard, enhancing the nightclub party atmosphere. Also listen for Agnetha in the second and final choruses, when she rocks out and her voice breaks through, highlighting some words.

In the *Mamma Mia!* musical and movie, the sexes were reversed, with the older woman addressing a much younger man. The score of the 2008 film also included a fun 'oompah' band instrumental version by members of the Benny Andersson Band.

The original recording of 'Does Your Mother Know' had a long instrumental opening, which was repeated after the first chorus, based on the chord pattern of the 'take it easy' section of the song. When ABBA performed 'Does Your Mother Know' on the television special *ABBA in Switzerland*, taped in February 1979, these were still part of the song. Sometime after returning home from Switzerland, the opening and refrain were ditched and the distinctive bass synth introduction added to the song. This was the first ABBA recording using Benny's new Yamaha GX-1 synthesizer. Benny had first encountered the instrument belonging to John Paul Jones of Led Zeppelin at Polar Music Studios, when that band was recording what would be their final album, *In Through the Out Door*, in November and December 1978.

The GX-1 would become the dominant sound of ABBA's recordings from now until the end. After restoration in 2015, the instrument is still in use today in Benny's Riksmixningsverket studio—one of the few examples of this rare synthesizer still in working order. Only twenty units were ever made.

On 5 June 2016, Benny and Björn celebrated the fiftieth anniversary of their first meeting with a party at Berns Restaurant in Stockholm. Many friends and collaborators performed the music of Benny and Björn during the evening, and towards the end of the night Benny and Björn joined the band onstage to perform 'Does Your Mother Know', one of just a handful of times since 1982 that Björn has performed on stage.

'If It Wasn't for the Nights'
Duration: 5.13

'If It Wasn't for the Nights' is ABBA's most distinctive example of late-'70s Euro-disco. It is another tale of broken relationships, so common to ABBA's *oeuvre* at this time. The lyric details a person who is throwing themselves into their work and daily tasks, but cannot avoid the lonely nights at home, where they do not have the daily distractions, spending the nights missing their lost lover. Björn once admitted: 'Those lyrics were written during a period when I was feeling really depressed. I was down as hell'. The song was recorded in October and November 1978, just as Björn and Agnetha's marriage was coming to an end—they would formally separate in December.

The song is designed for the dancefloor, with a long chorus and repeated instrumental breaks. It was planned to be ABBA's next single for release in early 1979, until they came up with 'Chiquitita' and dropped it.

In anticipation of the song's projected single release, ABBA performed 'If It Wasn't for the Nights' on the Japanese television special *ABBA Special* in November 1978 and *The Mike Yarwood Show* in the UK in December. The versions used for playback mixed out the strings and some other instruments, in an effort to fool the British Musicians' Union that ABBA were performing to a newly recorded track, which was a requirement by Musicians' Union rules. *The Mike Yarwood Show* performance can be seen on the DVD in the *Voulez-Vous* Deluxe Edition (2010), while the other can be seen on the DVD *ABBA in Japan* (2009).

'Chiquitita'
Written by Benny Andersson and Björn Ulvaeus. Spanish lyric by Buddy and Mary McCluskey.
Duration: 5.26
Released as a single 16 January 1979.

'Chiquitita' was introduced to the world at the gala televised concert *The Music for UNICEF Concert: A Gift of Song*, held in the General Assembly Hall in the United Nations building in New York City to launch UNESCO's International

Year of the Child. Due to the logistics of the concert, most artists lip-synced their performances or sang live over a recorded backing track, except for a couple of fully live acoustic performances. ABBA's performance was in the first category.

Not long after the concert, Björn said: 'It was great to be part of the UNICEF show in New York, especially as we knew the concert would be seen by a world wide audience'. Frida expanded: 'It's a very, very good feeling to do something, and especially for the children because … all of us have children and we're all aware of that situation in the world'. All royalties for 'Chiquitita' were donated to UNICEF in perpetuity, and to date, it has reportedly earned over $4 million.

In 2014, the campaign was relaunched, with royalties from 'Chiquitita' now being directed to UNICEF charities supporting young girls. With the relaunch, Björn announced that it was intended to release a new recording of 'Chiquitita' every year, but after just one by Swedish artist Laleh, the idea seems to have petered out.

'Chiquitita' means 'little girl' in Spanish. The lyrics are consoling, with a message of hope in the chorus to 'shine once more like you did before/sing a new song', making it the ideal song to donate to UNICEF.

Within weeks of the concert 'Chiquitita' was released as ABBA's next worldwide single, except in the US, where Atlantic Records was reluctant to release a new single without an album to release in its wake. At the time, the *Voulez-Vous* album was far from completion, with no scheduled release date. The single was finally released near the end of the year, when any impact from the concert was lost.

'Chiquitita' is another ABBA song that went through various lyrical choices. The initial version was titled 'In the Arms of Rosalita' with solo lead vocals from both Frida and Agnetha. A short fragment of that recording was played by Björn and Michael B. Tretow on the 1999 television documentary *The Winner Takes It All—The ABBA Story*. The song evolved with another lyric entitled 'Chiquitita Angelina', which in turn led to the finished version. '"Chiquitita" is another one of those percussive phrases, like "Take a Chance on Me",' Björn said. 'I think "Chiquitita" was the third title I had tried for the song. Never have I tried so many different complete lyrics, getting the girls to sing them, and still not been convinced.'

The song features the most complex backing vocal lines on an ABBA song since 'Knowing Me, Knowing You' three years earlier. The lyric both echoes and expands on the main lyric, with a counter melody that fits between and behind the main melody line.

'Chiquitita' was a return to form for ABBA, after the perceived failure of the previous single 'Summer Night City'. 'Chiquitita' was a No. 1 hit in several countries. In the UK, it entered at No. 8, ABBA's highest ever British chart entry position, though it was held off the top spot by Blondie's smash hit 'Heart of Glass'.

As the single was climbing the charts around the world, Buddy McCluskey of RCA Records, ABBA's licensee in Argentina, suggested to Stig Anderson that ABBA should record a Spanish version of 'Chiquitita'. ABBA had not enjoyed the same level of success in South America as they had in other parts of the world. McCluskey said: 'ABBA had been gaining popularity for a long time but "Chiquitita" is what really made the break for them. Mary, my wife and myself sat down and wrote a Spanish translation of the song and the girls recorded the vocals. The strange thing is that both versions, Spanish and English, were hits. Although the Spanish one was the biggest smash'. It was reported that the Spanish version was the biggest hit in Latin America in twenty-five years.

'Lovers (Live a Little Longer)'
Duration: 3.28

'Lovers (Live a Little Longer)' was the first song recorded for what became the *Voulez-Vous* album. It is one of the more adult, even sexual songs on the album. Björn said of the song on an Australian promotional record: 'It's rather special, you know. It's a song in a vein that I don't think we've done in ABBA before'.

'Lovers (Live a Little Longer)' was inspired by a real headline that Björn had spotted in a magazine, in which a physician had declared that lovers (presumably sexual) did indeed live longer. Frida gives a most sensual performance in the verses, though the shrill, high-pitched vocals in the chorus let the song down.

A hidden feature in the chorus is the high-pitched repeated line 'lovers live a little longer lovers live a little longer', buried to be almost inaudible in the mix, but can be more clearly heard through the OOPS process (out of phase stereo), which cancels out parts of a recording that are centred in the stereo mix.

'Kisses of Fire'
Duration: 3.16

The first verse of 'Kisses of Fire' is the most erotic piece of music in the ABBA catalogue, as Agnetha invites her lover to lay his head on her chest, touch her lips and 'see' with his fingertips. There is no mistaking the intentions of this invitation. The rest of the song is a 1979 ABBA disco banger, with Agnetha and Frida doing their best breathy Bee Gees impression in the second verse.

'Kisses of Fire' was the closing track on *Voulez-Vous*, as well as the B-side of the 'Does Your Mother Know' single.

In the film sequel *Mamma Mia! Here We Go Again*, 'Kisses of Fire' makes a somewhat interesting appearance, sung by actor Panos Mouzourakis fronting a ragtag Greek taverna band. On the film's soundtrack album, the song is completed in ABBA style, sung by actors Jessica Keenan Wynn and Alexa Davies as Tanya and Rosie, the younger versions of the characters played by Christine Baranski and Julie Walters in both *Mamma Mia!* films.

ABBA. *Clockwise from top left*: Björn Ulvaeus, Benny Andersson, Agnetha Fältskog, and Anni-Frid (Frida) Lyngstad. (*Photo: Bengt H. Malmqvist © Premium Rockshot*)

Above left: ABBA's first album *Ring Ring* (1973) was released under the banner 'Björn & Benny, Agnetha & Frida'. The album was released in a handful of countries at the time, only receiving full international release in 1992. (*Polar Music International*)

Above right: *Waterloo* (1974) was the first album released under the name ABBA, and in much of the world, it was the first ABBA album released. Highlights include the single 'Honey, Honey' and the alternate Eurovision selection 'Hasta Mañana'. (*Polar Music International*)

Below left: ABBA's self-titled third album (1975) included the worldwide hits 'SOS' and 'Mamma Mia'. Each member of the group had a featured spot on the album. (*Polar Music International*)

Below right: In August 1975, Polydor in the Netherlands released a compilation entitled *The Best of ABBA*, which was subsequently released in West Germany, Austria, and Switzerland. Around the same time, Vogue in France and Belgium released similar albums entitled *Greatest Hits*. In November, RCA in Australia also released *The Best of ABBA*. (*discogs.com*)

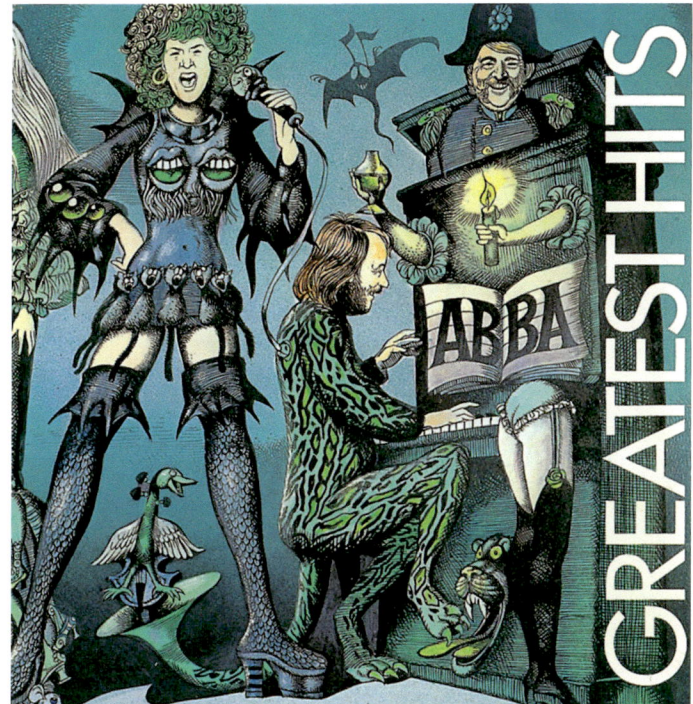

Greatest Hits was released in Scandinavia in November 1975. The album featured songs from ABBA's first three albums. The bizarre wraparound cover image was drawn by illustrator Hans Arnold. (*Polar Music International*)

Greatest Hits was released in the UK in March 1976. The brand-new single 'Fernando' was added to the album, though it was not listed on the first pressing sleeve seen here. Many other countries, including the US, copied this cover for their compilations in 1976. (*discogs.com*)

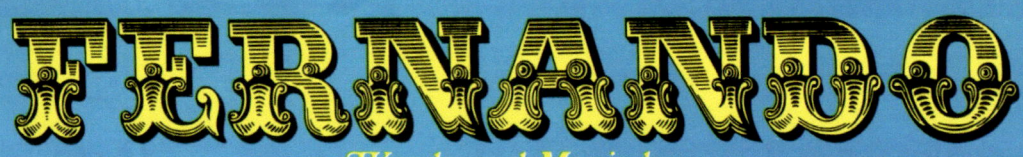

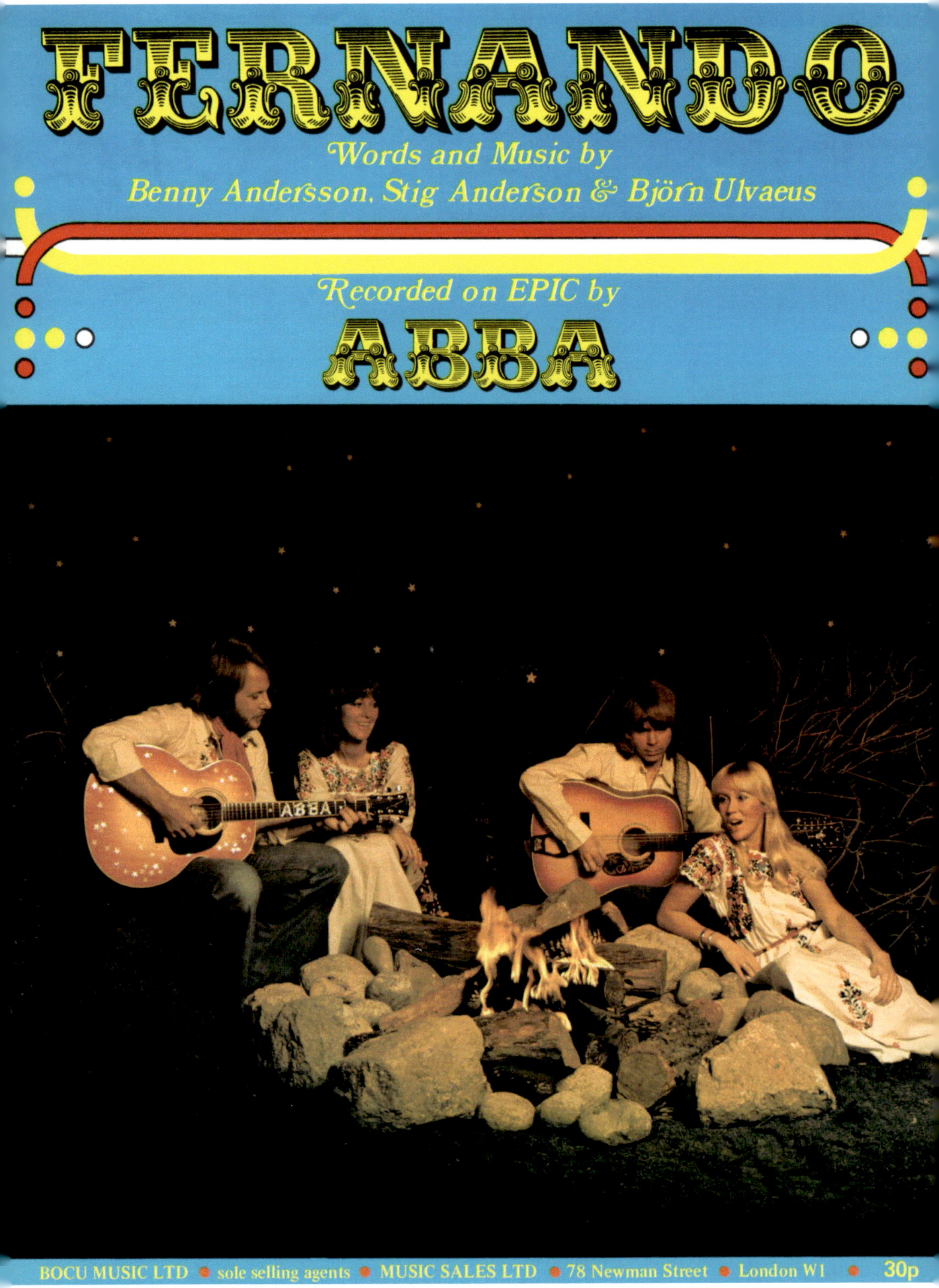
FERNANDO
Words and Music by
Benny Andersson, Stig Anderson & Björn Ulvaeus
Recorded on EPIC by
ABBA
ABBA
BOCU MUSIC LTD • sole selling agents • MUSIC SALES LTD • 78 Newman Street • London W1 • 30p

'Fernando', released in 1976, was never included on one of ABBA's studio albums. During the group's lifetime, it was their most successful single. The photograph on this British sheet music was taken during the filming of the promotional film. (*Andy Wetson collection*)

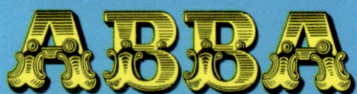

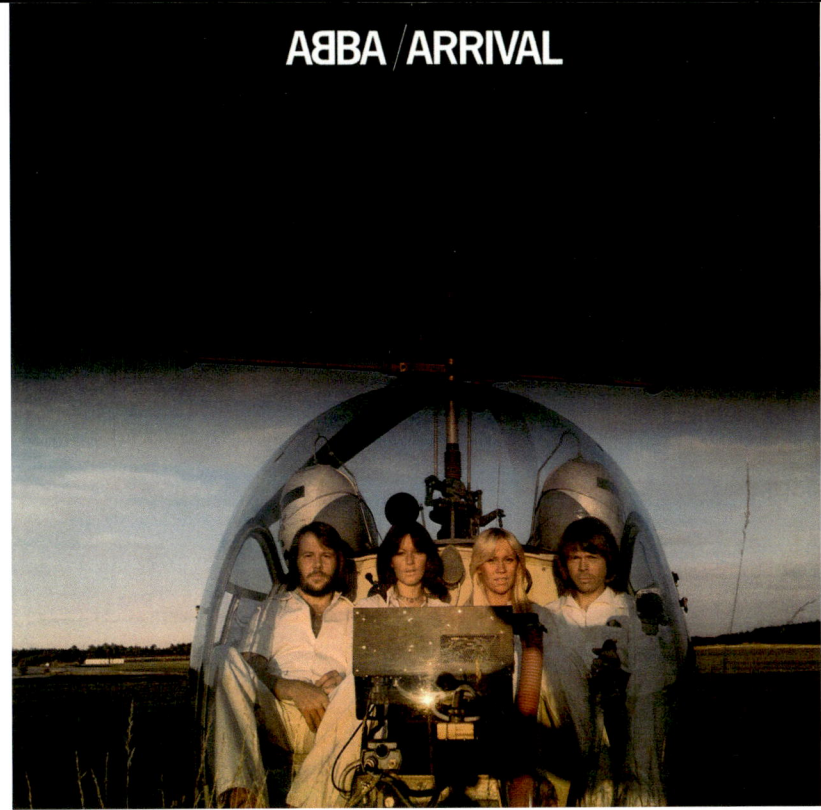

Above: Arrival (1976) is ABBA's first classic album and a worldwide No. 1, with hits 'Dancing Queen', 'Money, Money, Money', and 'Knowing Me, Knowing You'. The album's sleeve, featuring the four members crammed into the cabin of a Bell 47 helicopter, became an iconic image and one of the world's most recognised album covers. (*Polar Music International*)

Below left: ABBA's first major international concert tour took place between January and March 1977. ABBA performed in Norway, Sweden, Denmark, West Germany, the Netherlands, Belgium, the UK, and Australia. The tour programme features a vivid rendition of the ABBA logo, designed by artist Rune Söderqvist. (*Author's collection*)

Below right: ABBA's fifth studio album *ABBA: The Album* (1977) was released in conjunction with *ABBA: The Movie*. More ambitious than previous albums, it included the hit singles 'The Name of the Game' and 'Take a Chance on Me'. (*Polar Music International*)

ABBA on television, showing off some of their glamorous and memorable costumes. These bubble gum cards were available in Australia in 1976 and 1977, a popular collector's item. (*Author's collection*)

A rare postcard showing Frida and Agnetha in Metronome Studio, recording new lyrics for 'Fernando' for an advertising jingle for National electronics, 1976. Metronome was ABBA's favourite recording studio, until Polar Music Studios opened in 1978. The studio still operates today as Atlantis Studio. (*Author's collection*)

ABBA: The Movie (1977) was filmed primarily during ABBA's hugely successful Australian concert tour, with some additional filming in Stockholm. It premiered in Sydney, Australia, on 15 December 1977 and in Stockholm on 26 December. The original poster used the same artwork as *ABBA: The Album*, but some countries opted for this photograph, seen here on the cover of a Japanese souvenir programme. (*Author's collection*)

Polar Music Studios in Stockholm

Polar Music Studios officially opened in May 1978. The studio was built to specifications from Benny, Björn, and recording engineer Michael B. Tretow. ABBA recorded almost all of the tracks on their final three albums here. It was one of the first studios in Europe to install digital recording equipment in 1981. This pamphlet, with photographs by Anders Hanser, was produced to promote the studio when it opened. Polar Music Studios closed in 2004. (*Private collection*)

Chiquitita

Words and Music by
BENNY ANDERSSON
and BJÖRN ULVAEUS

Recorded by

ABBA®

on
EPIC
Records

channell

'Chiquitita' was presented to the world at *The Music for UNICEF Concert: A Gift of Song*, broadcast from the General Assembly at the United Nations' building in New York in January 1979. Royalties were granted in perpetuity to UNICEF. To date, the song has raised over $4 million. (*Author's collection*)

Above: Voulez-Vous (1979) is widely regarded as ABBA's disco album. Singles included 'Chiquitita', 'Does Your Mother Know', 'Angeleyes', 'I Have a Dream', and the title track. The album sleeve was photographed at the very 'in' Stockholm nightspot Alexandra's Disco. (*Polar Music International*)

Below: ABBA's second official compilation album *Greatest Hits Vol. 2* (1979) was released in the middle of ABBA's 1979 tour. It included hits from *Arrival*, *ABBA: The Album*, and *Voulez-Vous*, plus 'Rock Me' from the *ABBA* album, a 1976 hit in Australia and New Zealand, and the brand-new single 'Gimme! Gimme! Gimme! (A Man After Midnight)'. (*Polar Music International*)

ABBA's second international concert tour took in Canada, the US, Sweden, Denmark, France, the Netherlands, West Germany, Switzerland, Austria, Belgium, and the UK between September and November 1979, with an additional leg in Japan in 1980. The ice mountains image on the cover of the tour programme was also used as the stage backdrop on the tour and went on to become the logo for Polar Music. A stylized version of the logo is still used on Universal Music's ABBA releases today. (*Author's collection*)

In 1980, ABBA released the Spanish-language album *Gracias Por La Música* in South America and Spain. The album also had limited release in the US, the UK, Japan, South Africa, Israel, and Australia. It featured Spanish versions of ten ABBA hit singles and album tracks. (*Polar Music International*)

Above: *Super Trouper* (1980) saw a more mature, reflective ABBA. Its lead single, 'The Winner Takes It All', reflected on Björn and Agnetha's break-up, while other songs addressed world troubles. The title track, 'On and On and On', and 'Lay All Your Love on Me' all had single release. (*Polar Music International*)

Below: ABBA's final studio album, *The Visitors* (1981), saw an all new ABBA. Gone were the love songs of the past, replaced by paranoia, Cold War fears, and adult issues of children growing up and relationships ending. The album featured ABBA's last major international hit single, 'One of Us'. (*Polar Music International*)

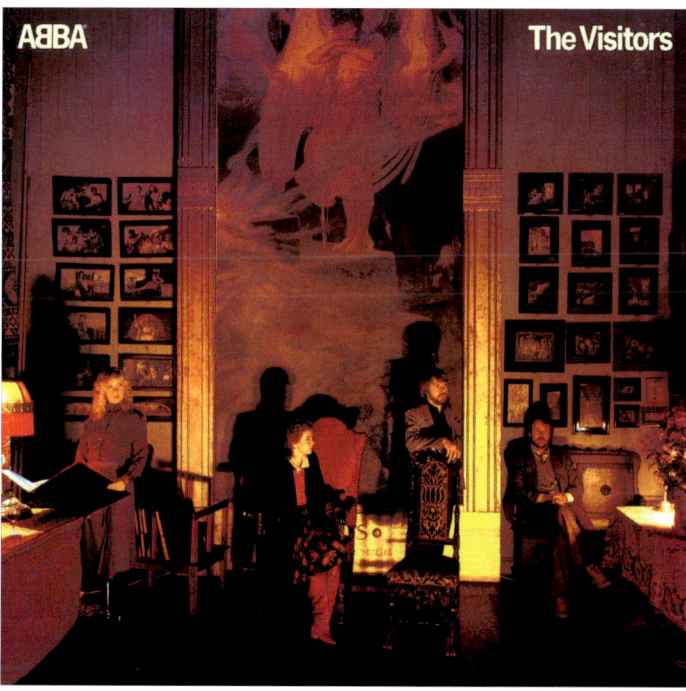

Above: ABBA's time together ended with the career-spanning compilation *The Singles: The First Ten Years* (1982), containing twenty-three international hits from 'Ring Ring' in 1973 to the final singles 'The Day Before You Came' and 'Under Attack'. (*Polar Music International*)

Below: ABBA's records were released around the world by different record companies, often with different sleeves. Here are sleeves for ABBA's classic 'Dancing Queen' from Sweden (Polar), France (Melba), Australia (RCA), German Democratic Republic (East Germany) (Amiga), West Germany (Polydor), and Japan (Discomate). (*Polar Music International, author's collection, discogs.com*)

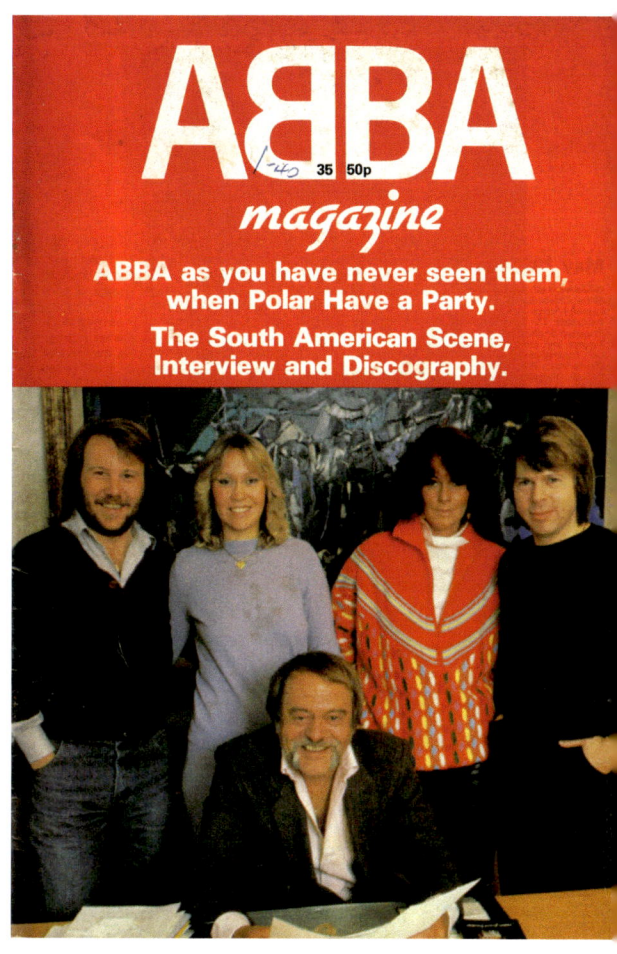

Right: Between 1977 and 1983, the official *ABBA Magazine* was published in Britain and distributed internationally (retitled *International ABBA Magazine* in 1981). The magazine ran for a total of sixty-five issues. Issue 35 seen here reported on manager Stig Anderson's fiftieth birthday party in January 1981. (*Author's collection*)

Below: In 1986, Polar Music released *ABBA Live*, a collection of concert recordings from the Australian tour in March 1977, London's Wembley Arena in November 1979, and the 1981 television concert from the special *Dick Cavett Meets ABBA*. Seen here is a rare promotional postcard—'AB' appeared on the front of the album sleeve and 'BA' on the back. (*Author's collection*)

The compilation CD *ABBA Gold: Greatest Hits* was released in September 1992 and spurred a worldwide ABBA revival. The CD features nineteen of ABBA's most popular hits. It has become ABBA's biggest seller, with over 31 million copies sold to date. (*Polar Music International*)

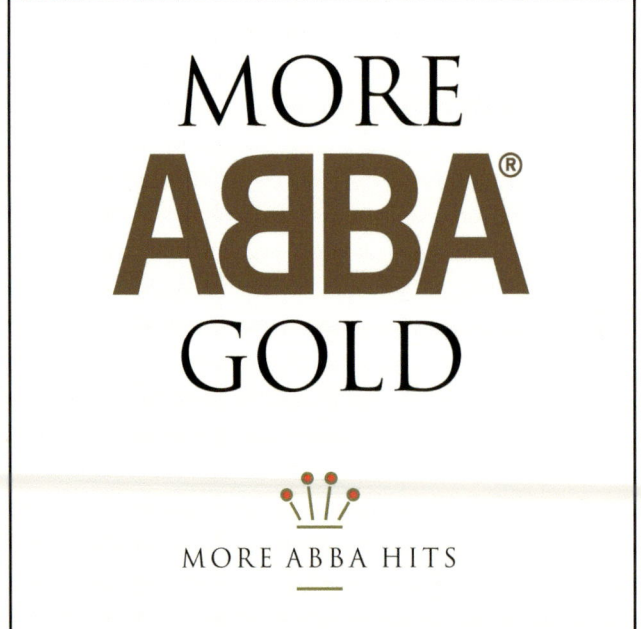

Following the success of *ABBA Gold*, in 1993, the follow-up compilation *More ABBA Gold: More ABBA Hits* was released. It included further hits not included on *ABBA Gold*, single B-sides, popular album tracks, and the unreleased 1982 recording 'I Am the City'. (*Polar Music International*)

Right: ABBA got the boxset treatment in 1994 with the four CD collection *Thank You for the Music*. The first three discs included ABBA hit singles, album tracks, and B-sides, while the fourth disc included hard-to-find rarities and a selection of previously-unreleased tracks. (*Polar Music International*)

Below: ABBA Live at Wembley Arena is a double CD/triple LP of a full ABBA concert recorded in London on 10 November 1979. It was released in September 2014, thirty-five years after it was recorded. The album features the first ever release of Agnetha's poignant ballad 'I'm Still Alive'. (*Polar Music International*)

THANK YOU FOR THE MUSIC

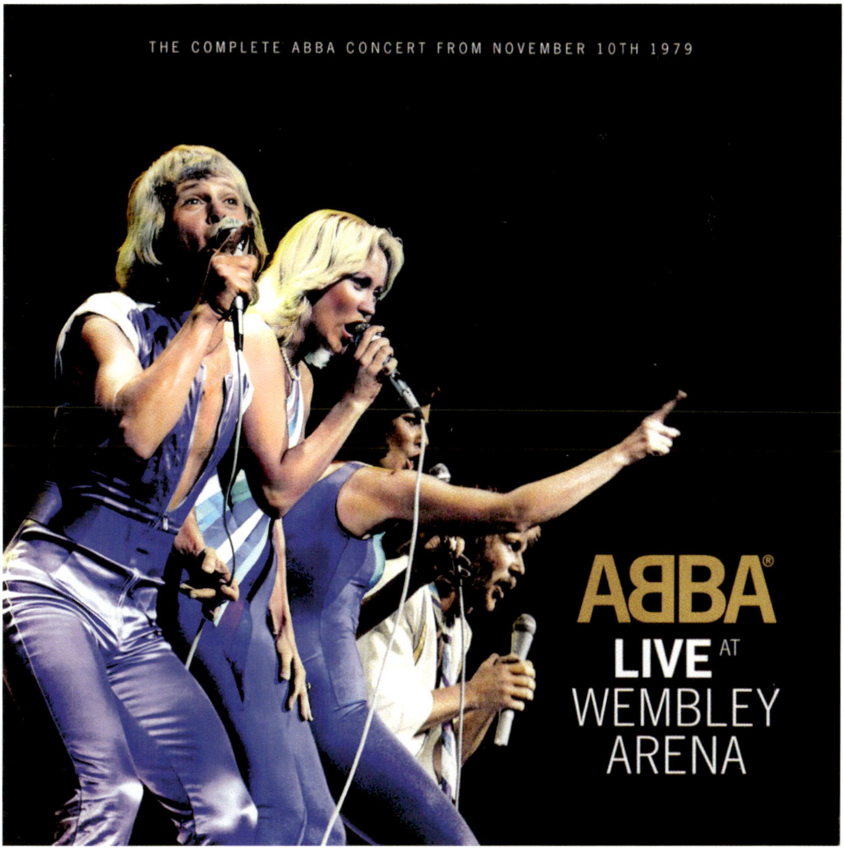

THE COMPLETE ABBA CONCERT FROM NOVEMBER 10TH 1979

ABBA®
LIVE AT
WEMBLEY
ARENA

BENNY ANDERSSON & BJÖRN ULVAEUS'

MAMMA MIA!

A NEW MUSICAL BASED ON THE SONGS OF ABBA®

Left: The musical *Mamma Mia!*, based on the songs of ABBA, opened in London in April 1999. It has played in over forty countries, been translated into over twenty-three languages, playing to over 65 million people. A movie version in 2008 broke records for movie-musicals, and a sequel in 2018 was also wildly successful. (*Author's collection*)

Below: Björn, Frida, Agnetha, and Benny standing together in January 2016 at the opening of *Mamma Mia! The Party* in Stockholm. This marked the first time the four had been seen together by the public in over thirty years. (*Photo: ©Tina Schuster*)

11

Non-Album Tracks, 1978–1979

'Summer Night City'
Duration: 3.34
Released as a single 6 September 1978.

Disco was huge in 1978. The film *Saturday Night Fever* was one of the most popular films of the year, while the Bee Gees-led soundtrack album was an enormous seller, spawning several chart-topping singles and inspiring a worldwide disco craze, though disco as a musical genre had actually been around as an underground movement since the start of the decade. At the time of the single's release, Björn said: '… everyone is doing that, really. It's the pulse of the Seventies'. Agnetha declared herself a fan of the Bee Gees' disco sound, saying in the *ABBA Magazine*: 'Yes, I think the influence affects everyone, because I haven't experienced anything like that since The Beatles. Whether or not their sound is commercial, it doesn't bother me. I love their disco sound because I feel it so much, most of the things you hear in discos have no melody'.

'Summer Night City' was ABBA's Bee Gees-inspired disco ode to city nightlife. For the first time since 'Honey, Honey' in 1974, an ABBA single featured vocals alternating between the male and female halves of the group.

Benny and Björn were never happy with the recording of 'Summer Night City'. It was the first song they recorded in their brand-new Polar Music Studios, which opened in May 1978. The studio, located on Sankt Eriksgatan in central Stockholm, would be where ABBA recorded almost all their songs from this point on. The studio sadly closed in 2004, due to an unaffordable increase in rent from the building's landlords. Björn, Benny, and engineer Michael B. Tretow made many attempts at mixing the track and adding more compression to make the song listenable to their ears. The recording also increases in tempo as the song progresses—try playing the song through, then before it fades out go back to the start and you can clearly hear it. 'Summer Night City' originally started with a dramatic forty-five-second prelude, but this was edited off the song before release. The full version was finally released in 1994 on the *Thank You for the Music* boxset, and also included on the Deluxe Edition of *Voulez-Vous* in 2010.

ABBA begrudgingly released 'Summer Night City' as a single in September 1978, as it was the only song from current recording sessions in a releasable state, and record companies around the world were clamouring for a new ABBA single. It had been four months since the previous single 'Eagle', and longer still in some countries such as the UK, where the most recent single had been 'Take a Chance on Me' eight months earlier. Agnetha, despite her stated enthusiasm for disco music, was not a fan of this song: 'I wasn't happy with "Summer Night City" to start with. I felt it wasn't "ABBA" but later on I began to like it'.

In the UK, there was minor controversy when some listeners heard during the fadeout the line 'fucking in the moonlight'. The line is actually 'walking in the moonlight', but with so much compression, the 'w' does have more of a 'v' or 'f' sound. Concerned about the controversy, and a threatened radio airplay ban, Epic Records released an edited promotional single that faded early, before the alleged offending section.

In ABBA's native Sweden, 'Summer Night City' was the group's final No. 1 single. It also topped the charts in Ireland and Finland, and in other ABBA-loving European countries it was a top five hit. In the UK, 'Summer Night City' was ABBA's lowest-charting single in three years, peaking at No. 5. The single release was cancelled in the US, as ABBA could not guarantee Atlantic Records that an album would soon follow (though it was released in Canada, where it peaked at No. 34). At the time, the next album, *Voulez-Vous*, was barely half finished.

'Summer Night City' is one of the few ABBA singles that was not included on a studio album, though the full-length version was originally planned to be on *Voulez-Vous*. In anticipation of its release, the full version had been presented on radio in Sweden in November 1978 by ABBA friend Claes af Geijerstam on his radio programme *Skivspegeln Special* (*Disk mirror special*). But with Benny and Björn's dissatisfaction with the recording, and its perceived lack of success thanks to its lower than usual British chart placing, it was left off the album.

'Lovelight'
Duration: 3.46
Released on the B-side of 'Chiquitita', 16 January 1979.

The first new ABBA recording of 1978 following the release of *ABBA: The Album* was destined to be only a single B-side, when it was released on the back of 'Chiquitita' in January 1979. Like other ABBA B-sides and unreleased tracks, the song seems quite disjointed, with the low-key verse clashing with a high-energy chorus and a guitar refrain that does not really gel with either.

The verse, with its acoustic guitars, melancholy vocal, and the downbeat tone of the lyric, sounds almost country and western. The electric guitar riff in the introduction and between verses sounds almost rock, while the chorus with its shrill vocals is heading towards the pop-disco rhythms that would impact ABBA's recorded output over the next couple of years.

For no apparent reason, the version released on the Polydor single in West Germany faded the track fifteen seconds early. A previously unheard alternative mix was included on the 1993 CD *More ABBA Gold—More ABBA Hits* and four-CD boxset *Thank You for The Music* in 1994.

'Gimme! Gimme! Gimme! (A Man After Midnight)'
Written by Benny Andersson and Björn Ulvaeus. Spanish lyric by Buddy and Mary McCluskey.
Duration: 4.45
Released as a single 15 October 1979. Also on the album *Greatest Hits Vol. 2* 29 October 1979.

This was ABBA's last dance on the '70s disco floor. It is Agnetha's plea for a man to love her and take her away from her boring life of watching late night TV, a theme that ABBA would return to in 1982. Its title and sense of yearning have made 'Gimme! Gimme! Gimme!' an obvious gay anthem.

Like many song titles and lyric themes, this title was inspired by Björn's reading. He said in 1979: '… that came about from reading a book. I don't remember exactly what happened but I was reading something and the lyric Gimme, Gimme, Gimme seemed to jump out at me and it grew from there'.

This late-1979 disco thumper is set to a driving beat with a memorable refrain that proved so enduring that American icon Madonna sampled it for her 2005 hit 'Hung Up', from her album *Confessions on a Dance Floor*. Benny and Björn are not keen on allowing samples of their songs. Björn stated: 'My attitude to sampling is essentially negative, especially if the people doing it are not really talented'. Benny explained that they gave their permission 'because we admire Madonna so much and always have done. She has got guts and has been around for 21 years. That is not bad going.'

Madonna declared herself to be something of an ABBA fan: she published a statement used to promote the ABBA compilation *Number Ones* in 2006: 'ABBA's timeless music continues to inspire me. It's joyous. Standing still when you hear ABBA's music is impossible'.

Listen to the eight-bar guitar refrain that opens 'Gimme! Gimme! Gimme!' It reappears at a lower volume under the vocals during the song's choruses. The song also features a long instrumental break that is one of the most unusual of all of ABBA's oeuvre; a forty-eight-second-long, bass guitar-led free-form passage with building strings and wordless vocalisation that does not really go anywhere, though it is eminently danceable.

The single was released to coincide with ABBA's North American & European Tour. It would be another of those few ABBA singles not included on a studio album, though it was the opening track on the simultaneously-released *Greatest Hits Vol. 2*.

Björn and Benny have different memories of ABBA's flirtation with disco music in 1978 and 1979. Björn recalls: 'We were in the era of disco. And "Gimme! Gimme! Gimme!" is very much a disco number'. Benny has a less than positive opinion of this era of ABBA's recorded history: 'Yeah, disco. Boring! I thought it was no fun to try to hang on to whatever was going on in the music industry at the time'.

The following year, 'Gimme! Gimme! Gimme!' would be recorded in Spanish as 'Dame! Dame! Dame!' for the *Gracias Por La Música* album, probably because it was ABBA's most recent single.

'Gimme! Gimme! Gimme!' inspired the title of a British comedy series starring Kathy Burke and James Dreyfus, who sang the chorus of ABBA's hit as the show's theme song. The programme ran for three series between 1999 and 2001.

American music and screen legend and star of the film *Mamma Mia! Here We Go Again* Cher released her dancetastic version of 'Gimme! Gimme! Gimme! (A Man After Midnight)' as the lead single from her ABBA-loving album *Dancing Queen* in 2018, and also an EP with no less than ten dance remixes.

12

Super Trouper

Sweden:	3 November 1980
UK:	21 November 1980
US:	December 1980
Current edition:	Universal Music/Polar CD 549 956-2
Personnel:	Benny Andersson: keyboards, synthesizers, vocals
	Ola Brunkert: drums
	Agnetha Fältskog: vocals
	Lars O. Carlsson: saxophone
	Rutger Gunnarsson: bass, string arrangements
	Janne Kling: flutes, saxophone
	Per Lindvall: drums
	Anni-Frid Lyngstad: vocals
	Janne Schaffer: guitar
	Åke Sundqvist: percussion
	Björn Ulvaeus: guitar, vocals
	Mike Watson: bass
	Lasse Wellander: guitar
	Katjek Wojciechowski: saxophone
Duration:	43 minutes

Recorded at Polar Music Studio, Stockholm, Sweden; February–October 1980, 'The Way Old Friends Do' recorded live at Wembley Arena, London: November 1979.

Produced and arranged by Benny Andersson and Björn Ulvaeus

Engineered by Michael B. Tretow

Chart position:	Sweden: 1
	UK: 1
	US: 17

ABBA's seventh studio album saw a more reflective collection of songs. A grown-up ABBA tackle marriage break-ups, high-society life, sexuality, psychological issues, and growing troubles in the modern world. Many listeners consider it ABBA's best album. It is certainly the most consistent-sounding, with Benny's synthesizers, particularly the huge Yamaha GX-1 that he had bought in 1979, dominating the soundscape. Recording engineer Michael B. Tretow says in the book *ABBA: The Complete Recording Sessions*: 'I think it stands up as an album in itself, not only as a collection of songs'.

The album sleeve was ABBA's most ambitious. The image of ABBA caught in a spotlight, dazzling in white, surrounded by circus performers, was most striking (sadly it loses some impact on CD). The cover photo shoot was made into an event, which was captured in dozens of photographs and on film. A specially commissioned documentary featurette on the photo session, *Somewhere in the Crowd There's You (On Location With ABBA)*, was created for the *Super Trouper* Deluxe Edition DVD in 2011.

Super Trouper is reported to be ABBA's highest-selling non-compilation album.

'Super Trouper'
Duration: 4.13
Released as a single 25 November 1980.

For the second time in their career, ABBA named a song after an album title, rather than the usual practice of naming an album after a song (the first was 'Arrival' in 1976).

With ABBA's new album scheduled for release in November, art designer Rune Söderqvist came up with the concept of 'circus' for the album sleeve. After the initial idea of a photo shoot in London's Piccadilly Circus was blocked by London authorities, citing bylaws preventing costumed people and animals in London's Theatreland district, and fearing the traffic chaos that an ABBA photo shoot would cause in the busy traffic hub, ABBA gathered at the Europafilm Studio in Stockholm, along with a real circus troupe and invited friends dressed in bright, colourful costumes.

The sight of ABBA dressed in white under a bright spotlight reminded someone of the large spotlights used at concerts. Super Trouper is a brand of spotlight then manufactured by the String Electric Corporation, popular for arena and stadium events. Thus the album now had a title.

At the same time, Björn and Benny were working on one final track for the new album, which could also be strong enough for single release: 'We had finished the album. Or so we thought. But listening to the songs again there was a nagging feeling it wasn't quite complete'. One fully completed song, 'Put On Your White Sombrero', had been shelved (see Appendix I), while 'Elaine', recorded during the album sessions, would remain as a single B-side only (see below).

As luck would have it, the title *Super Trouper* happened to fit this new song. 'The name of the album had been settled already, the big follow-spots we used on tour had provided that,' Björn recalled in 2014. 'It was only afterwards I found that the title of the album fitted the hook-line like a glove. And weaving the story around that title was no problem for a man, who had fallen in love again.'

That last comment from Björn indicates that the song could be interpreted as semi-autobiographical. At the beginning of 1979, following Björn and Agnetha's separation, Björn met his new partner, Lena Källersjö. In the *ABBA Magazine* in 1981, Björn explained: '... it is a very common situation that could come up very easily for anyone who is on tour, if their loved one is not around'. ABBA duties and concert tours kept them apart for long periods, though Lena did join the ABBA tour entourage in Los Angeles in September 1979, where ABBA had based themselves for several days, in Britain in November, and on ABBA's Japanese tour in March 1980. The couple married in January 1981.

In his book *ABBA: Let the Music Speak*, musician Chris Patrick observes that the chord sequence underneath the instrumental refrain following the chorus is exactly the same as in the chorus of 'The Winner Takes It All'. It is an unusual example of Benny and Björn recycling a musical fragment from a released song, rather than one they had rejected, though perhaps it was an unconscious reuse.

'Super Trouper' was released as a single in tandem with the album. It would be ABBA's ninth and last British No. 1 single. It also topped the singles chart in ABBA's faithful territories West Germany, the Netherlands, and Belgium, and reached the top ten in several other European countries. Footage from the album sleeve photo session was used in the promotional film clip and also in the clip for *Super Trouper* album track 'Happy New Year' and its Spanish version 'Felicidad'. Curiously, the spotlight that has a prominent place in the clip is not a Super Trouper, but a smaller CCT Silhouette follow spot.

(Fun fact: British rock band Deep Purple recorded a song entitled 'Super Trouper' on their 1973 album *Who Do We Think We Are*, which was a single in West Germany, the Netherlands, Belgium, and Denmark. In 2004, former Deep Purple keyboardist Jon Lord enlisted his friend and Zermatt neighbour Frida to sing 'The Sun Will Shine Again', which he had written specifically for her, on his album *Behind the Notes*.)

'Super Trouper' is one of the few songs to feature in the *Mamma Mia!* musical and film version, as well as the film sequel *Mamma Mia! Here We Go Again*. In the second film (spoiler alert), it is a spectacular finale sung by the all-star cast led by Cher, Meryl Streep, Lily James, and Amanda Seyfried. Benny, who produced the soundtrack music for the film, cleverly mixed motifs of 'Mamma Mia' and 'Gimme! Gimme! Gimme! (A Man After Midnight)' into the introduction of the song.

'The Winner Takes It All'

Duration: 4.55
Released as a single 21 July 1980.

'The Winner Takes It All', ABBA's first single of the '80s, is widely regarded as ABBA's greatest song. With a *tour de force* solo vocal from Agnetha, '"The Winner Takes It All" is something special,' Benny says.

Though the song sounds complex, it is actually built on two short melodies, one for the verse and one for the chorus, with a loose, descending piano figure from Benny holding the two sections together. Benny explained: 'It actually consists of very few notes. Two short phrases that go around and around'. It is the production of the recording, and Agnetha's bravura performance, that gives the song its emotional power.

The different arrangements for each verse and chorus provide variety and bring the listener along on the journey. The first verse and chorus feature only Agnetha's voice, backed by piano, acoustic guitar, and wordless backing vocals. The full band kicks in for the second verse and second chorus, with the backing vocals echoing the lines in the chorus. The full band is still there for the third verse, but Benny changes to staccato piano notes punctuating the vocal. At the end of the third chorus, the band goes quiet, and we return to Agnetha's voice, Benny's piano, and strings, until the end of the verse when the band comes back in force for Agnetha's vocal climax. Unusually, each chorus has a different lyric, rather than the usual pop song convention of the chorus repeating the same words. Agnetha feels it is one of her best recorded performances: 'I seldom listen to what I've recorded myself, but "The Winner Takes It All" is the exception. I listen to it when self-esteem is low. I did that well'.

In an oft-repeated story about the creation of the song, Björn admits that he had a few drinks as he was writing the lyric, which was one of the quickest he ever wrote: 'I did have help from a bottle of whisky, some Scotch. Not the whole bottle, but definitely a couple of big snifters'. It is often assumed that the lyric is about Björn and Agnetha's separation and divorce (which was not actually finalised until after the song was completed). Björn has admitted that their marriage breakdown may have coloured his lyrics, but it is '99% fiction' and not a literal depiction of their breakup: 'In our story, there was no winner'. In the book *Yeah Yeah Yeah: The Story of Modern Pop*, writer Bob Stanley gives a vivid description of the song: '… this is the story of someone put through the mill, pop's equivalent of [Swedish director Ingmar Bergman's 1973 television series] *Scenes From a Marriage*, with its grisly, unresolved feelings of love, memories, jealousy and confusion'.

The single was released in August 1980 and was a worldwide hit. It returned ABBA to the top of the British singles chart for the first time since 'Take a Chance on Me' in 1978. 'The Winner Takes It All' also topped *Billboard*'s Adult

Contemporary Chart (as had 'Fernando' four years earlier), making it ABBA's third American No. 1.

At the end of the year, French chanteuse Mireille Mathieu travelled to Polar Music Studios to record a French version entitled 'Bravo tu as gagné' ('Well done you have won'). The lyric was written by French singer Charles Level, and the recording was produced by Benny and Björn. The two ABBA men plus Frida sang backing vocals for that authentic ABBA sound, joined by French singer Françoise Pourcel (fun facts: Françoise was the wife of Alain Boublil, who coordinated this recording, had translated 'Waterloo' for ABBA's French version in 1974, and in 1983 would create the musical *ABBACADABRA*; see the entry for 'Arrival' above for more on that project. She was also the daughter of French bandleader Franck Pourcel, who in 1978 released an album, *Franck Pourcel Recontre ABBA*—Franck Poucel Meets ABBA. However, he did not actually meet ABBA until a photo session for the album sleeve at Polar Music Studios).

'The Winner Takes It All' features in the musical *Mamma Mia!* as the so-called eleven o'clock number, the big, show-stopping song in the second act. In the 2008 film version, Oscar winner Meryl Streep delivers a powerhouse rendition, partly sung live on location perched atop a Greek cliff.

'On and On and On'
Duration: 3.41

'On and On and On' details the flirtations of high society types at an A-list party full of celebrities and well-known people. First our protagonist meets a man, 'a minister, a big shot in the state' (a politician, not a minister of religion), who can only talk about the doom and gloom in the world. In the second verse, she spies another man who is 'kinda flirty'; they make eye contact and start chatting at the bar, though in the end, the only thing to do is 'keep on rocking'.

In press releases from Polar Music reporting on the progress of ABBA's 1980 album, the song had a different title: 'The title was originally "til the night is gone",' Benny explained. 'Both versions are now in the chorus, but we found that "On and on and on" was simpler and easier.'

'On and On and On' would be the last recorded ABBA song to feature the famous third voice of Agnetha and Frida singing in unison throughout the song. Though that sound would appear sporadically in ABBA's remaining years, the songs would mostly feature solo lead vocals by one woman or the other.

Listen closely to the backing vocals in the chorus. Primarily supplied by Benny singing in falsetto, they are highly reminiscent of the chorus of The Beach Boys' 1968 hit 'Do It Again'. Benny was and is an avowed fan of the Californian group. The favour was returned the following year when Beach Boy Mike Love covered 'On and On and On' for his solo album *Looking Back With Love*. In 2019, Love released a new version, more acoustic than his synth-heavy 1981 recording, on his album *12 Sides of Summer*. For ABBA fans, Love's original version was included in the American CD *ABBA—A Tribute: The 25th Anniversary Celebration* in 1999.

The song originally had a third verse, which does not really add anything lyrically; it was edited out for release on record: 'Standing up is scary/if you think you're gonna fall/Like a humpty-dumpty/'fraid of falling off the wall/I say if you ever wanna know what's going on/Gotta keep on rockin', baby/'til the night is gone'. However, earlier in the year, photographer and friend Anders Hanser, who had accompanied ABBA on their 1979 tour, was preparing a slideshow of his concert photographs and asked ABBA for some music to underscore the slideshow. Rather than giving him a concert recording, he was given the full version of this brand-new song.

At the end of 1980, 'On and On and On' was released as a single in Australia, New Zealand, and Japan. Polar Music provided Hanser's slideshow as the promotional film for the single, putting the full-length version out in the world. The clip would be included on ABBA video collections first on VHS and later on DVD, and it would finally be released on an audio format on the 2005 CD box set *The Complete Studio Recordings* (in glorious mono); the stereo tape was finally located and included on the *Super Trouper* Deluxe Edition CD in 2011 and *The Essential Collection* DVD in 2012

'On and On and On' is another of those songs that has been revisited by ABBA or their associates. Musician Mats Ronander, who was one of the guitarists on ABBA's 1979 and 1980 concert tours, gave the song a punkish makeover, sung in a faux-Cockney accent, with lyrics presumably tweaked by Ronander himself, throwing in a few 'fucks' and a butch gay twist. Ronander's version was released in 1992 on the Polar Music CD *ABBA—The Tribute*, which featured cover versions of ABBA songs by popular Swedish artists. In 2015, Benny joined musical collective FIRE! at a one-off concert event in Stockholm for a rather wild, free-form performance of the song, while the following year, Benny Anderssons Orkester performed 'On and On and On' during the band's summer tour in Sweden.

'Andante, Andante'
Written by Benny Andersson and Björn Ulvaeus. Spanish lyric by Buddy and Mary McCluskey.
Duration: 4.38

Andante is an Italian word meaning 'walking'. In musical notation, it is a term used to indicate the tempo a piece should be played at moderate tempo or at a walking pace.

'Andante, Andante' uses musical terminology as a metaphor for lovemaking. A woman asking her lover to 'take it slow', as he might when he is playing a musical instrument. Frida sings lead with a light, teasing sensuality that complements the lyric. An alternate interpretation of the lyric is less erotic (and less interesting)— that the song is the voice of a musical instrument talking to its player.

An early mix was inadvertently released in the box set *The Singles* in 2014, on which Benny's beloved accordion can be heard. On the version originally released on *Super Trouper* in 1980, Benny's synthesizers dominate and the accordion is inaudible.

Following the huge success of the Spanish singles 'Chiquitita' and 'Estoy Soñando' in 1979 and the 1980 album *Gracias Por La Música* in Latin America, ABBA decided to record two songs in Spanish for the *Super Trouper* album released in Spanish-speaking territories. 'Andante, Andante' was one of the two, with lyrics again written by Buddy and Mary McCluskey.

In 2016, Frida recorded the Spanish version with Cuban jazz trumpeter, pianist, and composer Arturo Sandoval. It was released in 2018 on Sandoval's album *Ultimate Duets*. Also released in 2018, Lily James sings a suitably sensual version of the song in the movie sequel *Mamma Mia! Here We Go Again*.

'Me and I'
Duration: 4.53

An unusual topic for an ABBA song, looking at a person with a split personality, and probably one of the few pop songs to reference Dr Sigmund Freud, the Austrian-born founder of psychoanalysis. Frida found inspiration in American singer Eartha Kitt and her 'catlike' way of singing for her lead vocal treatment of the song.

This inventive and progressive song is perhaps overly long, with a thirty-second, synth-based introduction that is repeated in part after the first chorus, and again after an instrumental repeat of the second chorus. Following another two chorus repeats, including a key change, part of the introduction melody returns, followed by a twenty-second, seemingly random synth noodling. At almost five minutes long, the song could have done with a bit of editing.

'Happy New Year'
Written by Benny Andersson and Björn Ulvaeus. Spanish lyric by Buddy and Mary McCluskey.
Duration: 4.24

'Happy New Year' had its origins in Benny and Björn's idea to write a musical based on events at a party on New Year's Eve. While on a second songwriting break in Barbados in January 1980 (they had first travelled in February 1979 to The Bahamas, seeking inspiration for the *Voulez-Vous* album), Benny and Björn met British funny man John Cleese, of *Monty Python* and *Fawlty Towers*' fame. Over dinner, they asked if Cleese would be interested in writing the book for such a musical, but he declined. The song 'Happy New Year', which started out with the intriguing title 'Daddy, Don't Get Drunk on Christmas Day', was the only outcome of that project. Imagine a song with that title as an ABBA song!

'Happy New Year' is one of several ABBA songs in this period that expressed concern about the state of the world and pleas for global peace. Upon the album's release, Björn said: 'There's one song on the *Super Trouper* album which is as close as we've come to writing something political and that is "Happy New Year". I feel one of the biggest problems in the western world today is the lack of confidence, and the way of looking negatively at the future. So the song is about trying to set up positive goals for the future. That's a political message in itself'.

It is one of the first ABBA songs that sounds like it lives in the real world, with its themes and lyric—'who can say/what we'll find/what lies waiting/down the line/in the end of/eighty-nine'—placing the song clearly in troubled early '80s. In the twenty-first century, Björn has expressed regret at that lyric in the third verse, which he feels locks the song in 1980. He has suggested replacing 'at the end of eighty-nine' with an alternate lyric, 'here's a toast to humankind'.

At one stage, Polar Music had planned to release 'Happy New Year' as a single. Polar's label manager Hans 'Berka' Berqvist told the *ABBA Magazine* in 1980: 'The only certain single release will be "Happy New Year" which will be out around October/November along with the album', but that was not to be. It was issued in single form in Portugal in 1980, and on an EP in Brazil and B-side in Australia in 1981, and has had limited single rereleases over the years, most notably in 1999 for the turn of the millennium. The song has become a perennial favourite, regularly appearing on Christmas compilation CDs. In these days of online music, 'Happy New Year' is one of the most popular downloaded and streamed songs on 31 December each year, even reaching the singles chart in some countries. Starting in 2018, Universal Music is releasing a different coloured vinyl 7-inch collectors' single each year; the 2019 issue topped the UK Vinyl Singles chart.

'Happy New Year' was the second song on *Super Trouper* to be recorded in Spanish for the Latin American market. The Spanish version was entitled 'Felicidad' ('Happiness'). The Spanish lyric expresses similar sentiments to the English version, but without the references to the new year; rather, it is a song of a general celebration.

Benny included 'Happy New Year' as one of six ABBA songs on his 2017 solo album *Piano*.

'Our Last Summer'
Duration: 4.18

In this charming song on side two of *Super Trouper*, Frida reminisces about a long-ago romance in Paris. Björn has described the song as being about 'the last summer of innocence' before settling down to marriage, children, jobs, and mortgages: '"Our Last Summer" is a true story. It's about someone I went to visit in Paris. It was one of those bitter-sweet, young love stories'. The same memory had inspired an early version of *Arrival*'s 'My Love, My Life' in 1976.

The lyric sets the scene with sites around the city: the Eiffel Tower, Notre Dame Cathedral, the Avenue des Champs Élysées, walking along the banks of the River Seine. There are croissants in the morning, drinks in cafés, philosophical conversations, Mona Lisa smiles, laughs in the rain. Benny says: 'There is a kind of nostalgic feel about the music as well as the lyric'.

In the end, we learn that the object of the singer's affection is now a family man and football fan named Harry. But is Harry a long-lost summer romance, or did they marry after that time in Paris, so now he is the singer's husband, the 'hero of [her] dreams'? That is the beauty of Björn's lyrics at this stage of ABBA's career—they are open to various interpretations, all valid.

'Our Last Summer' makes a prominent appearance in the first act of the *Mamma Mia!* musical. In the 2008 film, it is sung by Oscar winner Colin Firth as the character Harry, with Pierce Brosnan and Stellan Skarsgård, who do a creditable job despite none of them being singers.

'The Piper'
Duration: 3.25

One of the first songs recorded for the *Super Trouper* album was 'The Piper', in which lyricist Björn delved into subject matter more serious than anything that ABBA had attempted before. Inspired by the Stephen King novel *The Stand* (published in 1978), he wrote a lyric about the rise of a fascist-type leader. 'The lyrics deal with the fear that there will come a time when people will want such a leader again,' Björn later explained. The lyric also recalls the classic fairytale *The Pied Piper of Hamelin*.

The song sounds somewhat like a medieval madrigal, and it features a refrain with a melody played on flute by Janne Kling. The refrain ends with a phrase that initially confused listeners, who could not recognise the language. 'No, *sub luna saltumas* is not Swedish but Latin,' Agnetha explained. 'It means the last line of the chorus: we dance beneath the moon.'

'Lay All Your Love on Me'
Duration: 4.33

Though ABBA had ditched the disco beat at the end of 1979, they could still produce danceable music. With its synthesised sounds and apparently sequenced backing (actually played manually by Benny), 'Lay All Your Love on Me' is often regarded as a prototype of '80s dance music.

Björn expresses some pride in the lyrics. 'The song was inspired in part by Supertramp, who wrote songs like "The Logical Song" with lots of unusual words, rhyming on different, strange words that songwriters would normally not use,' he says. 'And I'm actually proud of the fact that I was able to include the word "incomprehensible" to rhyme with "sensible".' Not many songs squeeze in a six-syllable word!

The verses are sung by Agnetha at full pace, but the choruses at half speed, with multiple vocal overdubs replicating a huge choir. '"Lay All Your Love on Me" is definitely a hymn, but with 125 bpm,' Benny said.

The intriguing descending sound at the end of each chorus was created by engineer Michael B. Tretow, manipulating the sound by feeding the note through a harmoniser (an electronic device that can alter the pitch of a recording), lowering it a semitone on each repeat. It is curious to note that each time it sounds a little different, because each occurrence was done manually, and it was most successfully applied on the second verse. This stunning effect draws the listener into the chorus.

In mid-1981, with a lack of any new ABBA single in the pipeline, several countries (the UK, Ireland, West Germany, the Netherlands, and France) chose to fill the gap and release 'Lay All Your Love on Me' as a limited-edition 12-inch single. Judd Lander of Epic Records explained to the *ABBA Magazine*: 'That single was making waves before we released it! That's because DJs were playing it in discos on LP. In America they made an illegal 12″ single and that started selling through the grapevine. ABBA didn't want to release another track off *Super Trouper* but Stig thought wisely they shouldn't let bootleggers make money out of ABBA's material. So we went ahead and did it ourselves, a real disco-demand release that owes less of its success to radio'. However, the official single featured the album version, not an extended remix. The so-called illegal 12-inch single Lander refers to had actually been authorised by Atlantic Records and was only available to club DJs through a subscription service, not for sale to the public.

In the UK, 'Lay All Your Love on Me' became the biggest-selling 12-inch single to date (only surpassed by New Order's 'Blue Monday' two years later), and it remains the highest charting 12-inch single in that market. 'Lay All Your Love on Me', along with album tracks 'On and On and On' and 'Super Trouper', also reached No. 1 on *Billboard*'s Disco Top 80 Chart, though this chart was compiled from club playlists, not single sales. The single's British sales status garnered the song a place on the 1992 mega-compilation *ABBA Gold: Greatest Hits*, ahead of several bigger international hits.

'Lay All Your Love on Me' features in a man-ogling sequence in the stage musical and film *Mamma Mia!*, as a chorus line of buff young men dance in wetsuits and flippers.

'The Way Old Friends Do'
Duration: 2.53

Björn recalled in 1980: 'We wrote ["The Way Old Friends Do"] specially for the [1979] tour. We felt things needed cooling down if we did an encore. Happily we have never gone off without having to do one. It is a number we love singing and gives Benny a chance to play his favourite instrument'. ABBA's six concerts at London's Wembley Arena in November were recorded for a television special, broadcast in 1980 as *ABBA in Concert*, and for a potential live album, which was very belatedly released in 2014.

The basic recording of the track included on *Super Trouper* comes from one of those Wembley concerts. For inclusion as the final track on the album, the recording was subjected to vocal overdubs, plus percussion and Benny's synthesizers, which helps the live recording match the soundscape of the rest of the album.

A different night's performance without overdubs featured in the television special in some countries (it is a bonus track on the 2004 DVD release), and the final night's performance on the *Live at Wembley Arena* album in 2014.

Original vinyl pressings of *Super Trouper* included applause cross-faded over the end of the previous song, 'Lay All Your Love on Me', segueing into 'The Way Old Friends Do'. At the end of the song, an endless loop of applause played in the run-out groove, which would repeat forever for listeners without an automatic return arm on their turntable. On all CD pressings, the applause fades out quickly, and some CDs do not have the applause segue, giving 'The Way Old Friends Do' a clean start.

On 5 June 2016, at a party celebrating the fiftieth anniversary of Benny and Björn's first meeting, Frida and Agnetha took to the stage, singing 'The Way Old Friends Do' as a surprise to honour their former husbands and bandmates. The news spread quickly around the world but was wildly misreported: it was said that Benny and Björn joined the two women on stage during the song and the four sang together (they did not, the men took to the stage after the song, though all four did stand together), that they sang the *Chess* song 'You And I', or the *Super Trouper* song 'Me And I'. Bootleg video evidence confirmed the details of the performance.

To this day, 'The Way Old Friends Do' is the popular last song at ABBA fan gatherings, such as the annual International ABBA Day, run by the Official International ABBA Fan Club.

Non-Album Tracks, 1980

'Elaine'

Duration: 3.39
Released on the B-side of 'The Winner Takes It All', 21 July 1980.

Synth pop was the big new sound of 1980. The Buggles' synthesizer-driven single 'Video Killed the Radio Star' had been a hit in the last months of 1979. Bands like The Human League, Tubeway Army, and Ultravox were on the rise with electronic music created mostly (or completely) with synthesizers and drum machines.

ABBA embraced an electronic synth sound from 1980, thanks primarily to Benny's Yamaha GX-1 synthesizer, which he had purchased in 1979 and first played on 'Does Your Mother Know'. The GX-1 would be the dominant sound on the *Super Trouper* album, and most of ABBA's subsequent output. After arriving late to the disco with *Voulez-Vous*, ABBA was now on-trend.

The lyrics are a mystery. The song has been interpreted as the titular Elaine being a victim of kidnapping or, like 'I'm a Marionette' in 1977, an essay on being trapped by fame with 'nowhere to go', imprisoned 'like a goldfish in a bowl'. 'Elaine' was not to be on the next ABBA album; instead it only appeared on the B-side of 'The Winner Takes It All'.

The Visitors

Sweden:	30 November 1981
UK:	11 December 1981
US:	January 1982
Current edition:	Universal Music/Polar CD 549 957-2
Personnel:	Benny Andersson: keyboards, synthesizers, vocals
	Ola Brunkert: drums
	Agnetha Fältskog: vocals
	Rutger Gunnarsson: bass
	Janne Kling: flute, clarinet
	Per Lindvall: drums
	Anni-Frid Lyngstad: vocals
	Björn Ulvaeus: guitar, vocals
	Mike Watson: bass
	Lasse Wellander: guitar
	The Three Boys: mandolins on 'One of Us'
Duration:	38 minutes

Digitally recorded at Polar Music Studio, Stockholm: March–November 1981
Produced and arranged by Benny Andersson and Björn Ulvaeus
Engineered by Michael B. Tretow

Chart position:	Sweden: 1
	UK: 1
	US: 29

ABBA's final album is a new, bleaker ABBA. Gone is the sound of Agnetha and Frida singing together, creating that unique third voice. Solo vocals and Benny's mighty GX-1 synthesizer dominate the album. Benny and Frida's marriage had also come to an end, with that sadness reflected in the songs. Björn said at the time of the album's release, 'I don't feel that this LP is so much a departure from our usual style. After all, each of our albums is a little different from the last, and this one is equally different from *Super Trouper* as that was from *Voulez-Vous*.' Though, years later, he wrote: 'There is, if not a sinister, then definitely a very melancholic feel to that album as though somewhere in the back of our minds we knew the end was near'.

The album focuses on the Cold War between the 'west' and 'east' superpowers, adult problems of disintegrating relationships and children growing up. In 2014's *ABBA: The Official Photo Book*, Frida enthused: '*The Visitors* album is one of the best things we did. The quality of the songs! The lyrics Björn and Benny wrote! The level is fantastic all through. And everything we were going through at the time is reflected in the music, in a good way'.

This more mature ABBA did not seem to appeal to the world's record buyers. After each album outselling the one that came before, sales and chart action of *The Visitors* was much less than *Super Trouper*, though it did go straight to No. 1 in Sweden, Denmark, the Netherlands, Belgium, and the UK. At the time, no one knew it would be ABBA's last album, though privately Björn did say, 'We've emptied ourselves of everything we've got to give.'

The digitally recorded album was the first ABBA album to be released on the new Compact Disc (CD) format in 1982, though not actually the first CD ever, as has been widely reported*.

* The first test CD manufactured was a recording of Richard Strauss's *Eine Alpensinfonie* (An Alpine Symphony) in 1979. The first public demonstration of the CD was the Bee Gees' album *Living Eyes* on the BBC television programme *Tomorrow's World* in 1981.*The Visitors* was the first CD pressed for commercial release at Philips new factory in West Germany in June 1982. But the first CD to actually be released commercially was Billy Joel's *52nd Street*, in Japan in October 1982.

'The Visitors'
Duration: 5.49

The title track of ABBA's eighth and final studio album is probably the most intriguing, adventurous, and unexpected song ever released under the name ABBA. The verses, with their swirling synthesizers, Frida's seemingly random melody, and lyrics that do not rhyme, sounds like a cross between an Indian raga and early-'80s synth pop. The song's closest living relative would be 'Astradyne', the opening track on Ultravox's breakthrough 1980 album *Vienna*. 'It's a little bit different from the rest of the tracks,' Frida said. The chorus, with tightly-compressed vocals from all four ABBA members, is reminiscent of 1978's single 'Summer Night City'.

The lyric has been interpreted in many ways. Some listeners have thought the song was about an alien invasion and abduction, others about mental illness and the fear of being committed to an asylum, while still another interpretation has the singer is trapped in a haunted house. Frida said: 'It's a philosophical song. Anybody can have his own appreciation of it and then it won't be misunderstood'. At the time of the album's release, Björn did not want to explain what the song was about, letting the listener work it out for themselves. In Carl Magnus Palm's 1994 book *ABBA: The Complete Recording Sessions*, Björn admitted that he was trying to imagine the situation of Soviet dissidents, living in fear: 'I had a clear vision of that apartment, lots of bookcases on the walls.... Then suddenly the knock on the door'.

Phil Collins, producer of Frida's 1982 solo album *Something's Going On*, complained in the press that ABBA should have released 'The Visitors' as a single rather than 'Head Over Heels', which was the second single release after 'One of Us'. His words were prophetic: in the UK, where every ABBA single since 'SOS' in 1975 had been at least a top ten hit, 'Head Over Heels' stalled at No. 25. It is interesting to imagine how 'The Visitors' would have fared against the electro-pop stars of the day. 'The Visitors' was extremely popular in gay bars, always a dancefloor filler, especially in a semi-authorised extended version. Perhaps this marks the birth of ABBA's enduring popularity within the gay community, as ABBA's first generation of fans grew into adulthood.

Curiously, the title 'the visitors' is never sung in the song. At the end of the third verse, Frida sings 'I have been been waiting for these visitors', a phrase that is repeated over the final chorus and fade out. On the lyric sheet on the album's inner sleeve, the song is given the subtitle '(Crackin' Up)', the phrase that appears in the hook of the chorus. But that did not feel like the right title for the song, so 'The Visitors' it was.

'Head Over Heels'
Duration: 3.45
Released as a single 19 March 1982.

'Head Over Heels' is the story of a shopping- and fashion-mad woman with 'a taste for the world.' Agnetha takes the lead vocal here.

'Head Over Heels' was one of the first ABBA songs recorded after new digital recording facilities had been installed at Polar Music Studios. It was supposed to be a lighter song, but perhaps due to the new digital recording techniques, or possible tensions in the studio between the four individuals (Björn has said that it could be 'frosty' in the studio during *The Visitors* sessions), there is something 'cold' about the recording.

Agnetha had positive comments about the song in 1981: 'It's a different lyric. I think it is a very happy song. I can see this crazy girl in front of me. It felt very good to sing this song because it felt very cool, I think you can hear it, it is a different song'.

'Head Over Heels' was the second single from *The Visitors* in much of the world, released in March 1982. It was a chart hit in eternally ABBA-loving West Germany, Belgium, and the Netherlands (where it was ABBA's final No. 1 single anywhere), but it peaked at No. 25 in the UK, ABBA's lowest-charting single since 'I Do, I Do, I Do, I Do, I Do' in 1975, signalling a downturn in ABBA's popularity that would sadly continue with subsequent singles.

The promotional film clip cast Frida as the woman character, paired with Björn as her long-suffering husband, following her through shop after shop and the streets of Stockholm, with Frida modelling many designer outfits. 'All those clothes I borrowed from a very close friend of mine. Her name is Lillebil Ankarcrona and she has done a superb job in choosing exactly the clothes that suit my taste, and maybe broaden it a little,' Frida said upon the single's release.

(For ABBA trivia buffs: Ms Ankarcrona was at the time the common-law wife of Rune Söderqvist, designer of ABBA's record sleeves since 1975 and also of the ABBA logo. She was also the sister of Mona Nörklit, who would become Benny's second wife in December 1981).

'When All Is Said and Done'
Written by Benny Andersson and Björn Ulvaeus. Spanish lyric by Buddy and Mary McCluskey.
Duration: 3.20

If 'The Winner Takes It All' on *Super Trouper* was Agnetha and Björn's divorce song, then 'When All Is Said and Done' is the other couple's. 'It was Frida and Benny separating that triggered it and "triggered" is a better word because "inspired" doesn't come into the picture,' Björn wrote in 2014. 'I wanted to write something about them and what they went through. Something that gave credit to my friends' courage and dignity.' Frida said in in the book *ABBA: The Complete Recording Sessions* in 1994: 'All my sadness was captured in that song'.

The lyric is stoic. Here is the end of a relationship, but we accept that neither party is to blame, we are standing up and moving on, though 'there's no hurry anymore/when all is said and done'. The driving rhythm propels the song, suitably backing Frida's strong lead vocal. The vocoder, the go-to recording tool of the early '80s that gives a modern robotic sound to vocals, which had previously appeared on 'On and On and On', is effectively used for the harmonies in the third verse. The original recording had an additional verse, a repeat of the first, which was edited out before release.

A promotional film clip of 'When All Is Said and Done' was made in August 1981, indicating that Polar Music may have had plans to release the song as a single in advance of *The Visitors* album. Ultimately, no single was released until the album was completed near the end of the year. After the album's release, 'When All Is Said and Done' was released as the lead single in the US, Canada, and Brazil, and as the follow-up to 'One of Us' in Australia and Mexico, and third single from the album in New Zealand. It was ABBA's last American top thirty single.

Like *Super Trouper* the year before, two songs on *The Visitors* would be recorded in for the Latin American markets and Spain. 'When All Is Said and Done' was recorded in Spanish as 'No hay a quien culpar' ('No one to blame'), with lyrics written, as usual, by Buddy and Mary McCluskey.

Björn wrote new lyrics for the second verse of 'When All Is Said and Done' for inclusion in the movie version of the *Mamma Mia!* musical, with the original second verse then replacing the third verse, where it was sung by former James Bond actor Pierce Brosnan. The additional lyric, and the placement of the song in the movie (spoiler alert: it is sung at Donna and Sam's wedding reception), give the song a completely different context, one of feeling fulfilment after wasted chances in life: 'It's been there in my dreams/the scene I see unfold/true at last, flesh and blood/to cherish and to hold/Careless fools will suffer, yes/I know and I confess/once I lost my way when/something good had just begun/lesson learned, it's history/when all is said and done'.

For all that trouble, the new verse was not included in the final print of the movie. Contrary to rumour, this was not an effort to try to garner an Oscar nomination for Best Song. There are strict rules regarding songs submitted for Oscar consideration. Songs must be new, written for the film, and crucial to the storyline. For the same reasons, an unreleased song such as 'Just Like That' (see Appendix I for details of that song) could not be added to the film to be nominated, though there were unfounded rumours before the film's release that the song would be included.

At a 2009 ABBA tribute concert in London's Hyde Park, Australian singer Kylie Minogue sang 'When All Is Said and Done' with the movie lyric, accompanied by Benny on the piano. Benny had also played piano on a recording sung by Viktoria Tolstoy for trombonist Nils Landgren's 2004 album *Funky ABBA*, featuring modern jazz interpretations of ABBA songs. Landgren had a previous relationship with ABBA, playing trombone on the 1979 track 'Voulez-Vous'.

'Soldiers'
Duration: 4.38

'There's absolutely no reason in the world for us to begin to write political texts,' Björn said in 1976. He had obviously changed his mind by 1981. 'Soldiers' is an extremely political song. It talks of the fear of approaching war, which was a real concern for the world in the early '80s, with continuing Cold War tensions between superpowers the USA and USSR, the Islamic Revolution in Iran, the Soviet invasion of Afghanistan leading to threats of war from China, ongoing IRA terrorism in Britain, and despotic regimes in Asia and Africa committing genocide within their own borders.

Björn was usually reluctant to discuss the meaning of his lyrics, leaving them for the listener to interpret for themselves. However, 'Soldiers' was one song that he wanted to make sure the message was understood. 'Soldiers is not about ordinary fighting men, but about those on high rank. Those military men who make decisions that the politicians don't even know about,' he said in the official *ABBA Magazine*. Agnetha agreed with Björn's sentiments: 'I see the lyrics very seriously, and I think every human being is a bit afraid of what could happen in the world. This situation doesn't feel too good. It's about the fear of what can happen'.

Though all the songs ABBA recorded during 1981 featured solo lead vocals in the verses, the chorus of 'Soldiers' sees a welcome return of ABBA's third voice as Agnetha and Frida sing in unison, not heard since 'On and On and On' and 'The Piper' on the previous year's *Super Trouper*, and sadly not to be heard again. The drum pattern in the song's verses, devised by drummer Per Lindvall, manages to disguise the fact that the song is in 6/8 waltz time, while evoking both military drums and distant gunfire.

'Soldiers' is the fourth ABBA song that Benny and Björn allowed to be sampled, in the instrumental track 'Soldiers 2015' on the free download album *Peace Tracks*, celebrating International Peace Day in 2015 (the album also featured a song sampling 'SOS'). The track features the drum pattern and bass from ABBA's recording, supplementing musicians from six diverse countries, bringing the world's music together for peace.

'I Let the Music Speak'
Duration: 5.20

'I Let the Music Speak' is the most theatrical song in ABBA's catalogue, even more so than the songs in *The Girl with the Golden Hair* mini-musical in 1977. It is also an indication of Benny and Björn's future ambitions to write a musical for the stage. They have said that they thought the song was pushing the boundary of what could be included on a pop album, but it is certainly no 'Revolution 9'*.

Björn has explained that the lyric is about itself; it is a song about the creation of a song. The opening lines 'I'm hearing images/I'm seeing songs/no poet has ever painted' are a rather poetic description of the process of creation. Björn is saying that he lets the music speak to him when he is trying to to inspire a lyric. In the end, it is all about the music.

He explained his writing process in his book *You Are Who You Meet* in 2018: 'It starts with the tune. That's always been the case when Benny Andersson and I work together. When it comes to writing the lyrics, I play the demo of the song over and over again. Surprisingly often it tells me who the song is about. Sometimes as an image suddenly appearing in my head or even a kind of film sequence. All I have to do is transcribe what I'm seeing in my mind to lyric form'.

The theatricality of 'I Let the Music Speak', not to mention the title itself, made it the ideal opening track for Benny's 2017 solo album *Piano*.

* An eight-minute, twenty-second *musique concrète* sound collage, the penultimate track on The Beatles' 1968 eponymous double album, better known as the *White Album*. It is regularly nominated as the worst Beatles track, though it has its fans, including this author.

'One of Us'
Duration: 3.55
Released as a single 7 December 1981.

'One of Us' was the lead single from *The Visitors* album. Unusually, the single was actually released in Sweden one week after the album, even later in some other territories. For all previous albums, the lead single would be released two to three months in advance, with the second single released around the same time as the album, but 1981 had been a difficult year for ABBA. They had floated the idea of releasing 'When All Is Said and Done' in August, but in the end, no single was released until the album was completed.

The song is another song of regret on the end of a relationship sung by Agnetha. 'It's about a girl who has broken up from her man and she has to move into a new flat,' she said, a scenario shown in the song's promotional film.

'One of Us' would be ABBA's last major international hit single, peaking at No. 3 in the UK. It was the second-last of ten No. 1 singles in the Netherlands, and the last of nine No. 1s in West Germany, twelve No. 1s in Ireland, and sixteen No. 1s in Belgium, the nation where ABBA topped the charts most frequently. In Australia, due to bad timing of the release, when television music shows were on summer hiatus, it peaked at a lowly No. 48. In the US, where the single was not released until 1983 (to promote the compilation *The Singles – The First Ten Years*), it reached No. 33 on the Adult Contemporary Chart, but did not enter the Hot 100.

The sleeve of *The Visitors* bears an interesting credit: mandolins on 'One of Us' are played by a mysterious combo named The Three Boys. Björn explained the credit for curious listeners: 'That was just a stupid name we thought up. They don't exist as a group. In other countries, Eastern European ones especially, they call groups "The Three Comrades" or something like that. It is just making fun of that because it is really just Lasse [Wellander, guitarist], Rutger [Gunnarsson, bassist] and myself'.

'One of Us' is featured in the stage version of *Mamma Mia!*, but was dropped from the 2008 film adaption. It was resurrected in 2018 in the sequel *Mamma Mia! Here We Go Again* and also on Cher's *Dancing Queen* album. Critic Alexis Petridis wrote of Cher's rather understated version in *The Guardian*: 'She digs into the song's dark heart, stripping away the original's bouncy rhythm to produce an anguished depiction of romantic despair'.

'Two for the Price of One'
Duration: 3.36

'Two for the Price of One' is something of a throwback to the quirky story songs about unusual people that peppered ABBA's early years. Musically, it is also a flash forward to the recitative forms used in the musical *Chess* that Benny and Björn would create with British wordsmith Tim Rice in 1983 and 1984.

The lyric tells the story of an everyday man, who works as a cleaner at the local train station. He is lonely and scours the personal columns in the newspaper looking for love. He finds one intriguing ad, offering 'two for the price of one', and calls the number. In the end, he learns that the advertisement is for a woman and her mother. The final verse is open to interpretation: is the mother going to chaperone her daughter's dates or are the two women offering themselves up for a threesome? Curious indeed.

An earlier version of the lyric had a first-person narrative and was distinctly bleaker, where our protagonist cleaned the toilets, not the platforms at the railway station, and sometimes he wished he had a knife, rather than wife; possibly he is thinking of harming himself. It also lacked the punchline, instead just repeating the first two lines at the end.

The lead vocal is from Björn, his first since 'Does Your Mother Know' on *Voulez-Vous* in 1979. Agnetha and Frida join in as a sort of Greek chorus, echoing parts of the story and adding to the advertisement, as sung during the chorus.

The song ends with a brass band-like fanfare, courtesy of Benny and his synthesizers. Allegedly real tuba, trombone, and trumpets were recorded, but they are inaudible on the released recording, and the players were not credited on *The Visitors* album sleeve.

'Two for the Price of One' would be one of the few lighter moments on ABBA's final studio album. 'It's a nice little story about a guy who is a cleaner at a railway station who answers a lonely hearts ad from two girls looking for a blind date—the twist is that when they turn up its a mother and a daughter,' Björn recalled. It is a quite controversial song for ABBA's fans: they either hate it (seemingly most of them) or love it (a small, enthusiastic group).

'Slipping Through My Fingers'
Written by Benny Andersson and Björn Ulvaeus. Spanish lyric by Buddy and Mary McCluskey.
Duration: 3.51

'Slipping Through My Fingers' may be the most personal of all of ABBA's songs. While some songs were inspired by personal experiences but not being strictly autobiographical, 'Slipping Through My Fingers' is exactly about its inspiration. Björn wrote the lyric after seeing his and Agnetha's daughter, Linda, heading off to school in the morning. As she turned and waved goodbye ('with an absent-minded smile', the lyric tells us), he was hit by the fact that she was growing up, that this was the first step in her moving away from her parents, and that their time together was short.

Linda's mother, Agnetha, takes lead vocal on the song. 'It felt very … true to do,' she said. 'Although they are more or less Björn's thoughts, they are mine too I suppose. I think he has captured them very well.' In the second verse, she duets with herself, putting on a slightly childish voice in the harmony line to sound like she is singing with her child (some listeners have thought that she duets with eight-year-old Linda).

After the emotion of the verses, the choruses seem a little underwhelming, with overdone choral overdubs. Benny and Björn often cite a perceived mismatch between verse and chorus melodies as a reason for dumping a song on a single B-side ('Lovelight', 'Should I Laugh or Cry') or not releasing it at all ('Just Like That'). But here, they put a mismatched song on an album.

'Slipping Through My Fingers' was the first song from *The Visitors* album to be released, on a picture disc single and matching album as part of a series of records given away as prizes by Coca-Cola in Japan in June 1981. The two records were little known to ABBA's worldwide fan base at the time, but today they are prized collectibles.

'Slipping Through My Fingers' was the second song on *The Visitors* to be recorded in Spanish, titled 'Se me está escapando' ('It's slipping away from me').

'Slipping Through My Fingers' is one of the few 'deep cuts' from ABBA's catalogue to feature in the *Mamma Mia!* musical. In the 2008 film version, it is a touching duet between Meryl Streep and Amanda Seyfried, as mother and daughter, Donna and Sophie.

'Like an Angel Passing Through My Room'
Duration: 3.25

The final track on ABBA's final studio album was difficult for the group. Several attempts were made at getting the right sound throughout 1981 (see 'From a Twinkling Star to a Passing Angel' in Appendix I). Agnetha explained: 'You know we did two or three different backing tracks for that number and none of them came out that good…. Then they tried this very naked approach and I think it sounds a bit exciting'. The final attempt was the version included on the album. A simple recording that could be a lullaby or a requiem.

The recording features Frida's ethereal vocal, over Benny's music box-like synthesizer and an ominous-sounding ticking clock (generated by Benny's Minimoog) that had faded in over the end of the album's previous song ('Slipping Through My Fingers') and continues for several seconds after the music fades. The listener can imagine Frida sitting in a darkened room, illuminated only by the fireplace, as she contemplates a dying or dead relationship, or perhaps even death itself.

Frida recalled the recording with fondness: '"Like an Angel Passing Through My Room" is full of good memories for me. We were the only two, Benny and I, in the studio, alone with the "tic-tic" of the metronome sound … I love that sort of song'. Despite declaring the recording 'exciting', Agnetha had reservations: 'It is a strange number because you wait for something that never comes'. Or does it? Sometimes the end comes unexpectedly and quietly.

The song title inspired art director Rune Söderqvist for the sleeve of *The Visitors* album. He remembered a giant painting of the angelic figure Eros in artist Julius Kronbergs Ateljé (atelier, or artist's workshop) in Skansen, the open-air museum and zoo in Stockholm. He also thought an angel could also be a visitor, tying in with the album's title. ABBA was duly photographed in front of the painting, standing separately, perhaps subtly indicating the state of affairs within the group. The location has become a popular attraction for ABBA fans, though it is rarely open to the public.

Madonna recorded a haunting cover version with producer William Orbit around the time of her 2000 album *Music*, five years before the singer sampled ABBA on her international hit 'Hung Up' (see the entry for 'Gimme! Gimme! Gimme! (A Man After Midnight)' for more about that song). It remains unreleased officially, though the recording was 'leaked' on the internet on the singer's fiftieth birthday in 2008.

'Like an Angel Passing Through My Room' is the perfect ending for the album, and for ABBA, though they would record several songs in 1982 before calling it quits.

Non-Album Tracks, 1981

'Should I Laugh or Cry'
Duration: 4.29
Released on the B-side of 'One of Us', 7 December 1981.

'Should I Laugh or Cry' is a rather bitter song. The narrator is a woman who has grown tired of her man, who tries to impress, but fails. With Frida taking the lead, it is a curious song for her to sing within a few months of her and Benny's separation. How much personal experience is in the song and her performance?

'Should I Laugh or Cry' did not make it on to *The Visitors* album. Instead, it would be the B-side of the album's lead single 'One of Us', or 'When All Is Said and Done' in the US and Canada. The production values are certainly not up to the standard of the nine songs on the album. Benny has said that like many rejected songs, the verse and chorus do not go together. Many listeners disagree, feeling it would be a better fit on the album than 'Two for the Price of One', though just as many disagree with this assessment.

Final Sessions:
Non-Album Tracks, 1982

Personnel: Benny Andersson: keyboards, synthesizers, vocals
Agnetha Fältskog: vocals
Rutger Gunnarsson: bass
Per Lindvall: drums, percussion
Anni-Frid Lyngstad: vocals
Janne Schaffer: guitar
Åke Sundqvist: percussion
Björn Ulvaeus: vocals
Lasse Wellander: guitar
Digitally recorded at Polar Music Studio, Stockholm: May, June, and August 1982

'The Day Before You Came'
Duration: 5.50
Released as a single 18 October 1982. Also on the album *The Singles: The First Ten Years* 8 November 1982.

Here is where the story ends. ABBA's final recording, but penultimate single release. After the reportedly troubled sessions for *The Visitors* album in 1981, and Frida recording her first international, English-language album *Something's Going On* during February and March 1982, in May ABBA reconvened at Polar Music Studios to record a new album. After recording just three tracks, the group abandoned those album plans and instead announced a new career-spanning compilation double album *The Singles: The First Ten Years*, with a couple of new songs and a new single. 'The Day Before You Came', recorded in August, was the last of but six ABBA songs recorded in 1982.

'The Day Before You Came' is an almost six-minute epic tale of the boring, mundane things that happened to the protagonist on the day before a life-changing meeting: she leaves her house, catches the train to work, signs papers in the office, has lunch, smokes a cigarette, takes the train home, eats Chinese take-out food, watches TV, goes to bed, reads a book, and listens to the rain on the roof. There is a sense of pervading gloom, perhaps even doom, over the whole proceeding. What happened the next day? We will never know, but it might not have ended well. 'I really like that song,' Benny once said. 'It becomes extremely sad when you hear it like this. The recording is sad too, but the lyric itself is not sad, which is the genius of Bjorn. To me, when you read that lyric and take the music away it's just someone saying what they did that day—"I read a book", "I watched TV", "I took the tube", whatever; it doesn't say what it really is. But when you put that lyric onto that music you realise something not good has happened. It's a very intelligent lyric'.

As the protagonist prepares for sleep, she reads 'the latest one by [American feminist author] Marilyn French/or something in that style'. It is curious to note that French's latest novel at the time, *The Bleeding Heart*, is about a man and woman who meet on a train and instantly fall in love, though the relationship lasts for just a year after a bitter but passionate affair. Had voracious reader Björn read the novel? Had the directors of the song's promotional film, which featured Agnetha flirting with a handsome stranger on a commuter train.

For one of the few times in Benny and Björn's career as songwriters, this song was essentially written in the studio, based around a keyboard riff that Benny had created. The music track is dominated by Benny's massive Yamaha GX-1 synthesizer, only accompanied by a drum machine and a snare drum courtesy of percussionist Åke Sundqvist banging on the off-beat. Producers Benny and Björn had asked solo vocalist Agnetha to sing not as a singer, but as an ordinary woman, a move that generated some unfortunate criticism of Agnetha's alleged poor performance. Frida's only contribution was wordless backing vocals that come in with the second verse, notably the high operatic voice over the break (2.28 to 3.02) and the coda (from 4.32).

Upon release in October 1982, 'The Day Before You Came' was not a typical ABBA big hit. In a review in *Smash Hits* magazine, Fred Dellar predicted the single may not do well: 'There's a great lyric…. But the song's very wordiness may be its chart undoing'. It reached the top five in ABBA-loyal countries such as West Germany, the Netherlands, and Belgium, but only reached No. 32 in the important British market, which at the time was dominated by young synthpop bands (ironically, many of whom said they were inspired by ABBA). In recent years, the song has come to be regarded as one of ABBA's masterpieces. In the 2010 British television special *The Nation's Favourite ABBA Song*, it was voted by viewers as third favourite (only beaten by obvious hits 'Dancing Queen' and 'The Winner Takes It All'), while in 2012, *NME* described the song as ABBA's 'finest hour'. Björn has admitted: 'We were heading into something more mature, more mysterious and more exciting. But this time it was one step too far for our audience'.

British electropop duo Blancmange recorded a cover version in 1984. Their version famously charted better than ABBA's single in the UK, reaching No. 22. In their version, the protagonist is reading prolific romance novelist Barbara Cartland, then enjoying pop-culture fame.

Benny acknowledged the song's latter-day popularity with a solo version on his album *Piano* in 2017, reducing the song to the stark beauty of the melody. He revisited the song again during recording sessions for the soundtrack of the film *Mamma Mia! Here We Go Again*, creating a new version of the song sung by three-time Oscar winner Meryl Streep. Though the song was not part of the film's story, Benny explained: 'I felt I had to record it with Meryl'. He had the idea of the song playing over the end credits, but acknowledged: '… we cannot end the movie with the world's saddest song'. Nonetheless, the recording was released as an undeclared bonus track on the soundtrack CD. Björn updated the lyric for the second decade of the twenty-first century: the singer works longer hours, smokes less, reads Canadian writer Margaret Attwood (her latest novel *Hag-Seed*, a modern retelling of Shakespeare's *The Tempest*) and binge watches *House of Cards* on Netflix rather than '80s nighttime soapy *Dallas*.

'Cassandra'
Duration: 4.50
Released on the B side of 'The Day Before You Came', 18 October 1982.

Björn based the lyric of 'Cassandra' on ancient Greek mythology. Cassandra, daughter of King Priam and Queen Hecuba of Troy, had been blessed with the gift of prophecy by the god Apollo, but after she rejected his advances, she was cursed so that no one would believe her prophecies. Cassandra foresaw the invasion and fall of Troy, with its famous wooden horse that concealed Greek troops, and was subsequently enslaved by King Agamemnon of Mycenae. Later, she and the king were put to death by the king's wife, Clytemnstra, and her lover, Aegisthus, another event Cassandra had foreseen but was not believed.

Frida takes lead on 'Cassandra', one of the more successful tracks ABBA recorded in 1982. Her voice takes on new tones that she seems to have learnt while recording her solo album *Something's Going On* earlier in the year. Agnetha joins in the chorus, with her voice soaring on the lines 'but on the darkest of nights/nobody knew how to fight/and we were caught in our sleep'.

The musical arrangement in the chorus, but not the melody, is recycled from the unreleased 1980 song 'Put On Your White Sombrero' (see Appendix I).

'Under Attack'
Duration: 3.45
Released on *The Singles: The First Ten Years* 8 November 1982. Also released as a single 21 February 1983.

ABBA's final released single, 'Under Attack', is a bunch of melodies in search of a song. The melody of the verses is reused from the unreleased songs 'Just Like That', recorded earlier in 1982, and 'Rubber Ball Man'/'Under My Sun', created back in 1979 (see 'ABBA Undeleted' in Appendix I for details about those songs). In the book *Mamma Mia! How Can I Resist You?*, Björn said: 'Benny and I always carried this battery of little ideas around in our heads, thinking of ways to combine the old and the new. I don't know if that is a technique other songwriters use, but it was certainly ours'.

The backing is synth-heavy, while Agnetha's lead vocal has been compressed to the point of sterility. Interjections during the verses have been put through a vocoder to get that early-'80s robotic vocal sound, which had been used by ABBA quite effectively earlier, but here seems jammed in. 'The sound on the vocals of "Under Attack" is very much of the 1980s,' Björn admitted. The chorus literally shouts the title at the listener, and it offers so many overdubbed vocal layers that they cross over each other, obscuring the melody and making the lyrics near indecipherable.

In November, preparing for the single's release, Benny and Björn tried remixing the song, doubling the length of the introduction, changing the mix of some musical elements, and creating a cold ending. However, they weren't satisfied with the remix, and the version from *The Singles* was issued in 7-inch form.

It is possible that 'Under Attack' was not necessarily intended to be a single. An early press release announcing *The Singles* compilation album stated that it would include two new tracks, one of which would be released as a single. It would appear that following the lack of chart success for 'The Day Before You Came' in the UK (peaking at No. 32), 'Under Attack' was rush-released in the hope of improving on the previous single's chart placing—in the UK, it was released on 3 December, less than two months after the previous single, an unusually short timeframe between releases. Elsewhere, the single was released in January or February 1983. 'Under Attack' did do better chartwise in the UK, but only just, reaching No. 26.

'Under Attack' is a sad end to ABBA's glorious career, though reviewer Christopher Connelly inexplicably declared in *Rolling Stone* that the song was 'the best thing they've done in three years'. Only in the ever-ABBA-loving Belgium and the Netherlands did the single reach the top ten. In the promotional film, ABBA are seen in a deserted warehouse. At the end of the clip, they exit into blinding sunlight, walking away from the camera, the viewer, and from ABBA.

'You Owe Me One'

Duration: 3.29
Released as the B-side of 'Under Attack', 21 February 1983.

'You Owe Me One' was the first of three songs recorded in May 1982, before ABBA abandoned the plan to record a ninth studio album for release that year.

It is a bright, upbeat song, a return to an earlier, poppier ABBA, with some quite witty lyrics that could be disguising ABBA's internal conflicts ('buy me a ticket I'll go to the Bahamas/I need a rest from our petty little dramas'). It sees a brief return to unison vocals from Frida and Agnetha, though somehow they do not manage to get that famous third voice sound. Perhaps that was a sign that they had trouble gathering enthusiasm for the recording sessions. Like so many of ABBA's later recordings, Benny's synthesizers dominate the backing, notably his new Prophet-10.

It seems likely that had ABBA not needed a song for the B-side of 'Under Attack' at the end of the year, 'You Owe Me One' may not have been released at all. In a June 1982 Polar Music press release that announced the May sessions and the planned compilation album, the two other tracks recorded so far, 'Just Like That' and 'I Am the City' were described as 'LP-tracks', presumably for a new album promised in 1983, but 'You Owe Me One' was not mentioned at all. Recording and mixing of 'You Owe Me One' were not finished until the 'Under Attack' single was being prepared in November.

See Appendix I for more on 'I Am the City' and 'Just Like That'.

Epilogue

'If it ever stops being fun, we'll quit,' Björn had said many times over the years, as early as the press conference in Sydney at the start of ABBA's Australian concert tour in March 1977. In interviews in late 1980, he predicted that ABBA probably had two or three albums left in them. His prediction essentially came true.

Following the release of the compilation double album *The Singles: The First Ten Years*, the singles 'The Day Before You Came' and 'Under Attack', and some television promotion in West Germany, the UK, the Netherlands, and Sweden in November and December 1982, ABBA called it a day. Watching those television appearances today, the viewer can see the tension between the four and also the relief that it will soon be over. The official story at the time was that the group was 'taking a break', so that Benny and Björn could pursue their long-time dream of writing a musical, which they initially called a rock opera (a term that came into common use with The Who's *Tommy* album in 1969). *Chess*, written with British lyricist Tim Rice of *Jesus Christ Superstar* and *Evita* fame, was released on record in November 1984 and premiered on stage in London in May 1986. The musical spawned the hits 'One Night in Bangkok' sung by Murray Head with Anders Glenmark and 'I Know Him So Well' by Elaine Paige and Barbara Dickson.

Both Agnetha and Frida relished the opportunity to reignite their solo careers, each releasing several albums in English internationally between 1982 and 1987, with mixed success; Frida's single 'I Know There's Something Going On', produced by Phil Collins, was the most successful. In 1984, Frida recorded a song written by Benny and Björn, 'Slowly'—the only time one of the women recorded a new song written by the ABBA men in the post-ABBA era. By the end of the decade, both women had retired from public life.

The break never ended and ABBA never came back together, despite some outrageous offers to reunite.

For most of the '80s, ABBA was seen as out of fashion and largely ignored. A much-requested live album, *ABBA Live*, was released in August 1986 but barely made an impact anywhere, even in ABBA's home country. But late in the decade, an underground ABBA revival started, primarily in the world's gay communities, with ABBA-themed nights filling venues to capacity. Budget compilations were released that sold in respectable numbers, but not in enough mass to enter the charts. Some of the ABBA catalogue was released on CD, but these were mostly haphazard and uncoordinated releases by ABBA's licensees.

In 1990, the German-Dutch entertainment conglomerate PolyGram bought Stig Anderson's Sweden Music empire, including Polar Music. Two years later, once international licences had expired, the company released the compilation album *ABBA Gold: Greatest Hits* in September 1992, gathering nineteen of ABBA's biggest hits on a single CD. This led to a massive worldwide ABBA revival, with *ABBA Gold* quickly becoming a No. 1 album in many countries. Around the same time, British electronic duo Erasure released their *Abba-esque* EP, featuring four of ABBA's best-known hits—'Lay All Your Love On Me', 'SOS', 'Take a Chance on Me', and 'Voulez-Vous'—which took ABBA's songs back to the top of the singles charts. Australian ABBA tribute act Björn Again, which had formed in Melbourne in 1989, returned the favour with the EP *Erasure-ish*, featuring Erasure's hits 'A Little Respect' and 'Stop!' done in ABBA style. Björn Again's success spawned an ever-growing industry in ABBA tribute bands. The ABBA revival was further established in 1994 by the inclusion of several ABBA songs in two hit Australian films, *Muriel's Wedding* and *The Adventures of Priscilla, Queen of the Desert.*

The stage musical *Mamma Mia!*, a mother–daughter story featuring twenty-two ABBA songs, opened in London on 6 April 1999, on the twenty-fifth anniversary of ABBA's Eurovision Song Contest win, allegedly completely by coincidence (yeah, right). *Mamma Mia!* has since been translated into twenty-three languages, has played around the world to an audience of over 65 million people, and has grossed over $4 billion. A movie version starring Meryl Streep, Pierce Brosnan, Colin Firth, Julie Walters, Amanda Seyfried, Christine Baranski, Stellan Skarsgård, and Dominic Cooper opened in July 2008 (with the four ABBA members attending the Stockholm premiere) and became the highest-grossing movie musical of all time, as well as breaking DVD sales records. A sequel to the movie, *Mamma Mia! Here We Go Again*, featuring the original cast, new characters played by Cher and Andy Garcia, a younger cast led by Lily James, and more ABBA songs, premiered in July 2018 and came close to repeating original film's success.

An offshoot project, *Mamma Mia! The Party*, opened as an immersive dinner theatre experience in the Gröna Lund amusement park in Stockholm in January 2016. The opening night saw Björn, Frida, Benny, and Agnetha in attendance, and late in the evening (after media representatives had left the venue), they briefly stood together on stage in public view for the first time since 1986, much to the surprise and joy of those in attendance. Plans to open *Mamma Mia! The Party* in

London's suitably-named Waterloo were thwarted after complaints from locals in the primarily residential area, but the party lives on at The O2 in London, where it opened in September 2019. Further parties are planned in Europe and the US.

The touring exhibition ABBAWORLD opened at Earl's Court in London in January 2010, displaying ABBA's stage costumes, multiple awards, and other memorabilia. The exhibition featured brand-new video interviews with the four ABBA members, Görel Hanser (originally Stig Anderson's secretary, later vice-president of Polar Music, who today still represents Benny, Björn, and Frida individually as well as the ABBA organisation), and several of their musical and visual creative collaborators. In the following two years, the exhibition moved on to Melbourne and Sydney in Australia, Györ in Hungary, and Prague in Czechia. With lessons learnt from the tour venues, the exhibition found its final home in Stockholm as ABBA The Museum, which opened in May 2013 on the island of Djurgården, near popular attractions Gröna Lund amusement park and open-air museum Skansen. Visitors can see recreations of Björn and Benny's songwriting cabin and Polar Music's office and studio, examine ABBA's original costumes, be quizzed on ABBA trivia, and can join ABBA onstage via projected holograms. Today, ABBA The Museum is one of Stockholm's most popular tourist attractions, with over 1 million visitors in its first three years, and still attracting over 350,000 visitors per year.

A spin-off, Super Troupers: The Exhibition, which highlighted ABBA's impact on '70s Britain, was hosted at London's Southbank Centre in 2018. Curiously, the exhibition showed a copy of the *Ring Ring* album in one room to illustrate what 'a typical British family' might be listening to, despite the album not being released in the UK. Whoops! An expanded version of the exhibiton opened at The O2 in London in December 2019, adjacent to *Mamma Mia! The Party*.

Benny and Björn have continued to collaborate, writing the Swedish musicals *Kristina från Duvemåla* (*Kristina From Duvemåla*, 1995) and *Hjälp sökes* (*Help Wanted*, 2013). *Kristina*, a story of nineteenth-century Swedes emigrating to the US in search of a better life, has been translated into English and has played in concert versions in New York and London in 2009 and 2010. Alas, in the era of lighthearted jukebox musicals (thanks to fare like *Mamma Mia!*), it has been deemed 'too heavy' for theatre audiences looking for fun and escapism.

Benny has recorded three solo albums starting in 1987, and in 2001 formed Benny Anderssons Orkester (Benny Andersson's Orchestra, known as Benny Andersson Band on English-language releases), a flexible combination of Benny's musician friends, which has released nine albums to date and tours Sweden most summers. Benny has also recorded soundtracks for several Swedish films. Björn continues to write lyrics for Benny's songs, and in June 2016, they celebrated the fiftieth anniversary of their partnership.

Since retiring in the late '80s, Agnetha and Frida have both made sporadic returns to the recording studio, releasing occasional solo albums or making guest vocal appearances on other artists' songs. Aside from occasional appearances at public events, they have mostly stayed out of the public eye.

And the ABBA legacy lives on. In 2020, a new 'virtual entertainment experience' is expected to be unleashed on the world. The four ABBA members have been 'involved in the creative process', according to the initial media release. The so-called ABBAtars, digital representations of ABBA *circa* 1979, will perform to ABBA's original live and studio vocals in front of a live band. Benny said: 'We're inspired by the limitless possibilities of what the future holds and are loving being a part of creating something new and dramatic here. A time machine that captures the essence of who we were. And are'. The show will also include brand-new ABBA songs, the group's first recordings since 1982.

Despite the group coming to an end over three and a half decades ago, ABBA's music lives in the hearts and minds of millions of people all over the world.

Live Performances, Archival Releases, and Unreleased Songs

Here are the songs that got away. Between 1972 and 1982, ABBA performed several songs on television, radio, or in concert that were never released on record. There were a number of songs recorded during those years that for one reason or another were rejected and shelved at the time, but have been released on compilations and boxsets in the years since. The four former members have also surprised the world with occasional performances in the years after the group disbanded. Here are the songs that are known to have been heard in public. There are more, locked away in the vault, sadly never to be heard.

'Hej gamle man!'
Written by Benny Andersson and Björn Ulvaeus. German lyric by H. Bradtke
Personnel: Benny Andersson: keyboards, vocals
            John Cúonz: drums
            Agnetha Fältskog: backing vocals
            Gus Horn: bass
            Anni-Frid Lyngstad: backing vocals
            Björn Ulvaeus: guitar, vocals
Duration: 3.21
Released as a single *circa* October 1970. Also released on the Björn & Benny album *Lycka* in November 1970.

'Hej gamle man!' ('Hey old man!') is the first ever recording to feature the combined vocal contributions of Björn, Benny, Agnetha, and Frida, when Agnetha and Frida sang backing choir on this Björn & Benny song from their first and only duo album, *Lycka* (*Happiness*). Since first meeting in the late '60s, the four had gradually started working together, singing, playing, writing, and producing on each other's records but had never sung all together on one song until now.

The lyric tells the story of an old Salvation Army officer, standing in a town square every day, though he gives the appearance he has only been there since yesterday. The song itself is a *schlager*, a popular European style of music.

Björn and Benny went on to rerecord the song in German as 'Hey Musikant' ('Hey musician'), but it appears that Agnetha and Frida did not sing on this version. American singer Paul Evans recorded an English version, 'For Old Times Sake', with lyrics written by Evans and Paul Parnes, which was released on the B-side of his single 'Think Summer' in 1971—the first recording of a Benny and Björn compositon by a non-Scandinavian artist.

In 1994, 'Hej gamle man!' was included on the four-CD ABBA box set *Thank You for the Music*, the first time the song was made freely available outside Scandinavia. It was added as a bonus track on the *Ring Ring* Deluxe Edition CD in 2012. *Lycka* was rereleased on CD in 2006, with thirteen bonus tracks encompassing the complete released recordings of Björn & Benny as a duo, including 'Hey Musikant'.

'California, Here I Come'
Written by Al Jolson, Bud De Sylva, and Joseph Meyer
Duration: 1.00

'Red Roses for a Blue Lady'
Duration: 2.05
Written by Sid Tepper and Roy C. Bennet
Performed on the Swedish television program *5 Minute Saloon* in 21 October 1970

In October 1970, just weeks before making their stage debut in the *Festfolk* cabaret show, the fledgling quartet appeared on the Swedish television program *5 Minute Saloon*, singing two classic American songs. Björn, Benny, Agnetha, and Frida gave a rousing rendition of 'California, Here I Come', written in 1921 for the Broadway musical *Bombo*, starring Al Jolson. On 'Red Roses for a Blue Lady', which was written in 1948, musician and singer Gunnar 'Siljaboo' Nilsson joined the two couples. The performance of 'California, Here I Come' was included on the 2004 ABBA documentary DVD *Super Troupers—From Waterloo to Mamma Mia!*

'En hälsning till våra parkarrangörer'
Duration: 2.27
Released as a promotional single in January 1973

Not a song as such, 'En hälsning till våra parkarrangörer' ('A greeting to our park organisers') was a spoken-word record, with Björn, Benny, Agnetha, and Frida talking about the quartet's forthcoming tour of Sweden's *folkparks*. The record includes short excerpts of the quartet's first single 'People Need Love', Frida's first single for Polar Music, 'Man vill ju leva lite dessemellan' ('You've got to live a little every now and then'), and Agnetha's recent single 'Så glad som dina ögon' ('As happy as your eyes'). The B-side, a similar message from singers Lena Andersson and Ted Gärdestad, also featured a small contribution from Björn.

The single was distributed to Swedish *folkpark* promotors in January 1973. *Folkparks* were open-air entertainment venues in towns across Sweden. Every summer Swedish artists would tour the *folkparks*, often performing two or three shows per day. The record was packaged in a bespoke folder with photographs and biographies of the Polar artists, to encourage the promoters to book them in the upcoming summer *folkpark* season.

In 2012, the message from Björn & Benny, Agnetha & Anni-Frid was included as a bonus track on the *Ring Ring* Deluxe Edition CD.

'Alley Cat'

Written by Bent Fabricius Bjerre
Duration: 1.20
Performed on the Danish television programme *Omkring et flygel*, 27 May 1975 (broadcast 21 June 1975)

When ABBA appeared on the Danish entertainment programme *Omkring et flygel* (*Around a piano*) in May 1975, they sang a scat version of the show's theme song while gathered around Benny's piano. It was tradition for the show's guests to perform the theme song, which had been written by its host in 1961, at the end of each programme.

'Jingle Bells'

Written by James Pierpoint
Duration: 0.20 (1976), 0.28 (1977)
Performed on television in December 1976 (broadcast 25 December 1976) and December 1977 (broadcast 21 December 1977)

Benny and Björn played impromptu performances of this popular Christmas song twice during television reports about ABBA, on Swedish magazine programme *Rapport* in December 1976 (which also featured the first public airing of part of the melody of 'Thank You for the Music') and on the Dutch programme *ABBA Veronica Muziekspecial* a year later

'I Am an A'

Written by Benny Andersson, Stig Anderson, and Björn Ulvaeus
Duration: 5.20
Performed in concert on the European & Australian Tour 28 January to 12 March 1977

'I Am an A' was written for ABBA's 1977 concert tour as a light-hearted introduction of the four members. While the band and backing vocalists took a short break, Björn, Agnetha, Frida, and Benny sat on stools at the front of the stage, with Björn and Benny playing acoustic guitars as the song's only musical accompaniment. The lyrics introduce each of the ABBA members, with the other three offering snappy remarks: opening with 'I'm Frida, hello/I'm the star of the show' and Agnetha's retort 'that's what she thinks anyway', it goes on from there.

The song has never been released officially, though fans can hear it on bootleg audience recordings. The chorus melody was recycled in a demo tune, 'Free as a Bumble Bee', in 1978 (see 'ABBA Undeleted' below). The melody found its final home in 1984, as the chorus of 'I Know Him So Well', a highlight of the Benny Andersson/Tim Rice/Björn Ulvaeus musical *Chess*. That song gave Benny and Björn their tenth British No. 1 single, following nine No. 1s for ABBA.

'Get On the Carousel'

Duration: 5.53
Performed in concert on the European & Australian Tour 28 January to 12 March 1977. Released in *ABBA: The Movie*, 15 December 1977

'Get On the Carousel' was the fourth song in the mini-musical *The Girl with the Golden Hair*, the climax of ABBA's 1977 concerts. While the mini-musical's other three songs—'Thank You for the Music', 'I Wonder (Departure)', and 'I'm a Marionette'—were recorded for *ABBA: The Album* in 1977, 'Get On the Carousel' was never subjected to a studio recording.

It is not hard to see why: as performed in concert, the song runs for almost six minutes (following two minutes of percussion-driven vamping music, as Agnetha and Frida danced wildly, seemingly under someone else's control), it is highly repetitive, with just one verse and chorus repeated several times, a lengthy guitar riff played at the start of the song and again at almost the five-minute mark, and reprises of sections of 'I'm a Marionette' and 'I Wonder (Departure)'. The chorus is sung by the three backing singers, Lena Andersson, Lena-Maria Gårdenäs-Lawton, and Maritza Horn, with Agnetha and Frida interjecting over the top. Years later, Björn said: 'We were not happy enough with the song, although it worked in the context of the shows'. In the storyline, it essentially reiterates the theme of 'I'm a Marionette', which probably also contributed to its exclusion from the studio-recorded version of the mini-musical.

Despite not being recorded for *ABBA: The Album*, 'Get On the Carousel' is not completely unheard by the world. About four minutes of the live performance is included in *ABBA: The Movie*, probably filmed and recorded at the first of ABBA's three concerts in Melbourne. Later in the year, the melody of the chorus was reused as the middle section of 'Hole in Your Soul' on *ABBA: The Album* (the 'aha, you paint your world and use all colours' part).

The song ends with an eight-chord sequence rising one full octave. Interestingly, the exact same chord sequence ended the live version of 'Hole in Your Soul' when performed as the final song (before encores) on ABBA's North American, European, and Japanese tours in 1979 and 1980.

'Vi har ei tulle med øyne blå'
Written by Margrethe Munthe
Duration: NK
Performed in concert in Oslo, 28 January 1977

The opening night of ABBA's 1977 concert tour was held in Oslo, the capital of Norway, in January 1977, with the nation's Crown Prince Harald (now King Harald V) and Crown Princess Sonja in the audience. ABBA sang this traditional Norwegian children's song, which was written in 1917 and whose title translates as 'We have a child with blue eyes', in honour of the crown princess, who had recorded the song for a charity single the previous year. This is one that is unheard except by those attending the concert, as no bootleg audience tapes of this performance have surfaced.

'Johan på snippen'
Written by Gideon Wahlberg
Duration: 0.22

'Polkan går'
Written by Nyman
Duration: 0.20
Performed in Australia in March 1977. Released in *ABBA: The Movie*, 15 December 1977

These two Swedish folk tunes were played by Benny on accordion, along with other members of the tour band, in an impromptu moment backstage during ABBA's Australian tour in March 1977. It was captured on film in *ABBA: The Movie*. Other non-ABBA music heard in the film include the instrumental track 'Stoned' by Clive Hicks, and a jingle for Sydney radio station 2SM.

'Helan går'
Traditional
Duration: 0.20
Performed on French radio, 12 April 1978

ABBA offered up this popular Swedish drinking song 'Helan går' during an interview on French radio station Europe 1 in April 1978. The title literally translates as 'the whole [drink] goes [down]', but is more accurately expressed in this context as 'bottoms up', encouraging the drinker to take the whole shot of akvavit (a Scandinavian spirit) or vodka.

'(Remember the Days of the) Old Schoolyard'
Written by Cat Stevens
Duration: 2.05

'Help Me Rhonda'
Written by Brian Wilson
Duration: 1.11

'Barbara Ann'
Written by Fred Fassert
Duration: 0.43

'Una voce poco fa'
Written by Gioachino Rossini
Duration: 0.54

'Holiday'
Written by Barry Gibb and Robin Gibb
Duration: 1.10

'Jailhouse Rock'
Written by Jerry Leiber and Mike Stoller
Duration: 0.49

'What'll I Do'
Written by Irving Berlin
Duration: 1.20
Performed on the television program *Olivia!*, 8 May 1978. Broadcast 17 May 1978.

In an effort to promote ABBA in the US, Atlantic Records declared May 1978 'ABBA Month'. A massive billboard was placed on the Sunset Strip, opposite the busy Tower Records store in the heart of the entertainment district of Los Angeles, declaring ABBA as 'the largest-selling group in the history of recorded music'. The sleeve of the current release *ABBA: The Album* made a cameo appearance on the Robin Williams sitcom *Mork & Mindy*, though not in a particularly flattering light: a record store customer wants to return the album, though the album is not identified and only the back of the sleeve is seen.

The main event of the month was ABBA's appearance on the primetime television special *Olivia!* starring Olivia Newton-John, then riding high as the star of the movie musical *Grease*, and Andy Gibb, younger brother of the Bee Gees, in the middle of his own string of hit singles.

The show opened with the six stars being introduced, singing the Cat Stevens song '(Remember the Days of the) Old Schoolyard'. The second main section was a live medley by the three lead acts, including ABBA hits 'Dancing Queen', 'Fernando', and 'Take a Chance on Me'; Olivia's classics 'If You Love Me Let Me Know', 'Have You Never Been Mellow', 'Please Mister Please', and current hit 'Hopelessly Devoted To You'; and Andy's singles 'I Just Want to Be Your Everything', '(Love Is) Thicker Than Water', and 'Shadow Dancing'.

The final section of the special was a jam session, with the artists sitting in a circle facing each other on a stage surrounded by a small audience—this segment was inspired by a similar segment in Elvis Presley's famous 1968 'comeback special'. ABBA, Olivia, and Andy chat about life and music, and sing a variety of oldies: the Beach Boys' 'Help Me Rhonda' and 'Barbara Ann'; Frida sings a sample of opera from Rossini's *The Barber of Seville* (she can also be heard singing the same piece in backstage footage in *ABBA in Concert*, a documentary on ABBA's 1979 tour); Andy sings 'Holiday', from his brothers' back catalogue of hits; all six sing along to Elvis's movie hit 'Jailhouse Rock'; and it ends with Olivia singing Irving Berlin's standard 'What'll I Do'.

The special closed with all six stars singing ABBA's 'Thank You for the Music', excised from the second section.

The *Olivia!* special was released in the US on MCA Discovision, an early form of laserdisc, but has had no other home video release. An unedited version of the main medley section in true stereo (the original broadcast had been in mono) was uploaded on YouTube in 2011 by one of the editors who worked on the special.

ABBA month resulted in *ABBA: The Album* being the highest-charting ABBA album in the US, reaching No. 13, and 'Take a Chance on Me' becoming ABBA's most successful American single, peaking at No. 3 but reportedly outselling the No. 1 hit 'Dancing Queen'.

'Dream World'

Duration: 3.36
Recorded in September 1978. Released on the boxset *Thank You for the Music*, 31 October 1994.

'Dream World' was recorded in 1978 during troublesome sessions for what would become the *Voulez-Vous* album. This and a number of songs were recorded for the album and then shelved (see also 'Free as a Bumble Bee', 'Just a Notion', 'Hamlet III', and 'Crying Over You' in 'ABBA Undeleted' below). Like many songs written by Benny and Björn, parts of the melody were recycled, in this instance the last section of the chorus became part of 'Does Your Mother Know' (the 'take it easy' section). Benny says in the book *Mamma Mia! How Can I Resist You*: '... we decided that we didn't really like the song, but that section was worth keeping, and it found a home in "Does Your Mother Know"'. Other short snatches of melody were reused in 'Kisses of Fire' and 'I Have a Dream'.

'Dream World' was the first unreleased ABBA song to be semi-officially allowed out of the 'vault' after the group's demise, when recording engineer Michael B. Tretow played it on a radio show called *Sommar* (*Summer*) he was hosting in July 1986. The song was one of several previously unreleased songs to be included on the four CD boxset *Thank You for the Music*. Due to tape damage, this released version had a fade-in introduction, but in 2010, a version with the full introduction restored appeared on the *Voulez-Vous* Deluxe Edition CD.

'Ekorren'
Written by Eric Sandström
Duration: 0.07
Performed in the documentary film *ABBA in Japan*, 26 November 1978.

ABBA sang a snatch of this children's song about a squirrel, made famous by Swedish singer Alice Babs in 1955, for the cameras following them on their first visit to Japan in November 1978. It was included in the short documentary film *ABBA in Japan*, which was released on the DVD of the same name in 2009.

'Put a Little Love in Your Heart'
Written by Jackie DeShannon, Jimmy Holiday, and Randy Myers
Duration: 2.52
Performed at *The Music for UNICEF Concert: A Gift of Song*, 9 January 1979. Broadcast 10 January 1979.

When ABBA appeared at the all-star *The Music for UNICEF Concert* at the United Nations' building in New York in January 1979, at which they premiered the single 'Chiquitita', all the participating artists joined together for the concert's finale to sing Jackie DeShannon's 1969 hit 'Put a Little Love in Your Heart', though ABBA's voices cannot be discerned in the crowd of singers.

'Sång till Görel'
Written by Benny Andersson, Stig Anderson, and Björn Ulvaeus
Duration: 3.47
Released on a limited edition 12-inch single, 21 June 1979.

Görel Johnsen (later Hanser) had been hired as a secretary at Polar Music in 1969. She proved herself indispensable to the growing company and particularly to Stig Anderson, and by the mid-'70s, she was vice-president of Polar Music.

For Görel's thirtieth birthday in June 1979, ABBA recorded a song in tribute, 'Sång till Görel' ('Song for Görel'). The song was pressed as a special blue vinyl one-sided 12-inch single—the B-side was blank. Reports differ on the number of copies pressed, as low as fifty or as high as 200. Needless to say, it is one of the rarest and most sought after ABBA records.

The record was billed as ABBA & Stikkan on the label, as Stig sang one verse. Stikkan was Stig's stage name as a performer in the '50s, and the nickname by which he is still best known in Sweden. 'Sång till Görel' is the final song credited to the songwriting team Andersson/Anderson/Ulvaeus. In the song, ABBA and Stig praise Görel's abilities, her business dealings with Polar's international business partners, and how they cannot cope without her, even namechecking her then-fiancé photographer Anders Hanser.

To this day, Görel Hanser represents the interests of Benny, Björn, and Frida, as well as ABBA as an entity. She operates her own management company from Benny's Mono Music building on the island of Skeppsholmen in central Stockholm.

'Gammal fäbodpsalm'
Traditional, arranged by Benny Andersson
Duration: 1.36
Performed in concert on the North American and European Tour, 13 September to 15 November 1979, and the Japanese Tour 12–27 March 1980. Released on the album *Live at Wembley Arena*, 29 September 2014.

'Gammal fäbodpsalm från Dalarna' ('Old summer pasture psalm from Dalarna') is a eighteenth-century Swedish melody originally known as 'Psalm från Älvdalsåsen' ('Psalm from Älvdalsåsen'). It is best known in Sweden today through a 1936 arrangement for organ by Oskar Lindberg.

On ABBA's tours of North America and Europe during September to November 1979, and in Japan in March 1980, the haunting melody was played by Benny on his Yamaha GX-1 synthesizer as an introduction to the concerts, which segued into the opening number, 'Voulez-Vous'. The live recording was heard over the end credits of the 1980 TV special *ABBA in Concert* and released on the album *Live at Wembley Arena* in 2014.

'I'm Still Alive'
Music by Agnetha Fältskog, lyric by Björn Ulvaeus
Duration: 3.33
Performed in concert on the North American and European Tour 13 September to 15 November 1979, and the Japanese Tour 12–27 March 1980. Released on the album *Live at Wembley Arena*, 29 September 2014.

The poignant ballad 'I'm Still Alive' was written for and performed during ABBA's 1979 and 1980 concerts. The melody was written by Agnetha, her second and final composition for ABBA, with lyrics by her now ex-husband Björn. In concert, the song was presented as an Agnetha solo moment, when she took over piano duties from Benny. 'I was really knocked out with the warmth and appreciation I got from the audience after singing that number,' said Agnetha after the tour. Another song, 'Turn of the Tide', which may be the same melody with a different lyric, was also under consideration for the tour.

'The song she played as a solo spot—"I'm Still Alive"—will be on the next LP,' Björn said in 1980. 'It is a welcome departure for us, to have a number on an ABBA album that wasn't written, in part at least, by Benny or myself.' Ultimately, ABBA did not record the song, though its title made an appearance in the middle-eight of 'Super Trouper'. In 1981, Agnetha and Michael B. Tretow produced a Swedish version, 'Här är mitt liv' ('Here is my life'), with lyrics by Ingela 'Pling' Forsman, for Swedish singer Kicki Moberg. It was released on a Polar Music single backing her *Melodifestivalen* contender 'Men natten är vår' ('But the night is ours'), also written and produced by Agnetha.

For thirty-five years, 'I'm Still Alive' could only be heard on bootleg audience recordings, until it was finally released in 2014 on the *Live at Wembley Arena* album.

'Londonderry Air' aka 'Danny Boy'
Traditional
Duration: 1.20
Performed in concert in Dublin, 15 November 1979.

On the last night of ABBA's 1979 European tour, in Dublin, Ireland (which also happened to be Frida's thirty-fourth birthday), instead of the usual concert opening 'Gammal fäbodpsalm' (see above), Benny played the traditional Irish classic 'Londonderry Air'. With lyrics adapted to the existing tune in 1913 by Frederic Weatherly, song is best known the world over as 'Danny Boy'. The original tune dates back to the eighteenth century, and was first documented in 1855 in the book *The Ancient Music of Ireland* by George Petrie.

'Put On Your White Sombrero'
Duration: 4.28
Recorded in September 1980. Released on the boxset *Thank You for the Music*, 31 October 1994.

'Put On Your White Sombrero' was recorded during sessions for the *Super Trouper* album, though it was bumped from inclusion by the title track. The long introduction, which is the entire length of the song's melody, and the fairly nonsense lyrics, may have also consigned it to remain in the vault.

Frida takes solo lead vocal for the first two verses, with Agnetha joining in harmony on the third verse. The high volume of Agnetha's harmony vocal, overwhelming Frida's lead, gives the impression that the song changes key. The musical arrangement, but none of the melody, was reused almost two years later on 'Cassandra', one of ABBA's final recordings.

In 1994, 'Put On Your White Sombrero' was one of the few previously unreleased songs to be included in full on the *Thank You for the Music* boxset. Since its belated release, Björn and Benny have obviously had a change of heart about the song, approving its inclusion on CD rereleases of the *Super Trouper* album, and even on vinyl on a bonus disc of non-album singles and B-sides included in *The Vinyl Collection* boxset in 2010, selecting it ahead of actual single B-sides. In 2016, Benny Anderssons Orkester performed the song on their semi-annual summer tour of Sweden.

'Nu alla goda vänners skål'

Traditional
Duration: 0.26
Performed on the Spanish television programme *Aplauso #100*, 6 June 1980. Broadcast 14 June 1980.

During an interview taped in Stockholm for Spanish television programme *Aplauso* (*Applause*) in June 1980, ABBA burst into the traditional Swedish drinking song 'Nu alla goda vänners skål' ('Now all good friends, cheers'), ending with a hearty 'skål!'

'Hovas vittne'

Music by Benny Andersson and Björn Ulvaeus, lyric by Benny Andersson, Agnetha Fältskog, Anni-Frid Lyngstad, Rune Söderqvist, Michael B. Tretow, Björn Ulvaeus
Duration: 2.56
Released on a limited edition 12-inch single, 25 January 1981.

To commemorate Stig Anderson's fiftieth birthday in January 1981, ABBA recorded a special birthday song for their manager and former co-lyricist, 'Hovas vittne' ('Hova's witness', a pun on Jehovah's Witness, Hova being the town where Stig was born). Like 'Sång till Görel' in 1979, the song was pressed as a 12-inch single on red vinyl, the 200 copies given to guests at a huge celebration at Stig's home on his birthday. A sought-after collectible, in 2013, a copy of the single sold at auction for SEK42,000 (a little over £4,000).

The lyrics detail Stig's life and his many idiosyncrasies: his origins in rural Sweden, his dog Lukas, his love of sausages, his lyric-writing talent, the misadventures of international plane travel, his habit of starting up the vacuum cleaner at the end of a party to encourage guests to leave (now that is a trick we could all try), and his preference for raising a song by a semi-tone for the final chorus (which actually happens at that very point in the song). The lyrics were written by all four ABBA members, freelance designer of Polar's album sleeves Rune Söderqvist, and recording engineer Michael B. Tretow.

The day before the birthday party, ABBA recorded a video performance of 'Hovas vittne', directed by Kurt Hjelte, wearing the costumes that they wore when performing 'Waterloo' at the Eurovision Song Contest in 1974, for screening during the celebration. The video was subsequently screened on the Swedish television programme *O.S.A. Stig Anderson* in May 1982.

At the party, Benny and Björn presented the publishing rights of the song 'personally to Stig, for the world, forever', with the proviso that if the song were ever to be recorded, it must be with the original lyrics. Suffice to say, it is one of the few songs from the ABBA catalogue never covered by another artist.

A forty-five-second extract of 'Hovas vittne' was included on a promotional CD, *Gröna Huset Hova—Stikkan Anderson* (*The Green House Hova*) in 2000, when a memorial bust of Stig (who had died in September 1997, aged sixty-six) was unveiled in front of his childhood home. At the time, the building housed a florist, which closed in September 2018. Today, it is a second-hand shop, selling used goods, bric-a-brac, and even old ABBA records.

'Tivedshambo'
Written by Stig Anderson
Duration: 2.10
Released on the B-side of 'Hovas vittne', 25 January 1981. Performed on the television programme *Här är det liv*, 25 January 1986.

The B-side of the limited 'Hovas vittne' single was an instrumental version of Stig's first hit as a songwriter, 'Tivedshambo' ('Tivedian Hambo', Tived being the parish from which Stig hailed, a hambo being a traditional Swedish dance in 3/4 time dating from the late nineteenth century), written in 1947. Stig recalled in the mid-'70s: 'I was sixteen when I put together the first song I thought was something. It was called "Tivedshambo", and has become a classic of the old dance music and is still played a great deal today'. The melody on this recording is played by Benny on his beloved accordion and synthesizer.

In January 1986, Björn, Benny, Agnetha, and Frida were filmed singing 'Tivedshambo' at Polar Music's offices on Hamngatan in central Stockholm for Stig's *Här är det liv* (*This is your life*) television programme, with Benny playing accordion and Björn on guitar. They can be clearly seen reading the lyrics from cue cards (held off screen by the ever-supportive Görel Hanser), and from a sheet of paper in Agnetha's hand. This was the first time the four had sung together since December 1982, and reportedly the first time Frida and Agnetha had met in two years. To date, this is the last performance by ABBA seen by the general public, though not the last time they have sung together.

At this time, Frida was sporting stark white hair. After the relative failure of her second English album *Shine* in 1984, she retreated from public life, stripped her hair of colour so as not to look like 'ABBA-Frida', declined fan requests to be photographed or sign autographs, and had requested that her unofficial fan club close down as she had nothing more to offer the public. Tragically, her friend, the French singer Daniel Balavoine, with whom she had sung the duet 'Belle' a few years earlier (see the entry for 'Arrival' for details about that song), had been killed in a helicopter crash in Africa just the day before.

'Fanfare for Icehockey World Championships '81'
Duration: 0.35
Recorded in March 1981. Released on the album *Polargruppen—Ekonomipaket i ord och ton, circa* December 1981.

Benny and Björn composed this thirty-five-second fanfare for the Ice Hockey World Championships held in the Swedish cities of Stockholm and Gothenburg in April 1981. The recording sounds like the only musician featured is Benny, playing his Yamaha GX-1 synthesizer. The fanfare was also used as the opening theme of the 1981 television special *Dick Cavett Meets ABBA*, celebrating ABBA's tenth anniversary, and was released on the limited edition album *Polargruppen—Ekonomipaket i ord och ton* (*The Polar group—Finance package in words and sounds*) packaged with Sweden Music's 1981 annual company report. The album also included a selection of music released by Polar Music, including ABBA's 'Slipping Through My Fingers'.

'Ja må hon leva'/'Happy Birthday to You'
Duration: 0.34
Traditional/Attributed to Mildred and Patty S. Hill
Recorded *circa* March 1981.

Stig Anderson's wife Gudrun turned fifty in April 1981, a few months after her husband. ABBA recorded a special greeting, singing the traditional Swedish birthday song 'Ja må hon leva' ('Yes may she live') and the American song 'Happy Birthday to You'. The recording was allegedly made to be broadcast on BBC Radio 2 while Gudrun and Stig were visiting England in her birthday, though whether it was actually broadcast has been disputed.

The ABBA bootleg market has renamed this recording 'Sång till Gudrun' ('Song for Gudrun'), taking the title from 1979's tribute single 'Sång till Görel'.

'Don't Fence Me In'
Written by Cole Porter
Duration: 1.18 (in three segments)
Performed on the television program *Dick Cavett Meets ABBA*, 27 March 1981. Broadcast 12 September 1981.

In March 1981, ABBA convened at SVT Studio in Stockholm to film a television special commemorating the group's ten years together. The special consisted of two sections: an interview with American talk show legend Dick Cavett and a live concert featuring some of ABBA's greatest hits, including two unheard songs from *The Visitors* album that would be released at the end of the year.

An unexpected highlight of the interview section was ABBA's spontaneous performance of the American classic song 'Don't Fence Me In' in Swedish and English ('Ge mig en chans' in Swedish), which suitably impressed the host. The song was written by Cole Porter in 1934, the lyrics based on a poem by Robert Fletcher, but made famous in 1944 by cowboy actor Roy Rogers in the film *Hollywood Canteen*, and in a radio performance that same year by Kate Smith.

'Nu är det jul igen'
Traditional
Duration: 0.19
Performed on the West German radio programme *Mel Sondock's Hitparade*, *circa* December 1981.

ABBA sang this traditional Swedish Christmas song 'Now it is Christmas again' on West German radio in December 1981. The recording from the radio programme was released, with ABBA's permission, on the HIV/AIDS charity CD *Broadway's Carols for a Cure Volume 13* in November 2011 (though the song is not credited on the CD; it is tagged on to the start of 'Hark! The Herald Angels Sing' by the Broadway cast of *Mamma Mia!*).

'I Am the City'
Duration: 4.03
Recorded in May 1982. Released on the album *More ABBA Gold—More ABBA Hits*, 24 May 1993.

In May 1982, following the release of *The Visitors* album in November 1981 and recording sessions for Frida's first English-language solo album, *Something's Going On* (released in September 1982), ABBA reconvened at Polar Music Studios with plans to record a ninth studio album. After just three recordings, they abandoned the new album and instead aimed for a career-spanning compilation with a couple of new songs.

Of six songs that would be recorded in 1982, only four were released that year. Ironically, the only two that were not released in 1982, 'I Am the City' and 'Just Like That' (see the entry 'ABBA Undeleted' below for more in the latter song), were the only two that were mentioned in a Polar Music press release in June.

After the darker, serious songs and worldly themes on *The Visitors* album in 1981, 'I Am the City' was a return to the energetic, poppy ABBA of earlier years. The lyric personifies the city as a living, pulsing thing, enveloping its citizens.

After the predominantly solo lead vocals on the previous album, here Frida and Agnetha sing together in strong harmony and with solo lines from both.

In 1993, in an unprecedented move, the unreleased 'I Am the City' was included on the CD *More ABBA Gold—More ABBA Hits*, the follow-up to the huge international success of *ABBA Gold: Greatest Hits* the previous year. The song had been already circulating on bootleg cassettes in the ABBA fan community for a decade, so it was not unknown to hardcore fans. 'I Am the City', like most of ABBA's recordings in 1981 and '82, is dominated by Benny's synthesizers—the massive GX-1 that had featured prominently since 1979, plus his new toys the Prophet-10 and Yamaha GS-1.

'Der kleine Klaus'
Written by Benny Andersson, Tim Rice, and Björn Ulvaeus
Duration: NK
Performed in February 1986.

In February 1986, ABBA's friend and concert sound engineer Claes af Geijerstam turned forty. The four former ABBA members attended his birthday party, and together sang a rousing party song, 'Der kleine Klaus' ('The little Claus'), a rewritten version of 'Der kleine Franz' ('The little Franz'), an obscure song from the Benny Andersson/Tim Rice/Björn Ulvaeus musical *Chess*. It is not known if this performance was ever recorded or photographed for posterity.

The original version of 'Der kleine Franz', recorded in 1984 for the *Chess* concept album, remained unreleased until a deluxe thirtieth anniversary deluxe remastered edition of *Chess* in 2014. Bizarrely, the original recording is buried in the background, obscured by dialogue between two main characters. The song had featured in some productions of the musical over the years.

'ABBA Undeleted'
Duration: 23.31
A medley of songs recorded between September 1974 and June 1982. Released on the boxset *Thank You for the Music*, 31 October 1994.

Following the massive worldwide success of *ABBA Gold: Greatest Hits* in 1992, and the lesser but still healthy success of *More ABBA Gold* a year later, Polydor Records put together the four-CD boxset *Thank You for the Music*, released in November 1994. The compilers at PolyGram UK wanted to include previously unreleased music, as was expected on such a boxset. ABBA, particularly Benny and Björn, are famously reluctant to release songs that had been held back at the time. For the boxset, they relented, allowing the release of two completely unheard songs, unreleased alternate versions of two more, and a medley of studio outtakes, entitled 'ABBA Undeleted'.

The twenty-three-minute medley consists of excerpts from songs, some completed, others just demo recordings or early takes, interspersed with studio chatter (in Swedish, of course, but translations are available online). The medley was compiled by Michael B. Tretow, from original multi-track recording tapes, plus tapes he had recorded on the side of ABBA's studio sessions:

'Scaramouche', an instrumental dating from the first recording sessions for *ABBA: The Album* in June 1977. The non sequitur title was inspired by Queen's 1975 hit 'Bohemian Rhapsody'. No parts of this melody are known to have been reused in later Andersson/Ulvaeus compositions.

'Summernight City' (*sic.*), from a recording for a spoken-word greeting that starts with introductions from the ABBA members, then mingled the 1978 single with 'Money, Money, Money', until collapsing into laughter.

'Take a Chance on Me', a rocky, instrumental early take of ABBA's 1978 hit, originally entitled 'Billy Boy'.

'Baby', an Agnetha-led early version of 1975's 'Rock Me'. Some of the lyrics from this first take made their way into the final version.

'Just a Notion', an unreleased song from 1978. One of the few unreleased titles known during ABBA's time, thanks to an article in the official *ABBA Magazine* about the song's recording session, a rare and unique behind the scenes glimpse of ABBA at work: 'The girls go over a vocal phrase "right for me and you" and over, and over … to the backing track which Micke keeps running. Something isn't quite right,' wrote magazine editor Charlie Bates. It seems that it was obvious early on that the recording was not to Benny and Björn's satisfaction. In 1994, apparently it was planned to be included on the boxset in full, but Benny and Björn declared the recording 'unmixable.'

'Rikky Rock 'n' Roller', an unreleased glam rocker sung by Agnetha and Frida from 1974 that was recorded by veteran Swedish singer Jerry Williams (né Sven Erik Fernström) on his 1976 album *Kick Down*.

'Burning My Bridges', a country-style demo from 1980, sung by Björn. Had it been completed it might have added a little more variety to the *Super Trouper* album.

'Fernando' (written by Benny Andersson, Stig Anderson, and Björn Ulvaeus), the first take of Frida's original Swedish version, with a rigid, tango feel. This recording is a good example of Benny and Björn's continuing quest to find the best treatment for a song. Would this version have been a multi-million selling worldwide hit? Possibly not.

'Here Comes Rubie Jamie' (written by Benny Andersson, Stig Anderson, and Björn Ulvaeus), a working title for the unreleased song 'Terra Del Fuego'. The full recording featured solo passages sung by all four, joining together for the chorus, but this excerpt of one verse only has lines sung by Benny and Frida.

'Hamlet III Parts 1 and 2', two takes of the same melody recorded in 1978, one a full band instrumental, the other sung by Agnetha and Frida together over a lighter, guitar-led backing. The song would be recorded as the instrumental 'Lottis Schottis' for Benny's first solo album, *Klinga mina klockor* ('Ring, my bells') in 1987 (fun fact: Benny played the melody on accordion during the interview section of the television special *Dick Cavett Meets ABBA*, but it was cut from the broadcast).

'Free as a Bumble Bee', a 1978 demo sung by Björn and Benny, incorporating some melody from the chorus of 'I Am an A', from ABBA's 1977 tour (see entry above). That same melody would later be used in the chorus of 'I Know Him So Well' in Benny and Björn's musical *Chess*, which was a British No. 1 single in 1985. It shows that a good melody will come out in the end.

'Rubber Ball Man', an attempt for a new single in 1979 which would coincide with ABBA's North American and European tour. During rehearsals for the tour, ABBA tried out this song with a completely different lyric and rockier arrangement titled 'Under My Sun'. The second half of the verse melody would be reused in 1982 in 'Under Attack'. A distinctive synthesizer glissando is a major feature of 'Rubber Ball Man', appearing twice in this excerpt, but one can imagine it probably wears out its welcome on the full recording.

'Crying Over You', a Björn-sung experiment from 1978. Benny plays quite funky electric piano riffs, over a tape loop from Polar stablemates Svenne & Lotta's recording of The Box Tops' 1967 hit 'The Letter', from the husband and wife duo's 1978 album *Bring It On Home*, which had been produced by ABBA recording engineer Michael B. Tretow.

'Just Like That', the sixth song that ABBA recorded in 1982. 'Just Like That' is considered by many fans as the holy grail of unreleased ABBA songs. Agnetha sings lead on another song of lost love in a 'One of Us' soundalike. The song had apparently been proposed for inclusion on the 1993 CD *More ABBA Gold*, until it was vetoed by Benny and Björn. It was then hoped that it could be included in full on the boxset, but was vetoed again, and only the chorus was included in the medley. Benny later said: '"Just Like That" was a song we did record, but we never liked what we had done, so it remained unreleased'. In 1985, Benny and Björn wrote a new verse and rewrote part of the chorus for an album they co-produced by the brother/sister duo Gemini (Anders and Karin Glenmark), which they consider to be the definitive version of the song. The verse melody of ABBA's version with a new chorus was tried out for the musical *Chess* during recordings for the concept album in 1984; there are various instrumental and vocal demos (sung by Elaine Paige and Tommy Körberg, who had roles on the *Chess* album) with the new chorus melody, under the titles 'When the Waves Roll Out to Sea' and 'When the Stars are in the Sky'. A typewritten lyric sheet for the former title dating from this period is sardonically headed 'Nonsense Words to Flo's Final Song'. The melody finally found a home in the Swedish production of *Chess* in 2002 in the new song 'Glöm mig om du kan' ('Forget me if you can'). 'Just Like That' was featured in the musical *Mamma Mia!* during the creation and rehearsal period in 1999, as a love duet between the young leads Sophie and Sky. It was dropped just before the first previews, though the title and an explanation of the song were printed in the show's programme available throughout the preview period. Despite Benny and Björn's refusal to release ABBA's original recording, three different mixes have been circulating on bootleg cassettes, CDs, and online since the mid-'80s. The rather free-form saxophone refrain on 'Just

Like That' was played by British musician Raphael Ravenscroft, who had played the distinctive saxophone riff on Gerry Rafferty's 1978 hit 'Baker Street'. Ravenscroft happened to be recording a solo album, *Lifeline*, in Polar Music Studio B at the time ABBA were in the Studio A recording 'Just Like That'.

'Givin' A Little Bit More', an understated Björn-sung demo from 1981, a pleasant melody backed by synthesizer, piano, acoustic guitar, and drum machine.

'ABBA Undeleted' ends with a short, uncredited snippet of the end of 'Thank You for the Music', played solo by Benny on piano.

'Med en enkel tulipan'
Music by Jules Sylvain, lyric by Sven Paddock
Duration: NK
Performed 6 June 1999.

At Görel Hanser's fiftieth birthday in June 1999, held at the Moderna Museet in central Stockholm, guests were stunned when Björn, Benny, Agnetha, and Frida took to the stage to celebrate the milestone with a song. 'Med en enkel tulipan' (With a simple tulip) was written in 1938 by Swedish composer Jules Sylvain, though the four sang modified lyrics in honour of their longtime friend. 'It was very strange to me to see how we instantly picked up our places again with the ladies in the middle and Benny and I with the instruments alongside. It was weird when I looked beside me, to see the two women singing beside me,' Björn said later. The four had quickly rehearsed the song in a disabled toilet cubical, prior to appearing together.

Apparently the performance was photographed by party guests, including photographer Anders Hanser (then Görel's husband), and may have even been recorded on video, none of which have ever been seen or heard publicly, something that every ABBA fan is aching to see and hear.

'From a Twinkling Star to a Passing Angel'
Duration: 9.08
Various versions recorded between May and November 1981. Released on the album *The Visitors* Deluxe Edition 23 April 2012.

The final track on the final ABBA album, 'Like an Angel Passing Through My Room', was reportedly a difficult recording to get right. Several different attempts were recorded over several months during 1981, from disco thumper to hymn-like dirge. Agnetha talked about the experience in 1982: 'You know we did two or three different backing tracks for that number and none of them came out that good'.

In several modern-day interviews, Benny has said that it was one of his favourite melodies that he had written. This is probably what led to him creating a medley of five different versions for *The Visitors* Deluxe Edition CD in 2012. Benny compiled the medley himself, saying, 'It was fun to put this thing together, just to show what the process can be like. It's an interesting observation on how you labour over things before you reach the final result.'

The nine-minute medley opens with a Björn-sung demo, liberally borrowing the words from the nursery rhyme 'Twinkle Twinkle Little Star'. This leads into a simple demo with Benny on piano and Frida singing the early lyric 'Another Morning Without You'. This segues into an uptempo dance version with the 'Like an Angel Passing Through My Room' lyrics, with layers of harmonies and a lead vocal from Agnetha. This version was shelved because it did not really work, and it sounded too much like the previous year's 'Lay All Your Love On Me' (indeed, it does). A hint of an unreleased verse is heard before the medley segues to two excerpts from a dirge-like version, the first section featuring Frida partly speaking the lyric over a harmony-laden backing, before cutting to the final section of the song which features layers and layers of overdubbed vocals with Agnetha's high harmony piercing through. The final version in the medley is a full recording that is close to the version released in 1981, with just Frida's solo voice, Benny's synthesizer, and a faint ticking clock sound.

Another unreleased version is in circulation, an interim, uptempo recording with both the 'Another Morning Without You' and 'Like an Angel Passing Through My Room' lyrics on different tracks on the multi-track master track tape, obscured by the grunting of drummer Ola Brunkert. Apparently he often grunted quite loudly while playing, hence the gag in the credits on the *Arrival* album sleeve in 1976 'one day we're gonna let you hear him sing'. Michael B. Tretow revealed this recording on the radio show *Sommar*, the same programme in which he played 'Dream World' (see above) in 1986.

Hearing these alternate takes, it is clear that ABBA made the right decision with the version released on *The Visitors* in 1981, despite Agnetha's opinion that 'It is a strange number because you wait for something that never comes'.

'I Still Have Faith in You'/'Don't Shut Me Down'

Personnel: Benny Andersson: keyboards

Mats Englund: bass

Agnetha Fältskog: vocals

Lasse Jonsson: guitar

Per Lindvall: drums

Anni-Frid Lyngstad, vocals

Jörgen Stenberg: percussion

Björn Ulvaeus: vocals

Lasse Wellander: guitar

Recorded at Riksmixningsverket, Stockholm: June 2017

Produced and arranged by Benny Andersson and Björn Ulvaeus

Engineered by Bernard Löhr

Anticipated release 2020.

For a week in June 2017 Agnetha, Frida, Benny, and Björn secretly convened at Benny's Riksmixningsverket (RMV) studio in Stockholm to record two new songs, just a few months short of thirty-five years after ABBA's last recording sessions. The new songs came about as 'an unexpected consequence' during planning for the quaintly-dubbed 'ABBAtar' tour, where digital representations of the four ABBA members would perform ABBA's hits in concert with a live band. In an April 2018 statement, ABBA said: 'We all four felt that, after some 35 years, it could be fun to join forces again and go into the recording studio', adding that it was 'an extremely enjoyable experience' to be back in the studio together.

Later, Björn described the two songs: 'One of them is a pop tune, very danceable. The other is more timeless, more reflective, that is all I will say. It is Nordic sad, but happy at the same time'. He added: 'It certainly sounds like ABBA very much'. In another interview, he explained: '"I Still Have Faith in You" is in a way about ourselves, about the four of us'. Guitarist Wellander and drummer Lindvall are veterans from ABBA's original recordings, while percussionist Stenberg is a member of Benny Anderssons Orkester.

At the time of writing, the two songs have not been heard publicly. The songs are expected to be released in conjunction with the opening of the tour in 2020.

ABBA ended their announcement with a statement for a breathlessly waiting world: 'We may have come of age, but the song is new. And it feels good'.

Select Discography

During ABBA's ten years as an active group, in addition to the eight studio albums and dozens of singles detailed earlier, they released three official compilations, and an album of Spanish-language versions of their songs. In the years since, new compilations and boxsets have introduced ABBA to new generations of fans, affectionately dubbed 'Goldies' by ABBA's older fans, named after the 1992 compilation *ABBA Gold*. Home video releases on VHS and DVD have brought ABBA's television and concert performances right into the viewers' living room or mobile device.

Compilation Albums

Greatest Hits/The Best of ABBA

Sweden (Greatest Hits):	17 November 1975
UK (Greatest Hits):	26 March 1976
US (Greatest Hits):	24 August 1976
Current edition:	discontinued
Duration:	UK: 48 minutes
	US: 45 minutes
Chart position:	Sweden: 1
	UK: 1
	US: 48

UK: 'SOS/He Is Your Brother/Ring Ring/Hasta Mañana/Nina, Pretty Ballerina/ Honey, Honey/So Long/I Do, I Do, I Do, I Do, I Do/People Need Love/Bang-A-Boomerang/Dance (While The Music Still Goes On)/Another Town, Another Train/Mamma Mia/Waterloo/Fernando'
US: SOS/He Is Your Brother/Ring Ring/Another Town, Another Train/Honey, Honey/So Long/Mamma Mia/I Do, I Do, I Do, I Do, I Do/People Need Love/

Waterloo/Nina, Pretty Ballerina/Bang-A-Boomerang/Dance (While The Music Still Goes On)/Fernando'

Depending on what country you lived in, a twelve, fourteen, or fifteen-track compilation titled either *Greatest Hits* or *The Best of ABBA* (or something similar in your local language) was released in late 1975 or during 1976 or 1977, featuring tracks originally released between 1972 and 1975. A twelve-track album entitled *The Best of ABBA* was released by Polydor in the Netherlands in August 1975, which was soon released in West Germany and Austria. Around the same time, another album featuring the same twelve tracks in a different order, *ABBA's Greatest Hits*, was released in France and Belgium by Vogue. RCA in Australia also released *The Best of ABBA* in November, with the same tracks in a locally designed sleeve.

Copies of the West German album appeared on import in stores in Sweden, forcing Polar Music to rush-release its fourteen-track compilation *Greatest Hits* in November; initially, the album had been scheduled for release in March 1976. Epic Records in the UK released their version of the Polar *Greatest Hits* in March, with the addition of the brand-new single 'Fernando' and a new sleeve design. Over the next year or so, similar collections were released around the world, most of which also included 'Fernando' alongside the earlier songs, mostly packaged in either the Polar album sleeve (a horror cartoon image by illustrator Hans Arnold) or the Epic one (ABBA on a park bench, with Benny and Frida in passionate embrace, Agnetha looking forlorn as Björn reads a magazine). In Portugal and several South American territories, this compilation was the first ever ABBA album released, in a couple of cases packaged in a sleeve adapted from ABBA's self-titled 1975 album.

These compilations included ABBA's earliest singles—'People Need Love', 'He Is Your Brother', 'Ring Ring'—their breakthrough Eurovision winner 'Waterloo', and the international chartbusters 'I Do, I Do, I Do, I Do, I Do', 'SOS', and 'Mamma Mia'. Though many of the other included songs were not international single releases, by accident or design, almost every song had been a single A-side somewhere in the world, with one exception: 'Dance (While the Music Still Goes On)', which had only been a B-side.

Greatest Hits sold 2.5 million copies in the UK and was the second-highest-selling album of the '70s, behind Simon & Garfunkel's 1970 swansong *Bridge Over Troubled Water*. In the US, *Greatest Hits* was ABBA's first platinum seller. *The Best of ABBA* was the first album to sell over 1 million copies in Australia and held the record as the nation's highest-selling album for over thirty years.

Greatest Hits has had limited release on CD. It was released in the mid-'80s in the US. The European Polydor album *The Best of ABBA* also had a CD release, as did the Australian album of the same name, but these were all discontinued by the early '90s. A limited edition thirtieth anniversary replica of the Polar Music *Greatest Hits* was released in 2005, unusually on a black plastic disc, rather than the standard clear plastic CD.

Greatest Hits Vol. 2

Sweden:	29 October 1979
UK:	26 October 1979
US:	November 1979
Current edition:	discontinued
Duration:	58 minutes
Chart position:	Sweden: 20
	UK: 1
	US: 46

'Gimme! Gimme! Gimme! (A Man After Midnight)/Knowing Me, Knowing You/Take a Chance on Me/Money, Money, Money/Eagle/Rock Me/Angeleyes/Dancing Queen/Does Your Mother Know/Chiquitita/Summer Night City/I Wonder (Departure)/The Name of the Game/Thank You for the Music'

ABBA's second official compilation album features fourteen songs first released between 1975 and 1979. Eleven international hit singles from *Arrival*, *ABBA: The Album*, and *Voulez-Vous*—'Dancing Queen', 'Knowing Me, Knowing You', 'Take a Chance on Me', 'Chiquitita', 'Does Your Mother Know', etc.—plus the then brand-new single 'Gimme! Gimme! Gimme! (A Man After Midnight)', 1978's non-album single 'Summer Night City', and 'Rock Me' from 1975's *ABBA* album, which had been a hit in its own right in Australia and New Zealand in 1976. There is one one oddity in the tracklist, 'I Wonder (Departure)': it had not been a hit single anywhere, but a live version had been on the B-side of 'The Name of the Game'. The studio version from *ABBA: The Album* was included here.

Greatest Hits Vol. 2 was released in the middle of ABBA's concert tour of North America and Europe. *Cashbox* magazine called the album 'a brilliant summation of a group that is undoubtedly on the brink of even bigger breakthroughs'. In the UK, the album sold 1.2 million copies. It was also among the first three ABBA albums released on CD in 1983, but was deleted in the early '90s when it was superseded by *ABBA Gold*.

Gracias Por La Música

Sweden:	23 June 1980
UK:	18 July 1980
US:	1980
Current edition:	Universal Music/Polar CD 00602547040589
Duration:	Original LP 43 minutes, CD 62 minutes

Vocals recorded at Mike's Studio, Stockholm, Sweden
Engineered and mixed by Michael B. Tretow

'Gracias Por La Música [Thank You for the Music]/Reina Danzante [Dancing Queen]/Al Andar [Move On]/Dame! Dame! Dame! [Gimme! Gimme! Gimme! (A Man After Midnight)]/Fernando/Estoy Soñando [I Have A Dream]/Mamma Mía/ Hasta Mañana/Conociéndome, Conociéndote [Knowing Me, Knowing You]/ Chiquitita'

CD bonus tracks: 'Ring Ring/Felicidad (Happy New Year)/Andante, Andante/ Se Me Está Escapando [Slipping Through My Fingers]/No Hay A Quien Culpar [When All Is Said and Done]'

In 1979, ABBA recorded a Spanish version of 'Chiquitita', to facilitate the group's major breakthrough in the Spanish-speaking territories of South America. After the success of 'Chiquitita' and a follow up single, 'Estoy Soñando' ('I Have a Dream'), in January 1980, Frida and Agnetha recorded Spanish vocals for eight more ABBA songs for a full Spanish album, *Gracias Por La Música* (*Thank You for the Music*), for release in Latin America and Spain. The album was first released in Spain in April and Argentina in May. It was also released in parts of the US with prominent Hispanic populations, and had limited release in the UK, Japan, South Africa, Israel, and Australia. In Argentina, the album sold 130,000 copies, 50,000 copies in the US, and was a surprise hit in Japan.

The album was rebranded as *ABBA Oro—Grandes Éxitos* (*ABBA Gold: Greatest Hits*) on CD in 1993 (see below). For the next twenty-one years, *Gracias Por La Música* was the lost child of the ABBA catalogue. It was resurrected in 2014 with a Deluxe Edition with five bonus tracks: the Spanish version of 'Ring Ring' (recorded in 1973 but not released until 1994, on *ABBA Más Oro: Más ABBA Éxitos* [*ABBA More Gold: More ABBA Hits*]), two tracks recorded for Spanish and South American editions of *Super Trouper* in 1980, and two recorded for *The Visitors* in 1981. The Deluxe Edition also included a DVD of Spanish television performances and promotional clips.

The Singles: The First Ten Years

Sweden:	8 November 1982
UK:	5 November 1982
US:	December 1982
Current edition:	discontinued
Duration:	92 minutes
Chart position:	Sweden: 19
	UK: 1
	US: 62

'Ring Ring/Waterloo/So Long/I Do, I Do, I Do, I Do I Do/SOS/Mamma Mia/ Fernando/Dancing Queen/Money, Money, Money/Knowing Me, Knowing You/ The Name of the Game/Take A Chance On Me/Summer Night City/Chiquitita/

Does Your Mother Know/Voulez-Vous/Gimme! Gimme! Gimme! (A Man After Midnight)/I Have a Dream/The Winner Takes It All/Super Trouper/One of Us/ The Day Before You Came/Under Attack'

In 1982, ABBA planned to record and release a new studio album to follow *The Visitors*. After recording just three tracks, the group abandoned that plan and decided instead to release a career-spanning compilation double album to celebrate their first ten years together, which would include one or two brand-new songs, one of which they would also release as a new single.

An early plan was for ABBA to perform a few concerts at an undisclosed location (most likely Stockholm or London) to commemorate their tenth anniversary. Agnetha said in the *International ABBA Magazine*: 'We have discussed doing a live LP and in that case we will go to a place—maybe stay there for one week—do all the old and new songs and see what comes up'. Like the studio album, that idea soon lost momentum.

The Singles included twenty-three international hits, from 1973's 'Ring Ring' right through the next ten years of their greatest hits to two new 1982 tracks, the singles 'The Day Before You Came' and 'Under Attack'. Ultimately, there would be no second ten years, rendering the album's subtitle rather ironic, and ABBA came to an end within two months of the album's release.

ABBA Gold: Greatest Hits

UK:	21 September 1992
US:	21 September 1993
Current edition:	Universal Music/Polar CD 060251724732, DVD 980 755-7
Duration:	CD 79 minutes, DVD 99 minutes
CD chart position:	Sweden: 1
	UK: 1
	US: 63 (Top 200), 1 (Top Pop Catalogue)
DVD chart position:	Sweden: 1
	UK: 1
	US: 3

'Dancing Queen/Knowing Me, Knowing You/Take a Chance on Me/Mamma Mia/Lay All Your Love On Me/Super Trouper/I Have a Dream/The Winner Takes It All/Money, Money, Money/SOS/Chiquitita/Fernando/Voulez-Vous/Gimme! Gimme! Gimme! (A Man After Midnight)/Does Your Mother Know/One of Us/ The Name of the Game/Thank You for the Music/Waterloo'

With ABBA having something of a resurgence a decade after disbanding, PolyGram Records, the German-Dutch company that had purchased Stig Anderson's Sweden Music and Polar Music empire in 1990, put together *ABBA*

Gold: Greatest Hits, a single CD collection of nineteen of ABBA's biggest hits. Much research had gone into the creation of *ABBA Gold*, from the cover design to the track selection. Its nineteen tracks were selected from ABBA's biggest international hits, but with a bias towards the inclusion of British hits over some iconic European and Australian hits. However, the original Australian issue replaced three songs with others that had been bigger domestic hits, while in Spain, the Spanish versions of two songs replaced the English versions.

The compilation was an immediate hit around the world, topping the charts in many countries, selling 2 million copies in the first year, and it also brought about a critical reappraisal of ABBA's contribution to popular music. It continues to sell in amazing numbers to this day; it is ABBA's highest-charting and biggest-selling album in the US, and the longest-charting Top 100 album in the UK at 900 weeks, where it is also the second-highest-selling album of all time (after Queen's *Greatest Hits*). It has become ABBA's highest-selling album, reportedly selling 31 million copies to date.

The sleek, graphic-based artwork on the front cover inspired a generation of compilation albums, including several albums from PolyGram with almost the exact same cover, most notably *Carpenters Gold* (2000), plus others including The Beatles' *1* (2000), Bee Gees' *Their Greatest Hits: The Record* (2001), Elvis Presley's *ELV1S: 30 #1 Hits* (2002), and Nirvana's *Nirvana* (2002).

ABBA Gold has been rereleased several times in all available audio formats, usually coinciding with a significant ABBA anniversary, notably the twenty-fifth, thirtieth, and fortieth anniversaries of ABBA's Eurovision win, and the tenth and twenty-fifth anniversaries of the album's own release. The album has topped the charts again and again, particularly when the *Mamma Mia!* musical and film opened. *ABBA Gold* has also been released as a DVD collection with ABBA's famous promotional films and bonus features.

ABBA Oro—Grandes Éxitos

UK:	1993
US:	1994
Current edition:	Universal Music/Polar CD 543 129-2
Duration:	62 minutes
Chart position:	Sweden: —
	UK: —
	US: 38 (Top Latin Albums)

'Fernando/Chiquitita/Gracias Por La Música [Thank You for the Music]/La Reine Del Baile [Dancing Queen]/El Andar [Move On]/Dame! Dame! Dame! [Gimme! Gimme! Gimme! (A Man After Midnight)]/Estoy Soñando [I Have a Dream]/Mamma Mía/Hasta Mañana/Conociéndome, Conociéndote [Knowing Me, Knowing You]'

CD bonus tracks: 'Felicidad [Happy New Year]/Andante, Andante/Se Me Está Escapando [Slipping Through My Fingers]/No Hay A Quien Culpar [When All Is Said and Done]/Ring Ring'

In the wake of *ABBA Gold*'s release, the ten tracks from ABBA's Spanish album *Gracias Por La Música* (1980) were repackaged as *ABBA Oro—Grandes Éxitos*, initially for Spanish-speaking markets, but it also saw release in non-Spanish speaking territories. In 1999, the CD was rereleased with five bonus tracks, to collect all fifteen of ABBA's Spanish recordings on one disc for the first time.

More ABBA Gold—More ABBA Hits

UK:	24 May 1993
US:	1994
Current edition:	Universal Music/Polar CD 060251724733
Duration:	79 minutes
Chart position:	Sweden: 3
	UK: 13
	US: —

'Summer Night City/Angeleyes/The Day Before You Came/Eagle/I Do, I Do, I Do, I Do, I Do/So Long/Honey, Honey/The Visitors/Our Last Summer/On and On and On/Ring Ring/I Wonder (Departure)/Lovelight/Head Over Heels/When I Kissed the Teacher/I Am the City/Cassandra/Under Attack/When All Is Said and Done/The Way Old Friends Do'

Following the initial (and unexpected) success of *ABBA Gold*, a second collection of further hit singles, B-sides, and popular album tracks was compiled. *More ABBA Gold* included the first 'new' ABBA song released in eleven years, the 1982 recording 'I Am the City'. The first issue of the CD also included a previously unheard mix of 'Lovelight', the B-side of 'Chiquitita'.

Reportedly, the initial idea was to release a CD entitled *The Other Side of ABBA*, with non-album B-sides and fan-selected album tracks—several British ABBA fans were canvassed for their favourites. For commercial reasons, Polydor switched the concept to include several international hits that had not been included on *ABBA Gold*, alongside B-sides and album tracks from the original concept, creating a bit of a schizophrenic collection.

The Definitive Collection

Released:	CD 17 September 2001, DVD 15 July 2002
Current edition:	Universal Music/Polar CD 549 974-2, DVD 017 445-9
Duration:	CD 128 minutes, DVD 168 minutes
CD chart position:	Sweden: 28

DVD chart position: UK: 17
                       US: 186
                       Sweden: 1
                       UK: 2
                       US: 2

CD: 'People Need Love/He Is Your Brother/Ring Ring/Love Isn't Easy (But It Sure Is Hard Enough)/Waterloo/Honey, Honey/So Long/I Do, I Do, I Do, I Do, I Do/SOS/Mamma Mia/Fernando/Dancing Queen/Money, Money, Money/Knowing Me, Knowing You/The Name of the Game/Take a Chance on Me/Eagle/Summer Night City/Chiquitita/Does Your Mother Know/Voulez-Vous/Angeleyes/Gimme! Gimme! Gimme! (A Man After Midnight)/I Have a Dream/The Winner Takes It All/Super Trouper/On and On and On/Lay All Your Love On Me/One of Us/When All Is Said and Done/Head Over Heels/The Visitors/The Day Before You Came/Under Attack/Thank You for the Music/Ring Ring (1974 remix)/Voulez-Vous (extended remix)'

DVD: 'Waterloo/Ring Ring/Mamma Mia/SOS/Bang-A-Boomerang/I Do, I Do, I Do, I Do, I Do/Fernando/Dancing Queen/Money, Money, Money/Knowing Me, Knowing You/That's Me/The Name of the Game/Take a Chance on Me/Eagle/One Man, One Woman/Thank You for the Music/Summer Night City/Chiquitita/Does Your Mother Know/Voulez-Vous/Gimme! Gimme! Gimme! (A Man After Midnight)/On and On and On/The Winner Takes It All/Super Trouper/Happy New Year/When All Is Said and Done/One of Us/Head Over Heels/The Day Before You Came/Under Attack/When I Kissed the Teacher/Estoy Soñando/Felicidad/No Hay A Quien Culpar/Dancing Queen (at the Swedish Royal Opera)'

A two-disc, thirty-seven-track compilation CD including all of Polar Music's ABBA singles, plus several international single releases, essentially an update of 1982's *The Singles: The First Ten Years*. It was the first official CD release of two bonus tracks, the 1974 single remix of 'Ring Ring' and the 1979 extended remix of 'Voulez-Vous'. The Australian release added two more local hits as additional bonus tracks. A similarly packaged DVD released a year later compiled all thirty of ABBA's promotional film clips plus several bonus television clips.

In 2012, *The Definitive Collection* CD was selected as No. 179 in Rolling Stone's *The 500 Greatest Albums of All Time* issue, ABBA's only appearance on this prestigious list.

Number Ones

Released: 20 November 2006
Current edition: Universal Music/Polar CD 171 221-9 (UK), 0602517093195, DVD 170 971-5
Duration: CD 74 minutes, DVD 95 minutes

'Gimme! Gimme! Gimme! (A Man After Midnight)/Mamma Mia/Dancing Queen/Super Trouper/SOS/Summer Night City/Money, Money, Money/The Winner Takes It All/Chiquitita/One of Us/Knowing Me, Knowing You/Voulez-Vous/Fernando/Waterloo/Ring Ring (UK only)/The Name of the Game/I Do, I Do, I Do, I Do, I Do/Take a Chance on Me/I Have a Dream'

A CD and matching DVD collection of eighteen No. 1 singles, out of a potential twenty-eight worldwide chart-topping songs. The British version added one more song, 'Ring Ring', which had not been a local hit (let alone No. 1), making it an odd addition. It was released following the success of other compilations with the same concept by The Beatles (*1*), Elvis Presley (*30 #1 Hits*), and Michael Jackson (*Number Ones*). It may also have been a bit of a cash-in on the recent interest in the opening track 'Gimme! Gimme! Gimme! (A Man After Midnight)', with its sampling the previous year on Madonna's worldwide hit 'Hung Up'. Publicity material for the album included a quote from the American icon: 'ABBA's timeless music continues to inspire me. It's joyous. Standing still when you hear ABBA's music is impossible'.

The Essential Collection

Released: 21 May 2012
Current edition: Universal Music/Polar CD 00602527993720, DVD 00602527993744
Duration: CD 158 minutes, DVD 152 minutes

CD: 'People Need Love/He Is Your Brother/Ring Ring/Love Isn't Easy (But It Sure Is Hard Enough)/Waterloo/Honey, Honey/So Long/I Do, I Do, I Do, I Do, I Do/SOS/Mamma Mia/Bang-A-Boomerang/Fernando/Dancing Queen/Money, Money, Money/Knowing Me, Knowing You/That's Me/The Name of the Game/Take a Chance on Me/Eagle/One Man, One Woman/Thank You for the Music/Summer Night City/Chiquitita/Does Your Mother Know/Voulez-Vous/Angeleyes/Gimme! Gimme! Gimme! (A Man After Midnight)/I Have a Dream/The Winner Takes It All/Super Trouper/On and On and On/Lay All Your Love On Me/Happy New Year/One of Us/When All Is Said and Done/Head Over Heels/The Visitors/The Day Before You Came/Under Attack'
DVD: 'Waterloo/Ring Ring/Mamma Mia/SOS/Bang-A-Boomerang/I Do, I Do, I Do, I Do, I Do/Fernando/Dancing Queen/Money, Money, Money/Knowing Me, Knowing You/That's Me/The Name of the Game/Take a Chance on Me/Eagle/One Man, One Woman/Thank You for the Music/Summer Night City/Chiquitita/Does Your Mother Know/Voulez-Vous/Gimme! Gimme! Gimme! (A Man After Midnight)/On and On and On/The Winner Takes It All/Super Trouper/Happy New Year/When All Is Said and Done/One of Us/Head Over Heels/The Day Before You Came/Under Attack/Estoy Soñando/Conociéndome, Conociéndote/Gracias Por La Música/Felicidad/No Hay A Quien Culpar/The Last Video'

Another double-CD collection and accompanying DVD of all of ABBA's Polar singles plus other international hits, and all the promotional film clips, newly remastered, adding previously unreleased Spanish clips.

Before ABBA

Sweden:	June 2013
Current edition:	Universal Music/Polar CD 060253737771
Duration:	41 minutes

After ABBA

Sweden:	5 May 2018
Current edition:	Universal Music/Polar CD 060256741812
Duration:	150 minutes

These twin compilation CDs gather together songs from the ABBA members' solo careers and other projects before and after the group era. They offer a fascinating glimpse at how four diverse careers developed into ABBA, and where their interests took them in the years after the group split. Both are available exclusively at ABBA The Museum in Stockholm.

Boxsets

Thank You for the Music

UK:	31 October 1994
US:	April 1995
Current edition:	Universal Music/Polar CD 060251743234
Duration:	277 minutes
Chart position:	Sweden: 17
	UK: —
	US: —

'People Need Love/Another Town, Another Train/He Is Your Brother/Love Isn't Easy (But It Sure Is Hard Enough)/Ring Ring/Waterloo/Hasta Mañana/Honey, Honey/ Dance (While The Music Still Goes On)/So Long/I've Been Waiting For You/I Do, I Do, I Do, I Do, I Do/SOS/Mamma Mia/Fernando/Dancing Queen/That's Me/ When I Kissed the Teacher/Money, Money, Money/Crazy World/My Love, My Live/Knowing Me, Knowing You/Happy Hawaii/The Name of the Game/I Wonder (Departure)/Eagle/Take a Chance on Me/Thank You for the Music/Summer Night City/Chiquitita/Lovelight/Does Your Mother Know/Voulez-Vous/Angeleyes/Gimme! Gimme! Gimme! (A Man After Midnight)/I Have a Dream/The Winner Takes It All/Elaine/Super Trouper/Lay All Your Love On Me/On and On and On/Our Last

Summer/The Way Old Friends Do/The Visitors/One of Us/Should I Laugh or Cry/ Head Over Heels/When All Is Said and Done/Like an Angel Passing Through My Room/The Day Before You Came/Cassandra/Under Attack/Put On Your White Sombrero/Dream World/Thank You for the Music (Doris Day Version)/Hej gamle man!/Merry-Go-Round/Santa Rosa/She's My Kind of Girl/Medley: Pick a Bale of Cotton—On Top of Old Smokey—Midnight Special/You Owe Me One/Slipping Through My Fingers—Me And I (live)/ABBA Undeleted/Waterloo (French/Swedish)/ Ring Ring (Swedish/Spanish/German)/Honey, Honey (Swedish)'

In the 1980s and '90s, multi-CD boxsets were all the rage, often spanning an act's entire career, with hits, album tracks, alternate versions, and unreleased songs. PolyGram intended to give ABBA this treatment in 1992 as the company's first release of their newly-acquired ABBA catalogue, but instead took the safe road and released the single CD compilation *ABBA Gold*. Following that CD's massive success, the compilers revisited the boxset concept.

The first three discs of the four-disc, sixty-six-track set contained all of ABBA's singles, plus B-sides, and significant album tracks in chronological order. Disc 4 featured rarities and several previously unreleased songs, mostly excerpts collected in the medley 'ABBA Undeleted'. The original European-manufactured set had a limited edition number, reaching over 300,000 copies before it was discontinued.

The Complete Studio Recordings
Released: 7 November 2005
Current edition: Universal Music/Polar CD/DVD 0602498723272
Duration: CD 459 minutes, DVD 198 minutes

This nine-CD, two-DVD boxset encompasses all of ABBA's released studio recordings, including several rare alternate versions, plus DVDs of all of ABBA's promotional clips, a short documentary made in 1999, and five songs from the 1981 television concert segment of the special *Dick Cavett Meets ABBA*.

The Albums
Released: 27 October 2008
Current edition: Universal Music/Polar CD 060251774852
Duration: 368 minutes
Chart position: Sweden: 4
                      UK: 89
                      US: —

A budget-priced CD boxset including ABBA's eight studio albums plus a bonus disc of non-album singles and B-sides.

The Singles

Released:	5 May 2014
Current edition:	Universal Music/Polar CD 00602537649594
Duration:	301 minutes

Commemorating the fortieth anniversary of ABBA's Eurovision triumph, this forty-disc boxset collects all thirty-one of Polar Music's ABBA 7-inch singles, plus nine other singles from around the world, in replicas of their original sleeves.

Live Albums

ABBA Live

Sweden:	18 August 1986
UK:	9 April 1992
US:	1986
Current edition:	discontinued
Personnel:	Benny Andersson: keyboards, vocals
	Lena Andersson: backing vocals
	Ulf Andersson: saxophone, flute
	Ola Brunkert: drums
	Lars O. Carlsson: saxophone, flute
	Anders Eljas: keyboards
	Lena Ericsson: backing vocals
	Wojciech Ernest: keyboards
	Agnetha Fältskog: vocals
	Malando Gassama: percussion
	Rutger Gunnarsson: bass
	Lena-Maria Gårdenäs: backing vocals
	Maritza Horn: backing vocals
	Tomas Ledin: backing vocals
	Anni-Frid Lyngstad: vocals
	Mats Ronander: guitar
	Finn Sjöberg: guitar
	Åke Sundqvist: percussion
	Björn Ulvaeus: guitar, vocals
	Lasse Wellander: guitar
	Birgitta Wollgård: backing vocals
	Liza Öhman: backing vocals
Duration:	LP 46 minutes, CD 63 minutes

Recorded at The Australian Tour 1977, Wembley Arena, London 1979, SVT, Stockholm 1981

Engineered & mixed by Michael B. Tretow

Chart position: Sweden: 49

                    UK: —

                    US: —

'Dancing Queen/Take a Chance on Me/I Have a Dream/Does Your Mother Know/Chiquitita/Thank You for the Music/Two for the Price of One/Fernando/ Gimme! Gimme! Gimme! (A Man After Midnight)/Super Trouper/Waterloo'

CD bonus tracks: 'Money, Money, Money/The Name of the Game/Eagle/On and On and On'

ABBA had planned to release a live album several times during their career. In 1977, there was an idea to release a live album soundtrack for *ABBA: The Movie*, then to make *ABBA: The Album* a double LP, with a second disc of live recordings. In 1980, there was talk of releasing a live album from the 1979 tour, but as Björn said at the time: 'The point is any live LP now would contain the kind of material already out on *Greatest Hits Vol. 2*'. In 1982, ABBA planned a one-off concert to commemorate the group's tenth anniversary and to release a recording of that concert. All of these ideas were eventually dropped.

Due to continuing demand from ABBA's longtime fans, in 1986, Polar Music released a collection of live recordings with one song from ABBA's Australian concert tour in March 1977, seven songs recorded at Wembley Arena in London in November 1979, and three songs from the television concert portion of the special *Dick Cavett Meets ABBA* in March 1981. The songs were mixed together by engineer Michael B. Tretow to form a single 'concert', with overdubbed applause and elevated volume on the drums that give the album a bombastic mid-'80s sound. It is an unsatisfying listening experience.

ABBA Live was the first ABBA album released simultaneously on LP and CD, the CD version featuring three extra tracks (one each from 1977, 1979, and 1981). At the time, international interest in ABBA was at an all time low. The album barely entered the charts in those countries where it was released—it spent two weeks at No. 49 in Sweden—and the ABBA-faithful UK did not release it at all.

Live at Wembley Arena

Released: 29 September 2014

Current edition: Universal Music/Polar CD 00602537928644

Personnel: Benny Andersson: keyboards, vocals

                     Ola Brunkert: drums

                     Anders Eljas: keyboards

                     Agnetha Fältskog: vocals, piano on 'I'm Still Alive'

                     Rutger Gunnarsson: bass

Tomas Ledin: backing vocals
Anni-Frid Lyngstad: vocals
Mats Ronander: guitar
Åke Sundqvist: percussion
Björn Ulvaeus: guitar, vocals
Lasse Wellander: guitar
Birgitta Wollgård: backing vocals
Liza Öhman: backing vocals

Duration: 110 minutes
Produced by Ludvig Andersson
Mixed by Bernhard Löhr, Assistant engineer Filip Lindholm
Chart position: Sweden: 15
                          UK: 30
                          US: —

'Gammal fåbodpsalm/Voulez-Vous/If It Wasn't for the Nights/As Good As New/Knowing Me, Knowing You/Rock Me/Chiquitita/Money, Money, Money/I Have a Dream/Gimme! Gimme! Gimme! (A Man After Midnight)/SOS/Fernando/The Name of the Game/Eagle/Thank You for the Music/Why Did It Have To Be Me/Intermezzo no 1/I'm Still Alive/Summer Night City/Take a Chance on Me/Does Your Mother Know/Hole in Your Soul/The Way Old Friends Do/Dancing Queen/Waterloo'

Thirty-five years after ABBA's North American & European concert tour, the double CD/triple LP *Live at Wembley Arena* was belatedly released. The album contains a complete ABBA concert recorded on 10 November 1979, excluding backing singer Tomas Ledin's solo showcase 'Not Bad At All' (it came between 'Rock Me' and 'Chiquitita', after Frida declares 'What do you think of our band?'). Unlike previous live ABBA recordings, this album features no overdubs and minimal studio sweetening, only fixing technical faults. The album was produced by Benny's son, Ludvig Andersson, who said that he wanted to work on the recordings as he was too young to have experienced an ABBA concert (Ludvig was born in January 1982).

Live at Wembley Arena marks the first ever release of Agnetha's solo performance 'I'm Still Alive', and just for that, it is worth it.

Home Video

ABBA: The Movie

World premiere: 15 December 1977
UK: 16 February 1978
US: February 1979
Current edition: Universal Music/Polar DVD 0602498717004

Universal Music/Polar Blu-ray Disc 0602517793225

Duration:	95 minutes plus DVD extras
DVD chart position:	Sweden: 1
	UK: 1
	US: —

ABBA's only feature film is a pseudo-documentary, filmed primarily on their Australian concert tour in March 1977. Originally conceived as a television special, jokingly dubbed by ABBA as a home movie to remember the tour by, the idea soon grew into a Panavision cinema release.

Director Lasse Hallström added a story line about a naïve radio DJ Ashley Wallace (played by Australian actor Robert Hughes), who follows ABBA on their tour in Sydney, Perth, Adelaide, and finally Melbourne. He has been assigned to get an in-depth 'dialogue' with ABBA for a special to be broadcast on his radio station the day that the group leaves Australia. As he does not have an appointment, or his press card, he is thwarted at every step by ABBA's bodyguard (Tom Oliver). In the interests of authenticity, Hallström did not inform the ABBA members of the identities of the two actors until several days into the tour: 'I kept wondering who this odd, pushy journalist was. He kept desperately asking strange questions all the time and always wanted us to "go someplace where it was a little quieter"', Frida recalled. The film shows ABBA at airports, press conferences, hotels, and, of course, in concert, performing many of their hits, as well as illustrating ABBA's enormous impact on Australia.

Additional scenes were filmed in Stockholm in June, featuring new songs from the concurrent release *ABBA: The Album*, plus other scenes meant to emulate events in Australia. *ABBA: The Movie* is the only place you can hear the otherwise unreleased fourth song from the mini-musical *The Girl with the Golden Hair*, 'Get On the Carousel'.

It was reported that fifty hours of footage was filmed for the ninety-five-minute film. ABBA fans continue to hope that a full concert film can be compiled, but that seems unlikely. In different interviews over the years, Hallström has said that either the footage is probably stored somewhere in Stockholm, gathering dust, waiting to be found, or was destroyed after the film's premiere as surplus to requirements.

The film premiered in Australia and Sweden in December 1977 and was screened around the world during 1978. It had a limited release in North America in 1979 in the lead up to ABBA's tour in September. It even had limited screenings in Moscow cinemas around 1981, a rarity for a western pop film in those days. It was first made available on home video in 1980 and released on DVD in September 2005, with Blu-ray following in December 2007.

ABBA: The Movie was one of the top ten films of 1978 in the UK, the year of such blockbusters as *Star Wars*, *Saturday Night Fever*, *Grease*, and *Superman*, and multi-Oscar nominee *The Goodbye Girl*. In Australia, where the frenzied Abbamania of 1975 and '76 had subsided, the film was described as being 'reasonably successful'.

ABBA In Japan

First broadcast: 25 November 1978
Released: 26 October 2009
Current edition: Universal Music/Polar DVD 0602527102313
Duration: 54 minutes plus DVD extras

In November 1978, ABBA traveled to Japan to make a one-hour television special, featuring many of their hits, which greatly increased ABBA's profile and popularity in Japan. The special was released on DVD in October 2009, with bonus features including fascinating behind-the-scenes documentaries of this trip and ABBA's Japanese concert tour of March 1980.

ABBA In Concert

First broadcast: April 1980
Released UK: 1993
Current edition: Universal Music/Polar DVD 0044006564692
Duration: 51 minutes plus DVD extras
DVD chart position: Sweden: 1
                     UK: 2
                     US: 37

A one-hour television special with on-the-road scenes filmed during ABBA's first and only concert tour of North America in September 1979, and concert performances filmed at London's Wembley Arena in November on the European leg of the tour. The special was first released on home video in the 1980s and internationally on DVD in March 2004. Recordings from the Wembley concerts also formed the 1979 BBC Radio special *ABBA In Concert*, much of the 1986 album *ABBA Live*, and *ABBA Live at Wembley Arena*, a full-concert album released in 2014.

The Winner Takes It All—The ABBA Story

First broadcast: May 1999
Released UK: November 1999
Current edition: Universal DVD 060 998-9
Duration: 90 minutes
Chart position: UK: 3

This British television documentary commemorated the twenty-fifth anniversary of ABBA's Eurovision Song Contest win, and the 'coincidental' opening of the *Mamma Mia!* stage musical in London. Along with historical footage, Björn, Benny, and Frida were featured in new interviews, while Agnetha was filmed silently walking in Stockholm, recording a voiceover reading excerpts from her authorised biography, *As I Am*.

At the time, the four former ABBA members said this would be the last time they would be involved with an ABBA project. After television broadcast around the world, the documentary was released on VHS at the end of 1999 and on DVD in 2002.

The Last Video

First broadcast:	12 May 2004
Released:	17 July 2004
Current edition:	Universal Music/Polar DVD 0602498671542
Duration:	6 minutes plus DVD extras
Chart position:	Sweden: 4
	UK: 9
	US: —

The Last Video, originally titled *Our Last Video Ever!*, is a fun short film featuring a puppet version of ABBA auditioning for a sleazy record company boss, played by British comedian Rik Mayall, with several well-known Swedish actors and singers in other roles. The dialogue was cleverly created completely of lines from ABBA songs. The puppets were created by Jim Henson's Creature Shop, founded by the late Jim Henson of Muppets fame. During the film, the puppets 'perform' 'Take a Chance on Me', 'Dancing Queen', and 'Waterloo', and 'The Winner Takes It All' is heard at the end. The film includes cameo appearances from American singer Cher (who would later star in the ABBA-themed movie musical *Mamma Mia! Here We Go Again*), Eddie, the monstrous mascot of British metal band Iron Maiden, and Björn, Benny, Frida, and Agnetha themselves. Some digital trickery also has the puppet group encountering ABBA from 1977 in an elevator, in footage from *ABBA: The Movie*.

The film had its premiere during the semi-final of the 2004 Eurovision Song Contest, held in Istanbul, Turkey, in commemoration of the thirtieth anniversary of ABBA's song contest victory, and it was later released as a stand-alone DVD. It was directed by Calle Åstrand, son of Björn's Hootenanny Singers bandmate Hansi Schwarz. Again, this was announced as the last project the ABBA members would participate in, hence the film's title.

Super Troupers—A Celebratory Film from Waterloo to MAMMA MIA!—30 years of music

First broadcast:	September 2004
Released:	11 October 2004
Current edition:	Universal Music/Polar DVD 9824276
Duration:	89 minutes plus DVD extras
Chart position:	Sweden: 14
	UK: 2
	US: —

An updated version of the 1999 documentary *The Winner Takes It All*, *Super Troupers* is anchored around the fifth anniversary of the *Mamma Mia!* musical. New interviews from Frida, Benny, and Björn are added, plus interview footage of Agnetha from her own recent television special, which was made to promote her solo album *My Colouring Book*. The special is based around the anticipation of all four ABBA members appearing together on stage at the Prince Edward Theatre in London for the anniversary. Spoiler alert: Agnetha does not show, which everyone knew by the time it was broadcast, dulling the tension somewhat. Sadly, this documentary makes no mention of Stig Anderson, such an important part of the ABBA story.

Note: ABBA's classic promotional films, or music videos to use modern parlance, are collected together on the DVDs *ABBA Gold: Greatest Hits*, *The Definitive Collection*, *Number Ones*, and *The Essential Collection*, all discussed in the Compilation Albums section above. They are also available individually on download and streaming services.

Bibliography

Books

Andersson, B., Ulvaeus, B., Craymer, J., Dodd, P., *Mamma Mia! How Can I Resist You? The Inside Story of Mamma Mia! and the Songs of ABBA* (UK: Phoenix Illustrated 2008)

Borg, C., *The ABBA Phenomenon* (Australia: Horwitz Publications 1977)

Edgington, H., and Himmelstrand, P., *ABBA* (UK: Everest Books Ltd 1977)

Garau, M., and Tonnon, F., *ABBA: The Inner Circle Interviews* (UK: Bungalow Publishing 2010)

Gradvall, J., Karlsson, P., Wanselius, B., and Wikström, J., *ABBA: The Official Photo Book* (Sweden: Bokförlaget Max Ström 2014)

Halling, I., and Palm, C.M., *ABBA: The Backstage Stories* (Sweden: Bonnier Fakta 2014)

Lindvall, M., *ABBA: The Ultimate Pop Group* (Canada: Hurtig Publishers Limited 1977)

Palm, C. M., *ABBA: The Complete Recording Sessions—Revised and Expanded Edition* (Sweden: CMP Text 2017); *Bright Lights Dark Shadows: The Real Story of ABBA* (UK: Omnibus Press 2014)

Patrick, C., *ABBA: Let The Music Speak* (Australia: Christopher Patrick 2008)

Potiez, J-M., *ABBA: The Book* (UK: Aurum Press 2000); *ABBA: The Scrapbook* (UK: Plexus, 2009)

Russell, S,. *The ABBA Guide to Stockholm* (Sweden: Premium Publishing 2014)

Stanley, B., 'See That Girl: Abba' in *Yeah Yeah Yeah: The Story of Modern Pop*, pp 384-390 (UK: Faber & Faber 2013)

Tobler, J., *ABBA Gold: The Complete Story* (UK: Century 22 Limited 1993)

Ulvaeus, B., and Vale, P., *You Are Who You Meet* (Sweden: Björn Ulvaeus & Patrick Vale 2018)

Van Wymeersch, S., *Let's talk about ABBA* (Belgium: Dragonetti 2013)

Vincentelli, E., *ABBA Gold* (USA: Continuum 2004)

Wolf, Lutz W., (editor) and Bagnall, B. (illustrations), *ABBA: Take a chance on me Songbook* (West Germany: Deutscher Taschenbuch Verlag 1982)

York, R., *Abba In Their Own Words* (UK: Omnibus Press 1981)

Magazines and Newsletters

ABBA Appreciation Club/ABBA: The Fan Club/The Official Australian ABBA Fan Club (Australia: 1976–1983)
ABBA Intermezzo (Germany: 1990-present)
Official International ABBA Fan Club magazine (Netherlands: 1986-present)
Paul, P., and Bates, C. (editors), *ABBA Magazine/International ABBA Magazine* (UK: Poster Plus/The ABBA Magazine 1977-1983)

News Media

Classic Pop; *The Guardian*; *The Local*; MSN Encarta; News.com.au, *Pitchfork*; *The Quietus*; *Rolling Stone*; *Smash Hits*; Songfacts; *Vice*; Wikipedia.

Sleeve Notes and Audio Tracks

ABBA: The Singles (Sweden: Polar Music International/Universal Music 2014)
Stikkan Anderson väljer Polars pärlor: Pop-favoriter (Sweden: Polar Music International 1994)
Untitled ABBA promotional album for *Voulez-Vous* (Australia: RCA Victor 1979)

Websites

ABBA Omnibus www.abbaomnibus.net
ABBA On TV www.abbaontv.com
ABBA The Museum www.abbathemuseum.com
ABBA The Official Site www.abbasite.com
getabba: ABBA Picture Gallery and Collection www.getabba.com
icethesite—Benny Andersson News www.icethesite.com
Official International ABBA Fan Club www.abbafanclub.nl